The Classic Guide to FLY FISHING

The
Classic Guide
to
FLY FISHING

H. Cholmondeley-Pennell

AMBERLEY

First edition published 1889

This edition first published 2015

Amberley Publishing
The Hill, Stroud
Gloucestershire, GL5 4EP

www.amberley-books.com

Copyright © Amberley Publishing, 2015

British Library Cataloguing in Publication Data.
A catalogue record for this book is available from the British Library.

ISBN 978 1 4456 4723 4 (print)
ISBN 978 1 4456 4724 1 (ebook)

Typesetting and Origination by Amberley Publishing.
Printed in the UK.

Contents

Foreword

In consequence of the growing artfulness of man or of fish, or both, angling has come to be nearly as wide a field for the specialist as doctoring.

So begins Henry Cholmondeley-Pennell in his prefatory note to *Fishing: Salmon and Trout*. This is a revised edition of the original 1889 text, initially released with the object of producing a 'modern encyclopaedia to which the inexperienced man, who seeks guidance in the practice of the various British Sports and Pastimes, can turn for information.' Contained within are an eclectic collection of essays, anecdotes and guides written by some of the most prominent fly fishers of the day.

Henry Cholmondeley-Pennell (1837-1915), whose work makes up the bulk of this revised edition, was a renowned British naturalist, editor and occasional contributor to Punch known for publishing poetry and many volumes on coarse-fly and deep-sea fishing. The most notable amongst his titles *Badminton Library of Sports and Pastimes: Fishing. With contributions from other authors* and *The Modern Practical Angler: a complete guide to fly fishing, bottom-fishing & trolling*.

Major Traherne, widely regarded as being one of the most innovative fly tiers (and thus fishers) of all time, provides a seminal essay that draws heavily on accounts of his own experience in salmon fishing; and is 'induced to do so in the hope that it may be instructive to gentlemen who are inexperienced in the art, and also to a certain extent interesting to the angling public.' In his time, Major Traherne held a number of records for salmon catches in the late 1800's after fishing some of the best rivers in Ireland, Scotland, and Norway. In 1864 he caught 165 fish in fifteen days on the Namsen River in Norway; a record that still stands today and, it is said, is unlikely ever to be beaten.

Henry Ralph Francis (M.A.), who was educated at Brentford School and St. John's College, Cambridge before becoming Judge of the District Courts for the Northern District of New South Wales, presents an inspiring personal account of his angling exploits in 'Fly fishing For Trout and Grayling; or 'Fine and Far Off'. Soon after leaving Britain in 1858, he took a prominent role in the promotion of the National Mutual Life Association of Australia after its formation in 1869, at which he was later a director. Following deterioration in his health, he went on leave of absence without salary from 11 December, recuperating in Tasmania before returning to England in here he made his living writing about his hobby of fly fishing and Australia.

Elsewhere, the noted angler and fly fishing author Frederic Michael Halford (known also by the enigmatic pseudonym 'Detached Badger') writes with the British author and angling innovator on the relative merits and pitfalls of spinning and bait-Fishing for salmon and trout.

The Classic Guide to Fly Fishing is a re-mastered edition of one of the first ever 'manuals' of the sport, once considered to be a 'bible' for contemporary game fishermen.

The Editor

1

On Hooks, Tackle, and Fishing Gear

Ars est celare artem

The saying goes 'A good workman never finds fault with his tools,' but if by this it be meant that he can work as well with bad tools as with good, or produce equally satisfactory results, then it says little for the sagacity of those who made the proverb. It is especially in the more artistic descriptions of work that the importance of good tools is apparent. The fly-fisher is a workman in a highly artistic school, and, if he is to do his work thoroughly well, his tools, that is, his tackle – rods, hooks, lines, etc. must be of the very best.

There are still some 'happy hunting grounds' scattered throughout the British Islands on which 'the shadow of the rod or glitter of the bait' has but seldom fallen, small mountain lochs and moorland streams wherein fish are so guileless and simple in their habits that they will rise with delightful confidingness at the most rudimentary specimen of the artificial fly, offered to them in the least attractive manner. Such spots I have met with where it took weeks to impress upon its trout the melancholy fact that 'men were deceivers ever,' and where day after day the veriest bungler might fill his creel, and, for that matter, his pockets and his wading boots, with the unsuspecting fario, which came up gaily to his flies, three or four at a time, in blissful ignorance and apparently undiminished numbers. Such spots, however, are becoming rarer year by year. Even the most sequestered waters are now sought after, and generally found out, by the indefatigable tourist or the lessees of the sporting rights; and the inhabitants of such waters, however unwilling to be taught, are receiving the benefits of a sort of 'compulsory education 5 that is gradually opening their eyes to several little things going on in the wicked world around, with which it is to their advantage to be acquainted.

There are, of course, and probably always will be, degrees of advancement in 'trout knowledge.' The streams of Scotland and Ireland can never, in our time at least, be fished to the same extent as those of England, and especially of our southern counties. And it is very fortunate that it should be so, for many a man whose trout-fishing experience has been attained principally amongst the Scotch and Irish lakes and rivers, and who, not unnaturally, perhaps, considers himself a highly artistic performer, would be literally 'nowhere' if suddenly transferred with the same tackle and mode of fishing to the banks of the Itchen, the Test, or the Driffield Beck. Instead of finding comparatively few trout and those under fed, and predisposed to at least regard his lure with a friendly eye, he would see a water literally teeming with pampered and, therefore, highly fastidious, fish, whom his first appearance on the bank sent flying in a dozen different directions, and who, when his saturated nondescript did happen to pass over their noses, moved not a responsive muscle, and by their attitude conveyed the general idea of what Lord Randolph Churchill would call ineradicable superciliousness ...

But these are the products of 'centuries of civilisation,' and the ultimate outcome of the theory of the survival of the fittest.

In regard to salmon as well as trout the principle of the 'higher education' also holds good, although not quite in the same degree as in the extreme cases above referred to, inasmuch as such abodes of bliss in regard to salmon have unfortunately long ceased to exist cither in the British Islands or anywhere else within comfortable travelling range of Charing Cross. Every year the rent of a salmon river goes up; already it is but little less than that of a grouse moor, and what it may eventually come to, if we are not all ruined in the meantime, doth not yet appear.

Naturally, those who pay so dearly for their mile or half-mile of salmon water make up their minds to get the utmost possible out of it in the way of sport. The pools are assiduously fished whenever the water is in 'possible' condition. Often they are fished over two or three times a day, and sometimes by two or three different rods; and the consequence is that, at any rate after having been in the fresh water for some little time, and successfully resisted the first seductions thrown in his way, the salmon becomes much more shy and wary, and unlemptable by fly or bait unless presented in the most enticing fashion.

To this end the refinement of every part of the fishing gear is one of the principal, indeed, the chief means Like his 'star-stoled' cousin of the chalk streams, he scrutinises with a practised glance the object which is glittering before his eyes; and, however attractive may be the lure, if the 'line of invitation,' as someone calls it, with which it is presented be coarse or clumsy, or of flattened and, therefore, non-transparent gut, it is ten to one that he will 'decline with thanks.' In short, as 'fine and far off' might be taken, in the case of the trout fisher, as the password to success, so 'neatness and strength' should be the shibboleth of the salmon fisher.

I make no apology, therefore, for dwelling in some detail upon each item of the fly-fisher's equipment, and more especially on that which constitutes the alpha and omega of the whole matter, namely, the Hook.

HOOKS

Fish-hooks, as they have come down to us from antiquity, and are represented in bone or bronze in our museums and collections, appear to have been steadily improving from century to century, until in our own day the art of hook-manufacture, per se, may be considered to have reached its ultimate 'possibilities.'

Apart, however, from mere excellence of material and workmanship, the time is now apparently ripe for a sweeping change – so far, at least, as regards hooks used in fresh-water fishing – a change not of detail but of principle: the principle that is, of constructing the hook with a metal eye or loop, at the end of the shank by which the line is attached (knotted on) direct to the hook itself instead of by the old-fashioned process of gut lappings or gut loops. Consequently hook-making maybe regarded to this extent as at present in a transition state; and the angling world – the trout angler especially – is equally passing through a sort of interregnum between the old system and the new.

The realisation and completion of the eyed-hook principle was sure to come sooner or later, for an age which is 'nothing if not mechanical' could not but in the end rebel against the crude and unscientific method of procedure bequeathed to us by our ancestors, and adopted with scarcely a protest by generation after generation of succeeding anglers. The eyed-hook system was, in fact, the one great perfectionment in fly fishing that yet remained – in spite of previous incomplete or partially successful attempts – practically unaccomplished; and recognising the magnitude of the task, as well as the importance of its achievement, if achieved, I have for some years past thrown all my energies into the attempt, with results so far eminently encouraging.

The idea itself, of some sort of plan of attachment direct to the line by means of metal eyes or loops forming part of the hook, is by no means new. Mr H. S. Hall, whose charming contributions to these pages will be read with interest by all dry fly-fishers, was my immediate predecessor and pioneer on the somewhat thorny, though by no means untrodden, track; and long before him, both during the present century and still earlier, a perception of the advantages to be attained by a system of attaching the hook direct to the line has been present to the minds of several writers on angling and hook manufacturers, amongst whom Messrs Warner, of Redditch, are entitled to most honourable mention. But what I mean by saying that the perfecting of the idea yet remained to be accomplished is, that, however ingenious or admirable in themselves, these attempts and essays have failed in the one all- important respect of actually solving the problem; of solving it, that is, by producing such a system of hook-eyes and attachments as would obviate the various inherent difficulties and objections, and bring the invention into general practical use amongst anglers. Success – as I think it is now being perceived – depended, in fact, quite as much on the perfect' simplicity and strength of the knot by which the attachment is to be made as on the metal eye or loop itself.

This 'loop' might, theoretically, be either turned upwards or downwards, or 'needle-eyed' – that is, drilled perpendicularly through the end of the hook-shank like the eye of a needle; and in the first issue of these volumes each system was fully discussed, with the arguments pro and con. At present, however, it would appear – so far, at least, as the tackle makers may be supposed to feel the pulse of the angling and fly fishing world – that the arguments adduced in the earlier issues of this book, or other causes, have so far influenced public opinion in the matter that – firstly – eyed hooks are rapidly coming into more general use, primarily amongst trout-fishers; and – secondly – that only my own patterns of hooks with the eyes turned down enjoy any considerable or increasing popularity. I shall therefore, in the present revised edition, omit as far as maybe reference to argumentative or controversial matters, now possessing little beyond an 'academical' interest, and limit the scope of the following pages to explaining my own eyed-hook system in its most recent development, as applicable both to salmon and trout flies.

TO BEGIN WITH SALMON FLIES

Although in the case of the salmon fly – when dressed, that is, in the more ordinary way with a gut loop – the paramount and self-evident advantages for the eyed-hook principle that may be claimed in the case of the trout fly do not present themselves, yet there are several points, and those not unimportant ones, in which the metal-eyed salmon hook offers a distinct advance over 'lapped-on' hooks.

Take, for instance, probably the most obvious point, the question of durability. The life of the old-fashioned salmon fly, whether tied on a strand of gut or on a gut loop, is measured by that of the waxed lapping that binds the gut or gut loop to the hook-shank – the period, in other words, during which the wax retains its adhesiveness; and this, it is well known, it does not do for more than a limited – and, moreover, an uncertainly limited – time. The hook and the rest of the fly, on the contrary, when preserved from moth and rust, are for practical purposes indestructible, and if either should happen to give out the fact is easily discovered, and does not in its discovery entail losing the best fish, perhaps, of the season. The pleasure of possessing and keeping up a good stock of salmon flies is sadly alloyed by the reflection that after a few years prudence would counsel their being consigned to the nearest dust-hole.

Again, as regards the comparative neatness of the two systems, the verdict would probably be in favour of the metal eye, although the difference is but trifling.

There are no disadvantages of any kind that I am aware of as a set-off to the foregoing advantages, and therefore, weighing impartially the two systems – gut loops v. metal loops – it would seem that the balance inclines in favour of the latter. As observed, however, the fact that loops of some sort are in practice already very general in salmon flies, makes the question of less immediately critical importance to the salmon-fisher than to the trout-fisher, in whose case the change from lapped-on flies to flies attached by an eyed hook is nothing less than a revolution ... But to finish first with the subject of salmon hooks.

In the original design of the turn-down eyed salmon hook, it was alleged – no doubt with some show of reason – that, from imperfections almost necessarily incident to manufacture on a large scale, the pointed ends of the taper forming the loop were occasionally left so sharp, or incompletely 'closed' as to fray the gut of the attaching knot at this point; and in my newest patterns it will be seen this is effectually provided against by the tapered end of the wire, forming the eye or loop, being re-turned up the shank for some not inconsiderable distance. This gives a perfectly smooth and even surface of metal eye for the gut to work against, and its shape offers at the same time special conveniences to the fly-dresser.

The point of importance to be recollected in dressing flies on these hooks, whether for salmon or trout, is that the 'neck,' between the head of the fly and the loop, should be left clear to receive the gut.

It has been observed that my old turn-down eyed patterns of hooks, both salmon and trout, appear to be steadily pushing all other forms of eyes and loops out of the field – and this notwithstanding two very decided blemishes. One defect, so far as salmon hooks are concerned, has just been described, with its remedy; the other was inherent in the principle not only of my own turn-down eyed patterns, but in a still greater degree in the older models of hooks with eyes turned up. The defect is – or rather was – that the line did not, and could not, occupy a plane absolutely level with that of the hook-shank.

In the turn-down eyed hook the inaccuracy was of course reversed. The deflection was considerably less than that above illustrated; still it was a decided defect – one of its results being (in the case of my own hooks) to unduly narrow the 'gape' of the hook, and, in the turn up eyed hooks, to unduly widen it. That this must inevitably be the case, a glance at the last diagram will show.

To overcome the difficulty, I tried many experiments – indeed, I began experimenting on my own hooks almost as soon as the pages containing their original patterns were published – 1885, I think. It was really, however, a new principle, rather than a new pattern, that was wanted; and I only discovered what I was in search of after a wearisome succession of 'modified successes,' and an accumulation of abortive 'notions,' taking form in all unimaginable shapes of twisted and contorted steel. However, at last I did discover it, and having committed the folly of 'publishing' my old turndown eyed hook before getting it protected, I took the new one straight away to the Patent Office, and subsequently put the model into the hands of Messrs Wm. Bartleet & Sons, of Abbey Mills, Redditch, who soon turned out a sufficient quantity to try practical conclusions with, the results of practice fully bearing out the deductions of theory.

The principle embodied in the new hooks is, in effect, the bending of the shank-end first up and then down, into something like two sides, so to speak, of a triangle, of which one side is formed by the hook-eye, and the other by the turned-up end of the extremity of the hook-shank .The effect of this is to bring the line exactly into a plane with the hook-shank, whilst at the same time retaining all the advantages, in neatness and facility of attachment, etc., of the original turndown eye, together stick the full natural gape of the hook bend – and no more.

The new patent I have only hitherto had applied to my own special bends of hooks – the 'Pennell-Limerick' and 'Pennell-Sneck' bends (see illustrations); but it is, of course, equally applicable to all the other hook-bends of commerce, several of which are shown in the engraving a page or two on. Some or all of these will, I hope, be obtainable at the tackle shops before this volume is issued. To prevent fraud and to ensure the *bona fides* of the hooks sold as mine – many spurious and defective imitations of my

New Patent Salmon Hook with Up-Turn Shank and Down-Turned Eye.

earlier hook having, I am sorry to say, been made by unauthorised firms – I have also obtained a 'trade-mark,' and arranged that every packet of the hooks shall bear such trade-mark with my signature, and so affixed to each packet that it cannot be opened without the label being torn or destroyed.

Of the foregoing hooks all the larger sizes, intended primarily for salmon and grilse flies, from No. 8 upwards, 'New' scale (No. 7 upwards, 'Old' scale), are made with the wire of the loop or eye 're-turned' up the shank, as already explained. Sizes 8 to 10 'new' scale (7 to 5 'old' scale), inclusive, are made both with and without the re-turned eyes, so as to suit either light or heavy fishing; and from No. 8 'new' scale (No. 7 'old' scale), inclusive, and upwards, the hooks are made double as well as single.

Eventually, no doubt, all the smaller sizes will be manufactured both single and double, as the increase in the use of small double hooks for many descriptions of flies, including ordinary trout flies, where no one would formerly have thought of using them, is another comparatively recent advance in the science of fish-hooks. I have no doubt whatever that, especially for the smaller sizes of salmon hooks, the double pattern has considerable advantages, and I hear that on some rivers, the Tweed, for example, they are completely driving the single hooks off the water. It is obvious, indeed, that they greatly increase the chance both of hooking and of holding a fish; and against the small additional weight, which may be a slight inconvenience, perhaps, in casting, is to be set the fact that the extra weight has the effect of making the fly swim somewhat deeper, which in salmon-fishing is a generally desirable result.

The only correct mode of attaching salmon and grilse hooks with re-turned eyes, as well as the double hooks – in both of which the eye is made extra large for the purpose – is by the 'in-and-out' fastening, secured with a slip knot, double or single, here referred to as the 'slip-knot' attachment.

Although a 'single slip' knot is all that will usually be found actually necessary, especially with the smaller-sized grilse

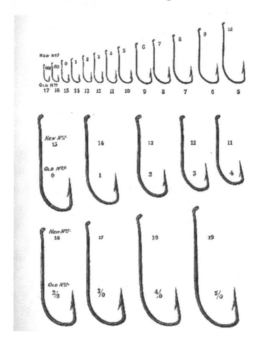

'Pennell-Limerick' Hooks, New Pattern with Turn-Down Eyes and Up-Turned Shanks

hooks, yet even in this case – and still more in that of the larger-sized salmon hooks – a 'double,' instead of a 'single,' slip knot makes 'assurance doubly sure.' Indeed, I myself almost invariably use the double slip knot, and recommend its adoption for all hooks of a size too large, or with eyes too large for the 'Jain Knot' attachment (hereinafter described) – and for all hooks with 're-turned' eyes. The 'double slip' (figured in the last cut) makes, when artistically tied on a large hook, a fastening quite as neat as, if not, indeed, actually neater than, the single slip; and is in many ways preferable. The following verbal instructions may perhaps assist the tyro, in attaching his casting line to a turn-down eyed salmon hook for the first time.

Take the hook by the bend between the finger and thumb of the left hand, with the eye turned downwards (in the position shown in the diagrams; then – the gut being first thoroughly well soaked – push the end, with a couple of inches, down through the eye, B, towards the point of the hook; then pass it round over the shank of the hook, and again, from the opposite side, downwards through the eye in a direction away from the hook-point. [The gut end and the central link will now be lying parallel] Make the double- (or single-) slip knot, A, round the central link, C, and pull the said knot itself perfectly tight; then draw the loop back until the knot, A, presses tightly into and against the metal eye of the hook, B, where hold it firmly with the fore-finger and thumb-nail of the left hand, whilst with the right hand – and 'humouring' the gut in the process, so as to clear the hackles, etc ... The central link is drawn tight, thus taking in the 'slack' of 'the knot. When finished, cut the superfluous gut end off nearly close.

To tie a double slip knot: first make a single slip knot, A, and, before drawing close, pass the gut end, B, a second time round the central link, C, and then again through the C loop, A when the knot will be like A in the diagram of double slip knot. To complete it, pull the end of the gut, B – gradually, and very tightly – straight away: in a line, that is, with the central link, C.

The slip knot is also the best for attaching the casting line to flies with gut loops, and should be tied in the same manner as that described for a turn-down eyed hook.

The same knot, for both gut or metal loops, may also be produced in another manner – when the loop is large enough – viz., by tying at the end of the casting line (separate from the hook) a 'noose,' with a slip knot (drawn tight), and afterwards passing from above, through the loop or eye, the 'apex' of the noose thus formed. The noose is then opened out and passed

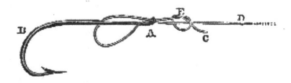

Turn-Down Eyed Salmon Fly Attached by Slip Knot.

upwards over the wholes fly, 'lasso-wise'; the knot is drawn to its place in the loop as already described, and the 'slack' taken in.

There is a mode of attaching casting lines to gut-looped salmon flies very commonly employed on account of its facility of manipulation, and the saving of trouble and time in changing flies. In consists in tying a knot at the end of the gut, and then passing the knotted end first through the loop from below, and, after giving it one turn round under the loop, finally passing the knotted end under the central link, and drawing the latter tight. It is in fact a 'jam knot' plus the knot at the end of the line. Excellently well as this knot answers for hooks of the smaller sizes with eyes turned down, as hereafter described, it does not and never can make a thoroughly 'ship-shape' knot for a salmon fly, inasmuch as the latter when thus attached invariably hangs – and therefore, of course swims – out of the horizontal: in other words, head downwards. If, on the contrary, the gut is passed through the loop from above and the turn taken over the loop, an opposite but equally inelegant effect is produced; the fly 'cocks up,' and might swim in almost any position conceivable, except the horizontal. There are several variations of this fastening; but I cannot say that I ever met with one entirely satisfactory for salmon flies. The best knot for gut-looped flies, or for plain hooks with gut loops, twisted or single, is, 'far and away,' that already recommended – the slip knot.

The 'Pennell-Limerick bend hooks,' before figured, p. 11, are also made plain (as shown over leaf) for the convenience of those who may still prefer the old 'lapping-on' system.

The bend of all these hooks, which is a variation of existing recognised bends, is one that I think will commend itself to the practised eye without much argument. The bend has been designed to combine in a mechanical form the three great requisites of penetration, holding power, and 'flotation.' The last-named, which sounds rather Irish, is a question of the general contour of the shank. It will be seen in the diagrams that the hook shank itself – or rather that part of it on which the fly is tied – is very nearly straight, whilst in the Limerick bend the shank is commonly slightly more curved, or, as it is termed, hog-backed, which when exaggerated, as it frequently is in the so-called Limerick hooks, supplied by the fly-tiers, has the effect of preventing the fly swimming or floating perfectly straight, and, indeed, when the stream is strong, an excessive 'hog-backedness' will not unfrequently cause it actually to spin.

It may be added that, as the greatest strain is always borne by the top angle of the bend, such angle should be formed, not 'square,' but in the strongest shape known to mechanics, viz., a curve (or the segment of a circle) sharper or more gradual according to the other conditions desiderated.

If it should appear that I am attaching undue importance to minute details, let it be borne in mind that 'the whole art and paraphernalia of angling have for their objects, first, to hook fish, and, secondly, to keep them hooked.' The difference in the penetrating powers alone of different bends of hooks is something enormous; between the extremes of goodness and badness (I am not speaking now of 'monstrosities') it amounts to certainly not less than a hundred per cent.

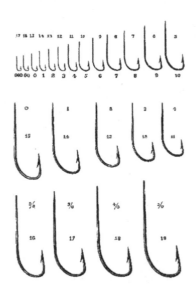

'Pennell-Limerick' Bend,
Tapered Shanks.

TROUT HOOKS

Eyed Hooks for trout flies, and the general idea of attaching them to the end of the casting line direct, are not, as already pointed out, in any correct sense of the term novelties, eyed hooks having been alluded to as early as Hawker's edition of 'Walton's Angler,' temp. 1760. No great attention, however, appears to have been paid to the subject of Eyed Trout-hooks until comparatively recent times, when the question – confined, at the particular period to which I am referring, to turn-up eyes – was ventilated at considerable length in the columns of the *Field* and the *Fishing Gazette* by Mr Hall. This was followed in the latter journal by a lively controversy on 'needle-eyed' hooks, initiated by myself; and finally I invented, and published, the turn-down eyed hook, of which so much has since been written, for and against, by partisans of the old and the new schools.

I have already explained why I feel released from the necessity of reprinting here the arguments *pro* and *con* these various systems – viz., that to judge by the success of my own turn-down eyed hooks, and the opinions of fly-fishers and tackle makers, so far as I am able to gather them, that system is in rapid course of superseding all others. If this is the case with the original imperfect patterns, how much more likely is it to be so now, when, by the introduction of the up-turned shank, the hook has been, so to speak, perfected ...

To return, therefore, to my text.

The considerations already adduced in regard to the proper form of a large salmon hook hold good, *caeris paribus*, and with increased cogency, in the case of a small trout hook, where of course the mechanical difficulties, first of hooking, and secondly of keeping hooked, are enormously increased. They are increased, in fact, exactly in the ratio of the size of the hook as compared with the size of the fish's mouth ... a number 000 is clearly much smaller in proportion to the mouth of a large trout than a number 17 or 18 is to the mouth of a well-grown salmon. The exact calculation I leave to the curious in figures. My system of eyed hooks is, however, applicable to all the ordinary hook-bends without exception, so that those who prefer one or the other of them to mine can reject the pattern ad yet adopt the principle.

The fly-fisher who is sufficiently interested in the subject of hooks to read this chapter at all will, I assume, have read the preceding pages which deal, under the head of salmon-hooks, with what I may call the 'natural theory' of my system. I need not, therefore, go again over the same ground. It may, nevertheless, be well to illustrate, on a smaller scale, more appropriate to trout-flies, the very important question of over- and under-draft in these hooks.

The general hanges in construction between the old and new forms of the hook will perhaps be most readily understood by contrasting some of the smaller sizes of each, including the sneck-bend form in which the patent is also manufactured of the sizes shown.

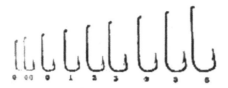

Fig. 1. Original Turn-Down Eyed Hook, with draft-line below true plane of hook-shank; Fig. 2. Turn-Eyed Pattern , with draft-line above plane; Fig. 3. New Bent Up-Turn Shank and turn-down eyed hook – correct draft-line.

Old Pattern of Turn-Down Eyed 'Pennell-Sneck' Hooks and New Pattern Ditto with Up-Turn Shank.

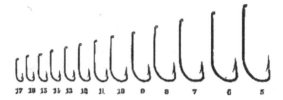

Old Pattern of Turn-Down Eyed 'Pennell-Limerick Hooks.

New Pattern Ditto with Up-Turn Shank.

I have used both bends – the Limerick and the Sneck – with nearly equal success, but my inclination is rather to prefer the sneck pattern for small river flies, and also for lake brown-trout flies; and the Limerick for anything larger, including sea-trout flies, and of course salmon flies.

The following diagrams show the appearance of the upturn shank and turn-down eye as applied to four of the most ordinary bends of commerce.

Round Bend, Kirby, Limerick Sneck Hooks

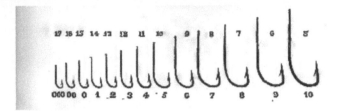

'Pennell-Limerick' Hooks with Plain Shank.

'Pennell-Sneck' Hooks with Plain Shank.

It may, perhaps, be well for convenience of reference to repeat here the smaller sizes of Limerick hooks with plain shanks, 'un-eyed' (upper figures, 'old' or 'Redditch' scale; lower figures, 'new' scale), as well as the tapered-shank sneck- bend hooks, which latter are made with points both straight and 'twisted,' or 'snecked.'

The diagrams represent two lake flies tied on the two different bends, – that on the sneck bend the 'Hackle Red' for brown trout, and that on the Limerick the 'Hackle Claret' for sea-trout. The formulas for dressing these, with some other patterns of my Hackle flies for sea- and brown-trout, which I have found very successful, are given further on.

Lake Flies Dressed on Patent Eyed Hooks with Up-Turned Shank.

A small stream trout fly ('Furnace brown') on a sneck-bend is also figured.

The great thing in dressing all flies on these eyed hooks is to leave clear the 'neck,' as shown in the diagrams, to receive the jam knot. The length of the hook-shank is specially designed to allow of this.

The great advantage – if I may venture so to speak of my own system – possessed by the turn-down eyed hook over all other forms of hooks whatsoever with eyes or loops, is the supreme simplicity and rapidity of its attachment to, and disengagement from the line by means of the Jam Knot. In from 10 to 15 seconds one fly can be taken off and another substituted; and that with unfailing certainty and malgre whatever the elements may operate to the contrary.

The engraving below – enlarged for the sake of readier illustration – exemplifies the principle of the Jam Knot attachment before the line is drawn tight – the tightening, of course, producing the 'jam.'

'Furnace Brown' Dressed on a Patent Sneck-Bend Up-Turn Shank Eyed Hook.

Principle of the Jam Knot on a Bare Hook, Magnified.

In practice the jam knot is produced 'automatically,' and is so perfectly simple, and quick in manipulation that, as I say, I can tie it complete in 15 seconds. The veriest tyro ought to master its principle at the first attempt, and after a few essays tie it by the water-side almost as rapidly as I can myself.

The fly being held in the left hand with the metal eye (A) turned upwards, 3 or 4 inches of the gut line are pushed through it from below. The fly is then 'let go' and a slip knot (C) made with the gut-end (C), round the line (D). [This is the point at which the process is seen in the cut.] The slip knot is not drawn quite tight, but left as shown – just open enough to pass comfortably over the metal eye. The fly is now taken again with the left hand, and the line pulled steadily by the right, until – aided when need be by the thumb and finger – the noose of the slip knot passes over the metal eye of the hook, when, on the line being pulled tight, the jam knot forms itself; and the process is completed by cutting off the waste gut-end 1 to within ½ or ¼ of an inch, according to the size of the fly and fineness of the gut. The finer the gut the longer should be the end left over.

There is no advantage with the jam knot in cutting off the gut too close, as the free gut-end which should be left over mingles naturally with the hackles of the fly. After cutting off the waste gut it is convenient to nip the free end down with the thumb nail in the direction of the hook-bend. This may be repeated whenever the flies are examined, which, of course – as with ordinary gut-flies – they should be at intervals, to see that the gut has not frayed at all at the head, and also that the free end has not by any accident been drawn in or shortened to the 'unsafe' point.

During the last few years, including the present season, 1889, I have caught, I should say, at least a thousand white and brown trout, weighing from a few ounces up to three or four lbs., in both stream and loch, with flies dressed on the turn-down eyed hook, and attached by the jam knot – sometimes on traces fine even to the fineness of 'Bullmer's gossamer gut'

– and I cannot call to mind a single instance in which the knot has been proved to have failed. Moreover (a hint to the novice) flies thus attached very rarely flick off.

With small flies the simplest way, when the gut becomes frayed at the head by wear and tear, is to cut or break the fly off close, disengage the waste end from the eye of the hook, and re-knot. With larger flies and stout gut the jam can generally be loosened by merely pushing the gut backwards through the eye, but this is a matter of unimportance, as in either case the operation is only one of a few seconds.

The perfecting of the jam knot for the trout-fly was the ingenious discovery of Mr Alexander J. Campbell, and without it I do not hesitate to say that the general acceptance of the system of turn-down eyed hooks which I am now sanguine enough to hope for, could never have been anticipated. The inconvenience – trifling though it was in comparison with previous methods of attaching eyed hooks – of tying the jam knot in the presence of the fly-wings and hackles, was originally one of the serious obstacles to be overcome. This 'knotting-on difficulty' has, in fact, hitherto had a large share in preventing the adoption of the eyed-hook principle.

Now, however, that this difficulty has been effectually overcome, and a perfect form of attachment as well as a perfect hook are within the reach of fly-fishers, the result can hardly be doubtful. Indeed, the advantages of attaching the fly direct to the casting-line are so obvious, and the disadvantages of the old lapped-on gut system so self-evident, that only one result could well follow. Amongst these disadvantages it may be instanced

That when once the 'gut hook' artificial fly gets 'worn at the head' – which in actual work very soon occurs – it becomes thenceforth worthless.

And when another fly is substituted, the gut must be soaked first (in practice generally in the saliva of the mouth) to enable it to be properly knotted on. If this soaking, or sucking, be not thoroughly done the fly will most likely whip off.

But even after properly knotting the two gut links together, it is ten to one that the link on which the fly or hook is lapped does not correspond with that at the end of the line: it is too thick, or too thin; too dark, or too light. From this results a linear disfigurement, or an inharmoniousness of tint (or both), at the very point where a perfect taper and complete uniformity of colour are of vital consequence.

These are some of the most salient defects of the system, almost universally adopted until the last few years, of lapping on hooks and flies to separate strands of gut. Of minor, but still serious drawbacks, must be reckoned the difficulty of carrying about a sufficient supply of 'gut hooks' – or still more of flies – of all needful sizes, and the destructive effects of time upon the contents of the 'store box.' Apart from 'moth,' this happens partly owing to the 'rotting' of the gut at the point of contact with the steel hook shank, and partly to the desiccation (drying up) of the wax on the lapping by which the gut is attached.

And all these defects – defects inherent in the principle of lapped-on hooks, and which cannot be gainsaid – are at once overcome by the new eyed-hook system.

It is to that system, then, to which I refer when I say that by it all the disadvantages attaching either to the artificial fly or plain hook lapped on separate strands of gut are entirely got rid of.

By knotting on the fly or hook direct to the main line ('gut-trace,' 'collar,' 'casting-line,' 'bottom-line,' 'foot-line') the fly or hook that has become worn at the head can be removed, and in a few seconds re-attached to the same already well-soaked, well-tapered, and evenly tinted line; thereafter remaining as serviceable as ever.

The minor drawbacks alluded to of the old system are also obviated by the new, as the necessary selection of flies and hooks can be kept in stock for years without any fear of deterioration. The economy in the matter of space, both in the stock-box and fly-book, is, moreover, considerable. As many flies or hooks as are required for a day's fishing could be carried, I might almost say, in the waistcoat pocket.

Published testimonies to the success of the eyed-hook principle generally are too numerous to attempt even to give a summary of them all here. Mr H. S. Hall, one of our very best clear stream fly-fishers, who has lately written an ably-practical essay on the 'Dry Fly,' has, it is well known, given his entire adhesion to eyed hooks, with which, indeed, his name has been long identified. Mr Frederic M. Halford, author of the lately published charming monograph on 'Floating Flies and how to dress them,' and also of a subsequent exhaustive treatise on 'Dry Fly fishing,' is another apostle of the new cult. His first chapter is devoted to eyed hooks, and the opening sentence runs thus:

> But before many years are passed the old-fashioned fly, dressed on a hook attached to a length of gut, will be practically obsolete, the advantages of the eyed hook being so manifest that even the most conservative adherents of the old school must, in time, be imbued with this most salutary reform.

After enumerating several of the more obvious advantages already noticed, Mr Halford continues:

> Flies dressed on eyed hooks float better and with less drying than those constructed on the old system... Another and, in my opinion, paramount benefit is, that at the very earliest symptom of weakness at the point of juncture of the head of the fly and gut (the point at which the maximum wear and tear takes place) it is only necessary in the case of the eyed fly to break it off and tie on afresh, sacrificing at most a couple of inches of the fine end of the cast; while in the case of the hook on gut, the fly has become absolutely useless and beyond repair. It must also be remembered that with eyed hooks the angler can use gut as coarse or as fine as he may fancy for the particular day, while with flies on gut he would require to have each pattern dressed on two or three different thicknesses.

Of course books on Fishing (I do not refer to catch-penny productions, or to trade circulars) do not appear every day, or every year, and those I have quoted from are, so far as I know, the most recent, and therefore authoritative, on subjects the importance of which has only lately begun to be recognised.

CASTING LINES

Next to the fly and its etceteras comes the Casting Line, involving matters connected with the selection, knotting, twisting, staining, etc ... of gut. The best gut is the longest and roundest, and the most transparent; an observation which applies equally to salmon and trout gut – natural and drawn. For practical purposes these desiderata must be considered in conjunction with, if not, indeed, made subordinate to, the question of the fineness or strength of the gut in proportion to the fishing for which it is to be used. To get salmon gut which fulfils all the conditions pointed out is becoming yearly a matter of greater difficulty, and, I might almost say, of favour.

A perfect hank of salmon gut can only be obtained, as a rule, by picking the strands out of a number of other hanks, which, of course, makes these considerably less valuable. Sixpence a strand – I have known a shilling a strand paid – for picked salmon gut is not at all an unusual or, indeed, unreasonable price, having regard to the difficulty of obtaining gut of really superior quality, and the all-important part it plays in a sport which, if not quite so expensive as deer stalking or grouse driving, is certainly becoming rapidly a luxury that only rich men can hope to enjoy. As the rent of a salmon river, to say nothing of incidental expenses, may probably be reckoned at seldom less than three figures, it is really the soundest economy to begrudge no expense connected with the tackle, rod, etc ..., upon which the sport obtained for all this outlay depends. Moreover, as regards gut, I believe that the best, and, consequently, the most expensive, is, in the long run, actually the most economical if proper care be taken of it. A thoroughly well-made casting line of carefully picked salmon gut will outlast three or four made of inferior strands, and during all its 'lifetime' will be a source of satisfaction. The breaking dead weight strain of a strand of the stoutest salmon gut, round, smooth, and perfect in every respect, ought not to be less than somewhere between fifteen and eighteen pounds.

Why in the case of salmon gut, as in that of all other commodities, the demand does not produce the supply, it is difficult to see. Caterpillars ought to be easily cultivated one would say. Think of the number of strands which might be produced by the inhabitants of a single mulberry tree!

> Millions of spinning worms That in their green shops weave
> the smooth-haired silk.

I stated to be frequently paid in Marseilles – this gut being, it appears, principally exported to Constantinople. Some samples of the 1884 crop, tested by my friend Mr R. B. Marston, broke at a dead strain of seventeen pounds. A writer under the signature of 'Creel,' mentions that some thirty years ago there could be found in the market a superior class of salmon gut now said to be unprocurable owing to the total extinction of the silkworm that produced it. 'Since this time,' he says, 'we have more than once been informed that a new breed of silkworm has been raised and encouraged in the South of France, introduced from Japan, possessing all the features of the former fine and strong gut which from its absence has caused the lament of many a veteran salmon fisher.'

In the selection of gut, aim first, as Chitty says, in his 'Fly Fisher's Text-book,' 'at that which is perfectly round,' to which end the best assistance the eye can receive is from the thumb and forefinger, between which the gut should be rolled quickly; if it is not round but flat, the defect by this process will be at once discovered. Next to roundness, colourlessness and transparency are the two points of most importance; and last – though, as some fishermen will perhaps suggest, not least – comes the question of length. Chitty, above named, gives for salmon gut – 'the part used' – 'sixteen to eighteen inches at least.' I can only say – I wish we may get it! In these degenerate days ten to twelve inches would be nearer the ordinary attainable mark, and for trout gut an inch or two more, say thirteen to fourteen, or, in exceptionally good strands, fifteen inches.

'Drawn gut,' as it is called, is simply gut that has been artificially scraped or fined down by being 'drawn' through a hole of a certain gauge or measure. For this purpose a steel plate is used having several holes or gauges diminishing gradually in size, and the 'face edges' of which are quite sharp. The gut is put through the holes in succession beginning at the largest, and ending with the smallest, when it has of course become of the desired fineness. The appearance of the gut after undergoing this process is not, however, so clean and transparent as the undoctored material, and though it looks beautifully fine – and, indeed, is so – it commonly frays and wears out very rapidly when exposed to moisture or friction of any sort. Drawn gut is, however, extensively used for many of the finer sorts of fishing, both with fly and bait. For my own part I prefer to pay almost any price, so to speak, for the natural gut whenever it can be obtained of the requisite fineness. This, however, is not always.

KNOTTING

There is a kind of 'endless' knot with which the casting lines prepared in some tackle shops are joined that seems for ordinary purposes to be about perfection; but how this knot is tied is a trade secret which I have failed to find out. Decidedly the best as well as the simplest knot 'open to the public' and one which is equally applicable to the finest and the strongest gut, is what is known as the single (and double) fisherman's

Fig. 1. Single Fisherman's Knot

knot (sometimes called 'water knot'), varied in the case of salmon gut, for heavy work, in the way described presently.

The gut having been thoroughly well soaked beforehand (in tepid water best) – which is, of course, a *sine qua non* in all gut knottings – the two ends of gut, A, A, are laid parallel to each other, being held in that position between the first finger and thumb of the left hand in the position in which they are to be joined. A half-hitch knot, it, is, is, is then made by the right hand with the end of each strand alternately round the strand of the other, and each separately drawn tight, the two separate halves of the knot being finally drawn closely together and the ends cut off.

It has been pointed out that the single fisherman's knot – varied as I have described in the case of salmon lines – is all that is required for any description of gut knotting. I should, perhaps, however, make an exception to this statement. In the case of drawn gut, and also in natural gut of exceptional fineness, the extreme limpness of the strands makes the single fisherman's knot very liable to 'draw' if the ends are cut at all close, as they should be on the score of neatness. In such cases it is, therefore, better to make the knot with two double, instead of two single, half-hitches; the end, that is, with which each half-knot is tied is passed twice instead of once round the central link and through the loop, in the manner shown in the engraving.

This is the 'double' fisherman's knot. With very fine gut the increase in the size of the knot is so small as not to be worth considering, whilst the increase of strength obtained is of importance.

Fig. 2. Double Fisherman's knot.

Except for salmon fishing, if a drop-fly is used it is not a bad plan to pass the end of the gut-link of the fly between the two strands of the joining gut and between the two halves of the knot before drawing the latter close. The drop-fly will then stand out at right angles to the casting line, a result which it is desirable to attain. A single knot tied in the link of the drop fly at the required distance outside the knot in the casting fine prevents its slipping.

Another and still simpler attachment for the drop-fly, which in practice I usually adopt as being much the quickest, is, with a double half-hitch (k of the knot in fig. 2), to knot on the drop-fly – fly uppermost – to the casting line (fig. 5). On this knot being pulled tight, and slipped down as far as the next juncture on the line, it will be found to answer exceedingly well, although the point of junction is one which will always have to be carefully looked at from time to time, as the friction of the drop-fly knot is apt to fray away the link to which it is attached. For salmon fishing I never myself use a second fly, unless by any chance the river or lake I am fishing be also tenanted by white trout, and then, of course, the fly is a comparatively small one, for which the last-named attachment, fig. 5, will answer every purpose; or slightly better, perhaps, the fly may be attached above one of the knots with a loop, as shown in fig. 6; or, stronger still, as in fig. 7, an attachment which also gives the maximum stand-out-at-right- angle inclination to the fly, and the principle of which, as applied to casting lines with the ordinary splice, fig. 8.

Nothing can well be more clumsy than the knots usually employed in joining the strands of a salmon casting line, and their inefficiency in the matter of strength is on a par with their unsightliness. In the *Book of the Pike*, 1865, I gave diagrams and explanations of the buffer knot above referred to, in which the objectionable features of the old method of splicing are got rid of, whilst a very great additional strength is obtained. To tie it lay the two strands side by side and proceed in exactly the same manner as already described for tying the single fisherman's knot, with the exception of the final drawing together of the two separate half-hitches. Instead of drawing these two half-knots together and lapping down the ends on the outside, as was the old manner, draw the knots only to within about three-sixteenths or one-eighth of an inch of each other, as shown in the engraving at A, and lap between them with light waxed silk, or, still more artistic, with very fine (soaked) gut. This 'between lapping' relieves the knot itself of half its duty, and on any sudden jerk, such as striking, acts as a sort of 'buffer' to receive and distribute the strain. Tied in the old-fashioned way I find that, on applying a steady pull, a salmon gut casting line breaks almost invariably at the knot.

Drop Fly Attachments for Trout Casting Lines.

Fig. 6.; Fig. 8.; Fig. 7.

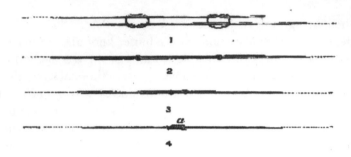

Fig. 9. The Buffer Knot for Salmon Gut.

Tied in the manner I suggest it will probably break at any other point in preference.

Major Traherne, whose almost unequalled experience as a salmon fisher entitles his opinion to the utmost weight, wrote as follows on the buffer knot for salmon casting lines:

Not long ago I fondly imagined I had invented a plan for untying the links of a casting line without knots, and was on my way to the *Fishing Gazette* office to unfold my secret. My friend Mr. Cholmondeley-Pennell happened to accompany me on a different business, and on my letting him know what mine was turned round and said, 'My dear fellow, I am very sorry for you, but I brought that out years ago in the "Modern Practical Angler,"' and as we were passing Farlow's shop at the time he took me in and soon convinced me that he was right, and that his principle and mine are the same, although differently carried out. Therefore, although I can lay no claim to be the inventor of the 'buffer knot,' I can honestly say that I had never seen or heard of it before.

It is impossible to invent a better method of fastening gut together than that which makes the fastening the strongest instead of the weakest part of the casting line, and it is surprising to me that this method has not been adopted.

I am glad to see that this knot *is* at last being adopted, after being some twenty years before the angling public; and though 'I say it that should not say it,' Major Traherne's frank testimony in favour of its superiority as applied to extra stout salmon casting lines (or for gut spinning traces where extra strength is required) does not go at all beyond the fact. If salmon fishers reading this chapter acquire nothing in return but the knowledge of this one apparently trifling piece of information, their time will not have been wasted.

The difference between my original knot, as above described, and the variation of it alluded to by Major Traherne is very trifling; such as it is, however, I am of opinion that as regards neatness and simplicity of manipulation my knot is distinctly preferable, and I have lately had letters from Major Traherne saying that he has come to the same conclusion.

Except for salmon, and then not when they run decidedly small, no lapping of any sort is required in any part of the casting line. The lapping that used to be applied at the tackle shops gives no additional strength whatsoever, whilst the effect is to exaggerate that which must always be a disfigurement.

For casting lines of all kinds single gut, tapered, is the only material that I ever think of employing, and I find it quite strong enough when obtained of the best quality. Between the top of the casting line and bottom of the reel-line, however, it will generally be found convenient – always in the case of salmon lines – to interpose a couple of feet or so of some thicker medium, and for this purpose twisted tapered gut 'points,' as they are called, with the lengths neatly spliced (not knotted) together, can now be obtained. The old-fashioned 'points' made in separate lengths, and joined with a huge unsightly knot, are distinctly objectionable.

This twisted 'intermediary' materially increases, I think, the ease and nicety of the cast in the case of both trout and salmon lines. . The thick end of the twisted point should be neatly lapped on to the end of the reel-line, and is most conveniently terminated by a knot, as small as may be, which is attached to the loop of the gut casting line by a sort of modified 'jam,' readily admitting of detachment. For very light trout or grayling fishing, a few strands of stout salmon gut, tapered., may be substituted for the twisted point, the casting line being knotted on by the ordinary fisherman's knot, and cut apart at the end of the day, or – where an extra finely tapered reel-line is employed – both gut and twist may be dispensed with.

STAINING

All sorts of stains are recorded by different authors and adopted by different fishermen according to individual taste and fancy. I used personally to fancy what is known as the red water stain for rivers where the water took a darkish or porter-coloured tint after a fresh, and for 'white' waters a light bluish or cloud colour. I am by no means clear, however, that in the case of the fly-fisher there is any sufficient warranty for this nicety of refinement, if, indeed, it be a refinement at all in the proper sense of the word. When we see a porter-coloured water we forget that we are looking down from above, whilst the fish we wish to catch is, in all probability, looking up from below, and that our line being 'flotant' is but a few inches below the surface of the water. The result is that when he comes up to take the fly the stratum of water interposed between the gut and the sky is really, when viewed by the human eye at any rate, almost colourless. It is the depth of water which produces the depth of colour. The same thing again applies to the clear streams which after a flood become merely slightly thickened with mud and never take the red or bog-water stain under any circumstances.

In order as far as might be to satisfy my own mind as to what practically was the best stain, I arranged an experiment in which the actual conditions of the floating line were as nearly as possible reproduced – substituting my own eye for that of the fish. A glass tank was obtained with a glass bottom, and I found that with about three inches of water in it the difference between water stained with tea or coffee to about the same extent as the red water of a river, or slightly clouded to represent the waters of a chalk stream, was, for practical purposes, nil, and, after trying various experiments, the general conclusion appeared to be that the stain which was most like the colour of the sky was the least visible; also, that the very lightest stain was better than a dark one, and that in the case of perfectly sound clear gut no stain at all seemed practically to be required, as the negative colour, or rather approximate colourlessness, of the gut harmonised, on the whole, very well with most kinds of sky tint.

Probably a light ink-and-water, or 'slate,' stain is as good as any, taking one day with another. To produce it, mix boiling water and black ink, and soak the gut in it – rinsing it thoroughly when it has attained the desired colour. This, indeed, is a precaution that should never be omitted in staining gut, which is otherwise apt to lose its transparency. When too dark a stain has been given it may readily be reduced in intensity by soaking the gut in clean boiling water.

For the common 'red water stain an infusion of tea leaves, boiled down until a teacupful of black tea in a quart of water becomes a pint, gives a nice clean transparent tint; or coffee that has been previously charred in a frying-pan and ground, will answer instead of tea.

When the gut is not entirely round and clear, or, in other words, is 'stringy' it is very apt to have a sort of gloss, and, when the sun is shining upon it, glittering effect in the water, which is highly undesirable. In such a case I have tried, with apparently good effects, slightly rubbing down the gut with dryish cobbler's wax. This also has the effect of making the gut flotant – a hint for the 'dry-fly'.

I once at Loch Leven met with the friend of a fly-fisher who never used to stain gut, but took off the glitter by simply pulling it once through a piece of fine emery paper ... This is drawn gut with the 'chill off.'

For dressing flies, where gut is used in the bodies, Judson's aniline dyes, kept by most chemists, will produce any sort of stain required. The directions are given on the bottles, but I recommend the use of only one-half the proportion of water. Some of the stains produced by the aniline dyes, however, destroy the texture of the gut.

Hair, which I cannot recommend for any sort of fly fishing, and which when used should be taken from the tail of a stallion, is seldom stained, being generally preferred of the natural brownish tint. If, however, it is required to stain it for the purpose of fly-tying or otherwise, the animal greasiness must be first removed by slightly boiling the hair in a 'mordant' obtained from an ounce of alum dissolved in a pint of water. This is also a good preparatory mordant for feathers before they are dyed.

The length for the casting line itself, shown by general experience to be the most convenient, is about three yards. In the case of salmon fishing with a second fly, or lake trout fishing with three flies and a double-handed rod, an extra foot – making, say, ten feet in all – is sometimes added, but it may be safely said that fifty 3-yard casting lines are made for one over that length. Where eyed flies are used, which have of course no separate link of gut belonging to them, the casting line becomes practically a link shorter.

I rarely myself use more than two flies in trout or any other fishing – except occasionally when experimenting on the best flies for a new water – and therefore three yards is an ample allowance. Not that, as 'Box and Cox' expresses it, I have any 'violent animosity or rooted antipathy' to three flies, but that for ordinary purposes I find two preferable. Two flies can be cast better than three; two flies can be 'worked' better than three; two flies are not so liable to entanglements as three; and when they do get 'mixed' the tangle is less inextricable. By 'working better,' what I mean is that whilst the upper dropper, which, a second or two after the cast, hangs – or should hang – clear of the line, and, barring the fly, nearly clear of the water also, – and whilst the tail fly is of course always swimming clear, the lower or second dropper, by the action of drawing in the flies, gets of necessity more or less muddled up with the casting line (which the nose of a rising fish is very likely to strike), and cannot be worked, like the top dropper, cross-line or 'otter' fashion, dribbling along, that is, amongst the ripples.

The argument applies also to river fishing, though perhaps in a somewhat less degree inasmuch as the action of a current – often nearly smooth – does not lend itself so readily to the artistic working of the dropper as the streamless and generally wind-wrinkled surface of a lake.

All this, however, is fairly a question of practice as well as theory, and, as I say, many excellent fly-fishers – perhaps a majority – prefer three flies to two. Their contention is that it gives a greater chance of the flies being seen, and a greater choice to the fish when he does see them.

Passing from the gut to the reel, or running line, I find so wide a field open before me that I despair of being able to do justice to the numberless different descriptions of lines, dressed and undressed, silk, hemp, hair, and what not, which compete for the fly-fisher's favour. When I served my apprenticeship to the craft almost everybody used a line composed of a mixture of silk and hair, and this has still some votaries left, amongst whom, however, I am decidedly not one. It had, in fact, only one good quality, lightness; perhaps I should say half a good quality, because the lightness which is of advantage in the water is a great disadvantage in casting against the wind. For the rest, this silk- and-hair line possesses pretty nearly every drawback that can well be combined. The moment it is not-tightly stretched, in other words, that it has a chance of kinking, or crinkling up, it promptly does so the protuberant points of hair impart a disinclination, almost amounting sometimes to a positive refusal to allow itself to pass through the rod rings, whilst, even under the most careful treatment, it gets rotten, or so much weakened as to be untrustworthy, after the shortest term of service. So much for 'silk' and 'hair.'

Hair by itself may be dismissed in a very few words. As contrasted with the silk mixture, it possesses its virtues in a greater and its faults in a minor degree. It is still more flotant in the water, where also it is much less visible, and it never gets rotten. But as a set-off the difficulty of casting against the wind and the friction in the rod-rings are, of course, exaggerated. On the whole, although I have used reel-lines entirely made of brown horsehair for trout fishing in calm and bright weather with considerable satisfaction, I decidedly prefer a dressed – i.e. waterproofed – line, whether silk or hemp, which is suitable for windy as well as calm weather, and which with proper care will last quite long enough for all practical purposes.

For salmon fishing, of course, lines made of hair or of silk and hair, would be put out of court on one ground alone, namely, a want of sufficient strength.

With regard to the question of hemp or silk, I must say that when the 'Manchester Twine Cotton Spinning Company' first started they sent me some lines, both dressed and undressed, which were exceedingly perfect, and which I believe, after fourteen years' occasional service, to be still as strong as ever – in fact, so strong that on trying one of them just now with both hands a friend of mine failed to break it. This line, however, is what is termed 'cable-laid' – twisted, that is, in the same manner as a ship's cable – the principle of which is that whilst the cable itself is twisted from right to left, the separate ropes of which it is composed are twisted from left to right. The result of this is that the two twists counteract each other in their mutual inclination to kink, and when wetted, the cable, instead of swelling, hardens and contracts. Of the plaited hemp lines issued by the same company I have nothing good to say, neither did any of the dressings of those that I have seen properly affect their object, and if they did so temporarily, my experience is that they would not stand.

In the case of the particular line to which I refer, no semblance of dressing of any sort now remains, or did remain after the first few months, or, perhaps, weeks, of real 'service in the field,' on any part of the line which had come into actual use. The strength, however, was and is, I think, bulk for bulk, unequalled by any lines that I have met with made of silk. The latter, however, possess the great advantage of taking the dressing, or waterproofing, perfectly, and admitting afterwards of a smoothness and polish which facilitate very greatly the running out and the reeling in of the line.

These dressed silk lines also, if not absolutely so strong as those made of hemp (and they have improved of late years), can be made quite strong enough for all practical purposes. I say advisedly 'can be made,' because I have found the most unexpected differences in the strength of different so-called silk lines of the same thickness, and where they have been said to be of the same manufacture. The best rough and ready method of testing is to take a foot or two of the line between the hands and ascertain, by breaking or trying to break it, what is its actual strength.

It appears, then, that on a computation of advantages and disadvantages our support should be given to dressed silk lines for fly fishing; and as these are made of every thickness, from that of an ordinary piece of stout sewing cotton almost to that of a bell rope, everyone can, without difficulty, suit his particular objects and tastes. Dressed silk has in rough weather a 'driving' power which cannot be obtained with any undressed material, and nothing but silk appears to be capable of taking the dressing properly.'

Then comes the question: Shall the dressed silk line be 'level' – that is, of equal substance throughout – or 'tapered,' which means in ordinary parlance, getting finer towards the end at which the casting line is to be attached ? The latter is sometimes what is called 'double tapered,' that is, the line is tapered at both ends – or it may be only a 'single taper,' when, of course, the taper is made at one end only. As between level and tapered lines, each have its advantages and its disadvantages, but, on the whole, I think nine fly-fishers out of ten prefer, in practice, a line more or less tapered towards the casting end.

So far as the actual casting is concerned, apart from 'fine fishing,' these details are of little importance on quiet days, but in stormy weather, when the wind is blowing half a gale, perhaps right in the fly-fisher's teeth, the case is radically altered, and the man whose line is properly tapered and balanced and in weight exactly suited to his rod will be able to go on casting with comparative efficiency, while his neighbour, less perfectly equipped, will find his flies blown back in his face every other cast.

The importance, to the salmon fisher especially, of a line which will cut its way through a fierce March squall has been so well recognised that in order to give greater 'cutting' power line-makers have even gone to the extent of manufacturing reel-lines with wire centres. My friend Mr Senior now informs me that some he tried, made by Foster, of Ashbourne, answered exceedingly well. I have used them myself also, and in squally weather they certainly possess great 'cutting' power against or across the wind.

The salmon line that seems to command the greatest number of suffrages amongst connoisseurs is what is known as the 'swelled line.' This line is gradually tapered thicker from the end up to a point which it is calculated will generally come near about the top of the rod in making a cast. Thus the average length of the taper from the finest to the thickest part is usually, for a salmon line, 15 to 20 yards, then tapering off backwards until it reaches its finest point again at another 15 or 20 yards – i.e. 30 or 40 yards in all, where it is attached to the 'back' line. This is the line recommended by Major Traherne (see article on salmon fishing).

I find I get capital casting with the swelled line, both as applied to trout and salmon fishing – in the former case the swell or thickest point should be reached proportionally quicker, say, for a single-handed rod in about 9 or 10 yards from the end. The quantity of line, clear of the rod-point, that can be continuously used with the maximum of effect in lake trout fishing with a ten-foot rod is, I find, about 18 or 20 feet – or nearly twice the length of the rod – plus the casting line: i.e. 9 or 10 yards altogether. Deducting 3 yards for the casting line, this would leave 6 or 7 yards as the point in the reel-line at which, for ordinary lake work, the thickest point of the taper or 'swell' should be reached; but as longer casts are often required, and as, moreover, the same line will probably do duty for river fishing as well, probably from 8 to 10 yards of taper will be found the most convenient length. For a double-handed trout rod, something between the proportions of a salmon line and those last-named are applicable. If a level (untapered) line be used, the interjection of 2 or 3 feet of twisted gut point – an advantage in almost all cases – will be found highly desirable, breaking as it does the otherwise abrupt transition from reel line to gut.

Dry-fly fishers, who generally use stiffer rods than common, have canons of their own on these questions, and the latest science of reel-lines for the floating fly will be found in Mr F. M. Halford's able article.

Let me, in quitting the subject, emphasise one parting caution: The thickness (and swell) of the line must absolutely be proportioned to the capacities of the rod if the most artistic results are to be obtained. A heavy line demands a stiff rod (and top), and vice versâ, and a light whippy rod with a fine top a line of corresponding lightness. A transposition of these conditions – either way – will produce failure.

One other hint – if a reel-line is not absolutely smooth, reject it unhesitatingly, no matter what its other qualifications may be. I know of lines admirably strong, capitally tapered, long wearing – 'conscientious' lines in fact in every way – but of which I would have none at any price. With such, every time you want to lengthen or shorten your cast there is friction on the rod-rings, and an impediment more or less to free passage; in giving line to a fish ditto (often the cause of losing it); whilst both in casting through the air and lifting out of the water, such a line entails at every cast of every day, from its 'cradle to its grave,' a certain small comparative disability, which to willingly subject oneself to is stupid, because wholly unnecessary.

This naturally applies to any kind of line, dressed or undressed.

REELS AND REEL FASTENINGS

The Fisheries Exhibition of 1883 was prolific in new reels, many of which, it must be confessed, were not only highly ingenious as inventions, but really excellent in their adaptation to different sorts of fishing. Indeed, if reels have not in the matter of 'improvement' quite kept pace with the improvements in rods, they are yet prodigiously in advance of the unmechanical windlasses with which our forbears, in the not very distant past, were content to reel in the victims of their prowess. But I will not slay the slain twice over, or evoke, merely for the purpose of exorcising them, the ghosts of 'Pirns,' 'winch-winders,' 'multipliers' (*horresco referens*!) and other similar abominations, which if not actually as extinct as the dodo, soon will be ...

Of modernised improved reels or winches that which presents, perhaps, the greatest actual novelty is Slater's 'Combination Reel,' so called because uniting the qualifications of a Nottingham reel and an ordinary plain or check reel. This it does without, so far as I can judge, diminishing the efficiency of either. Further – speaking with due diffidence of a speciality of fishing which I have had very little opportunity, or perhaps taste, for acquiring – it would appear to be vastly superior to the old-fashioned open Nottingham reel, in that, being confined to the barrel by transverse bars, the line cannot be perpetually 'winding off' – or I should say 'twisting off' – the reel when not wanted, and hitching its loose coils round the reel itself and everything else in its vicinity.

Nottingham fishing apart, however, the reel is of very general applicability, and being exceptionally light, as well as simple in construction, presents advantages in many directions.

For all kinds of fishing, for example, in which the bait is commonly, or occasionally 'cast from the reel,' it is excellent.

So also it is in some branches of fly fishing, such as (to mention one in which I have used it with much satisfaction) in lake fishing with a double-handed rod. Indeed, even for light salmon fishing, I have both used it myself and seen it used successfully by others. No doubt the speciality of the reel is for pike spinning, in which connection it is figured and described in Vol. II, but for the convenience of trout and salmon fishers the illustration is here repeated.

In order fully to adapt the Combination Reel to the requirements of the ordinary fly- and float-fisher, as well as to the troller, the winder and axle, instead of being entirely of wood, as formerly – necessitating, of course, a large diameter – are now also made, in the form shown in the woodcuts, of wood and metal combined, by which the diameter of the axle is reduced, and the reel so far in all respects assimilated to the ordinary patterns of brass and bronze, – its speciality in regard to the Nottingham style of casting being of course retained. The insides of the barrel plates on both sides are, in this later pattern, composed almost wholly of metal, rotating freely on a fixed steel pivot or centre-pin. Attached to the non-revolving (left-hand) plate is a brass frame or cage supporting the horizontal bars, between which, of course, as in ordinary reels, the line passes, whilst this immovable framework is 'recessed' into a groove in the revolving barrel. The object of the revolution of the whole right-hand side-plate – made exteriorly of wood – is to enable a 'drag' to be placed upon the running-out of the line, without which, as a means of regulating the length and direction of the cast, casting from the reel in the Nottingham style would be practically impossible. The two portions of the reel readily come apart when it is desired to oil or clean them; and it was when in this separated condition that the upper figures in the cut were taken, the lower figure showing the reel when put together. By shifting with the finger a button or 'catch' the action can be changed to a 'check.'

The diameter of the reel from which the engraving was made is 2½ inches; inside width between barrel plates, inch; weight, 6 oz. This size and pattern is suited for any kind of fishing, but for lake trout fishing I prefer a 4-inch reel of the original wooden pattern, the increased diameter of the axle, unaccompanied by any increase of weight, giving a more rapid and powerful winding-in power. For light salmon fishing a 4½ inch Slater's wooden reel will be found about the most convenient size. After continuous wetting, these reels should be taken apart and carefully dried and oiled all over, otherwise they are apt to swell and 'stick.'

Another comparatively recent introduction is Mr Heaton's 'Strike from the Winch' Reel, which has its advocates for trout and even for salmon fishing; though, I confess, I should not be inclined to put any great faith in it – or rather in the principle it embodies – as applied to the latter purpose. The object of the reel is primarily to soften or relieve the 'jar' of the stroke by keeping the hand clear of the line and allowing the reel (the resistance of which can be made weaker or stronger) to do the work instead. It has no 'check,' in the technical sense, of any sort, and the graduated pressure is obtained by the application of a screw working over, and against, the end of the axle. It is important that the end of this regulator should be kept carefully oiled.

For Salmon reels proper we have, if not an *embarras de choix*, at least several excellent varieties to select from.

First there is 'Farlow's Lever Reel' – a solid brass (bronzed) reel. It is made in all sizes, but it is distinctly as a salmon reel that it finds its most natural place.

Its speciality is the mechanism in which a lozenge-shaped piece represents a convex spring plate, which by means of a screw-nut can be loosened or tightened at pleasure, so as to offer exactly the resistance to the running out of the line that may be desired. This takes the place of the ordinary check, which is, however, attached to a second variety of the reel for those who may prefer it. In this latter model the regulator-spring is transferred to the left-hand, or opposite, plate, and replaced on the right-hand plate by the check machinery.

There is also a little supplementary plate for lubricating

purposes.

Chevalier and Bowness manufacture a very similar reel, in which the 'pressure nut' is turned on and off by the fingers, instead of by a knife-blade or screwdriver.

These are both strong and thoroughly serviceable reels; and for salmon fishing, where it seems – or I should perhaps rather say, seemed till recently – to be the general theory – or, at any rate, practice – that weight is subsidiary to strength and durability, can be safely relied on. A 'lever' reel of 4½ inches, with a proper complement of line, weighs 2 lbs. 1 oz.

Another capital reel, which I have found excellent for all sorts of boat work, is Malloch's 'Sun and Planet' Reel. This is a check reel, and its peculiarity is that unless, and until, the handle is taken hold of, the line runs out without any movement of the side plate (or, of course, of the handle), so that, when trailing, for instance, the rod can safely be left with the reel resting on the bottom of the boat, and in case of a 'run' there is no danger of a contact between the reel-handle and boat-gear causing one of those sudden checks on the line which are apt to produce inopportune results.

In the reel which I have of this pattern the right-hand plate is made of some white metal lightly bronzed, or rather 'greyed,' and the left-hand plate of ebonite. The ebonite plate, in my opinion, renders it less suitable for bank fishing, where a knock on a stone is very likely to happen, entailing very probably a fracture of the ebonite.

To those who desire light reels made entirely of metal, where very rough work is not to be expected, Hardy Brothers' 'Revolving Plate Reel' will commend itself.

The 4½ -inch reel will take comfortably too yards of fine hemp backing and forty yards of medium dressed silk taper suited for a salmon rod up to sixteen feet in length.

The lightest reel in the world is probably that made entirely of aluminium. An aluminium reel 2½ inches in diameter weighs less than 3 oz., but the price is alarming – at least 1*l* per oz.

This, of course, is carrying things to an extreme; but clearly the question of weight in reels is of the utmost importance if the rod is to be properly balanced – which is only another word for saying, 'if the maximum and perfection of work are to be got out of it.'

There can be no question, however, that, whether with the idea of 'balancing' or otherwise, the weight of reels ordinarily used, especially in salmon fishing, is greatly overdone. The reel has always to be supported 'at arm's length,' so to say, where every ounce tells its tale during a day's fishing. Another vitally important point in a salmon reel for genuine hard work is the winding-in leverage, as every salmon fisher knows who has had the experience of 'reeling up' – or trying to reel up – half a dozen heavy fish in as many half hours. Again, the ideal salmon reel must be strong enough to run no risk from chance collisions with rocks or other 'jeopardy of war '; and, further, the check machinery should be as simple as possible, and readily accessible in case of accidents or for purposes of lubrication. A narrow barrel or winder and (of course) a corresponding narrow groove are desiderata which, happily, it is now hardly necessary to insist upon. In salmon reels, however (though hardly in trout reels), this last point may be overdone, having regard to the convenience in carrying line in the most compact form.

As I could not find any salmon reel completely fulfilling these several conditions, I set about constructing one, and in doing so unhesitatingly pressed into my service the best points I could find in any existing reels, well-known or otherwise. The outcome is shown in the reel figured below, in which I believe it will be seen that the desiderated requirements are combined ... But let me, in the first place, acknowledge my indebtedness to the other inventors of whose several systems I have taken advantage.

The form of the side plates of my reel, with a rim all in one solid piece of metal, is due to General Sir Daniel Lysons, G.C.B. This rim not only enables the exterior end of the handle to be 'guarded,' or counter-sunk, so as both to protect it and prevent the

Pennell Reel,
Fig. 1.

line hitching round it, but at the same time makes it practicable to dispense altogether with the second or exterior side plate.

The handle of the Lysons reel terminates inside the rim, so that the leverage is only about the same as that of a handle attached in the ordinary way to a revolving side plate; and to gain the maximum of possible leverage (point two) I have adopted in a modified form the handle which is said to be the invention of Colonel Latour – or which, at any rate, is known as 'Colonel Latour's handle.' This, in a 4½ -inch reel, gives an increased leverage, or winding-in power, of half an inch in actual measurement, or, mechanically speaking, some-where about doubles it (?). The doubled leverage will tell, from the first putting together of the rod until the gaffing of the last fish of the day gives the wearied muscles of the right arm and back a not unwelcome respite.

The last point is the check mechanism, shown in drawing, fig. 2, which ought to be simple, and at the same time easily accessible – accessible, that is, without any 'taking to pieces' of the reel. In my 'combined reel' the check machinery is merely covered by a hinged lid (A, B, C), sufficiently close- fitting to be practically water-tight, while admitting of being opened at once by giving the catch, c, a turn with the point of a knife-blade.

In all the foregoing reels the handles are so attached as, in one way or another, to prevent the line getting caught round them.

Pennell Reel, Fig. 2. Outside of left hand plate, showing check mechanism and lid.

There is still, however, something left to be desired in this matter of reel and line hitching. The snake is 'scotched,' not killed. In whatever manner the handle may be attached, the line still is left free to hitch round behind the back of the reel itself – a freedom of which, it is almost needless to say, it seems to have a provoking determination to avail itself to the utmost. It appeared, therefore, that a stop might be put, once for all, on this never-ending worry, by partly covering over the space at the back of the reel with a 'protector' or guard of some sort. The mechanical realisation of the idea was easy; the protector springs from the middle bar of the posterior curve, over which (bar) it 'clasps,' – the exterior end pressing close on to and against the rod, whilst the 'interior' end is fixed to the metal support of the foot plate.

Messrs Bernard, of Church Place, Piccadilly, have also recently made a 'protector' on the same principle, but differently applied: as it is attached – always, of course, by the middle bar – with a separate spring, forming an equally effectual prevention of 'line-hitching.' Indeed, in one respect, it is even more absolutely 'undefeatable' than my original device, as it occupies the whole width of the reel-barrel. Per contra it adds appreciably to the weight, which the original pattern does not. The annexed cut shows Bernard's modification as applied to one of their excellently proportioned silver-bronzed trout-reels.

To show how really serious an annoyance this hitching of the line round the reel is recognised to be, Messrs Foster, of Ashbourne, have actually gone to the trouble of constructing a reel in an enlargement of the rod-butt itself, a plan which, whatever may be its merits in other respects, it is needless to say effectually overcomes the difficulty.

Some beautiful reels are now made in America, for a specimen of the most perfect of which I am indebted to the courtesy of the inventor, Mr Chas. F. Orvis, of Manchester, Vermont, U.S.A. This reel, with its extraordinarily narrow barrel, and side plates perforated throughout for lightness, seems to me to comprise theoretically all the points of a perfect trout reel, and I find in practice its performance is equal to its promise, its great diameter enabling a fish that runs in' to be wound up so fast that the evils of a 'slack line' need seldom be felt.

Besides lightness, the perforation of the side plates, allowing the air to get to the line, are intended to prevent the latter rotting if left damp, and I must say that though the line has been – day after day, and in fact since I began to use it some months ago – left wet, it does not seem so far to have suffered any deterioration whatever in consequence. The only imperfection in the reel was that owing to the old-fashioned 'crank' form of handle the line not unfrequently got hitched round it, and to remedy this I have had a handle fitted to mine, as shown in the engraving, which effectually overcomes the 'hitching' tendency, whilst at the same time increasing the leverage. The double handle is also of considerable advantage in real work, as the handle is more rapidly found, and consequently less time is lost in winding in – this is an advantage possessed by the Slater reel also; and it has saved me many a fish, more especially in boat work, when the boat has been drifting before a wind, and the hooked fish, as before pointed out, 'runs in.'

The reels described in the foregoing pages represent the latest advances that have been made, and amongst them neither the salmon nor trout fisher need, I think, find any difficulty in selecting a reel suited to his taste, – observing again that the question of weight is one demanding most serious consideration, especially on the part of fly-fishers who are not burdened with superfluous muscular development. If the lower (untapered) portion of the reel-line – otherwise the 'back line' – which is not used in casting, and which undergoes comparatively little wear and tear, is made to consist of either fine undressed silk or (better) hemp, the total weight may be sensibly reduced without loss either of efficiency or 'compass.'

Allowing, say, forty yards – either of the ordinary taper, or of the swelled taper, as already described, for casting purposes, sixty or seventy yards of hemp line strong enough to hold anything that swims can be got comfortably upon a three and three-quarter or four-inch reel (according to the width of the barrel), and this length will usually be found sufficient for all ordinary purposes. In 'big rivers,' however, as the editor truly observes in the foot-note, this length may be advantageously increased to 120 or even 150 yards, in which case the size of the reel will, of course, have to be increased also. On to a four-inch reel of my pattern I can get 100 yards of back line, consisting of very fine, solid plaited, superficially dressed, hemp, and forty yards of medium-sized swelled dressed silk taper, as thick as is suitable for casting with any rod up to fifteen or sixteen feet. The hemp backing is about as fine as a fine trout reel-line, and I found one yard of it drew out the steelyard to twenty-three pounds before it broke. This hempline will also last right well. The 'back line' and the tapered, or casting, part of the line should be very carefully and neatly lapped together with fine waxed silk at the place of junction, so as to obviate any danger of the line getting stuck in the rings at that point when running out with a fish. If small stiff steel rings ('snake' pattern best, see p. 80), such as I use myself and advocate for every description of rod, are adopted, the chance of a 'hitch' at the critical moment will be reduced to a minimum.

In the foregoing observations on reels generally I have assumed that all practical fishermen will use a reel which is either normally a 'check,' or that can be made into a check at pleasure. The old-fashioned 'plain reel,' as it is called, possessed certainly the merit of being plain – very plain, indeed, we should think nowadays! – and simple, in the sense of not being likely to get out of order. But there its merits end. When there is no 'check' to interfere with the rapid rotatory motion of the wheel set going by a heavy fish, there is nothing in the mechanism to prevent the line 'over-running,' the result of which is usually a complete stoppage at the critical moment.

Multiplying reels are at least equally objectionable upon another ground, namely, that, when 'winding in' a fish, the old mechanical axiom of 'what is gained in speed is lost in power 'is apt to come into operation with disastrous results. No one can fairly wind-in a heavy fish with a multiplying reel of the old type, and now that reels with deep narrow barrels, giving increased speed and power, are almost universally manufactured instead of the antiquated shallow, broad-grooved pattern, there is no practical advantage gained by further rapidity of action.

RODS

With regard to fly rods I shall say but little. *Quot homines tot sentetitiae.* Some fly fishers like hickory, others prefer green-heart, or lancewood. Some like a rod made all of one wood, others give the preference to a rod with the butt of one sort of wood and the top joints of another, and a great many of the modern school, especially those with whom price is not a matter of importance, have given in their adhesion to the spliced-cane rods, which are supposed to owe their origin to our enterprising cousins on the other side of the 'Herring Pond.'

In the 'form' of the rod again, as in regard to the wood of which it may be constructed, it is rare to find two fishermen of the same opinion. Many still hold to the old-fashioned straight-butted rod, which tapered away with almost mathematical precision from the reel to the point, alleging, amongst other advantages claimed, that with this shaped rod a spare top can always be carried in case of accident without the inconvenience of a separate top case. Of late years, however, many practical fly fishers – indeed, I think I may say the majority – favour some modification or other of the form of the rod which owed its birth, or, at any rate, its christening, to the habitues of Castle Connell – preferring the swishy play obtained by fining or tapering away the butt rapidly from above the reel …

On all these subjects, were I to go into them in detail, I might easily double the length of this chapter, without carrying conviction, or probably amusement, to anybody but myself. I, therefore, refrain from doing more than touching thus lightly on the mere superficial aspect of the question, leaving every man to remain, as, indeed, he ought to be, and would be for anything I could write to the contrary, his own counsel, judge, and jury.

With regard, however, to the now fashionable split-cane rods, a few words on the method of their construction, and on their two principal varieties, may possibly not be uninteresting to those who are not already initiated into the mysteries of this interesting branch of rod-making.

In the *Art of Fly-Making* published by Mr Blacker about thirty years ago, second edition, occurs, I believe, the first notice of split cane rods. Mr Blacker says:

> The beautiful rent and glued-up bamboo-cane fly rods, which I turn out to the greatest perfection, are very valuable, as they are both light and powerful, and throw the line with great facility. The cane for these rods must be of the very best description, or they will not last any time. They will last for years, however, if really well made, and, taken care of.

The wood employed in their manufacture is the 'male bamboo', procured from India; great care and experience being required in selecting only such canes as are of the finest quality and have been cut at the proper season.

This is a matter of great delicacy and difficulty, as will be understood when it is borne in mind how troublesome it is to properly balance a rod constructed of even the ordinary solid woods where the plane can be used after the joints are fixed. Either from want of knowledge or proper machinery, many so-called cane rods are put together so that they have to be subsequently filed or planed to get the requisite spring, thus removing the most essential part of the cane. These inferior rods are then painted, or burnt over again to imitate the natural colour of the original skin, from which, however, they are easily distinguished by experts.

Probably one of the reasons why it has been supposed by fly fishers that these rods will not stand the heavy work brought to bear upon them in salmon fishing is the use of inferior cement in the process, and the glue subsequently oozing out of the joints in wet weather, thus tending to make them come loose afterwards. In Mr Kelson's report on the collection of salmon rods in the Fisheries Exhibition (*Field*, October 27, 1883), he observes that 'this is always the case sooner or later with these hand-made rods for salmon; but if eleven years' experience with them be admitted sufficient, I may say that the rods made with the machinery used by Messrs Hardy, who obtained the first prize for these split-cane rods at the Fisheries Exhibition, for cutting the cane perfectly true, obviate the difficulty satisfactorily.'

The ordinary butts of split-cane rods, as well as the upper joints, are hexagonal, and are simply made of six V-shaped strips, glued together in the manner described. In the highest class of rods, however, the butt is built double, both the centre and external wall being constructed of separate layers of the hardest part of the cane. The centre is made first in the usual way, and after it has dried the second, or external, layer or wall is built up round it. Messrs. Hardy inform me that although the labour and expense involved in this double construction are, of course, infinitely greater, the strength gained by the process is enhanced to such an important degree that they make all their split-cane salmon rods in this fashion as to the thicker parts.

Complaints have often been made to me that the ordinary split-cane rod is deficient in casting power as against a wind, and I must say that my experience tends to confirm the truth of the statement. In order to meet this objection, however, the above-named manufacturers and others have endeavoured to make the split-cane rods with a steel centre to each joint, so as to increase their 'stiff springiness,' so to speak. The spring is first tapered and then tempered in the same manner that the main spring of a watch would be. After this it is coated with a waterproof and finally built up into the centre of the rod.

I have a light salmon rod made for me on this principle by Messrs Hardy with which I find I can get plenty of power, whether the wind is high or low, and from whatever direction it blows. In the case of a strong head wind especially, I am disposed to think I can make better casting with this rod than with any I ever used, and it is withal a very handy and fairly light weapon, but quite stiff enough for any ordinary fishing. Its length is fourteen feet. I find that on a calm day I can cast, with heavy salmon line, over thirty measured yards on the level grass, and this, in my opinion, represents as much as is often wanted to be done in practice; in fact, most casts with the salmon fly will, if measured, be found, I am satisfied, nearer twenty than thirty yards. Of course, I am aware that there are some rivers and, perhaps, some casts here and there on most salmon rivers, in which a longer rod would enable the fisherman to reach some favourable point otherwise inaccessible, but when this cannot be done by wading I am content to put up with the loss of an occasional good cast in exchange for the constant comfort and convenience which I find in a rod of the proportions indicated.

It is all very well to talk lightly of casting forty yards, and so forth, with a twenty-foot Castle Connell, but the man who wishes to do it, and to go on doing it all day, must be of stronger mould or greater height than the ordinary run of mortals. In my opinion a twenty-foot rod requires a seven-foot fisherman to wield it with comfort, and I am quite satisfied that for all ordinary purposes the salmon fisher would get more comfort and more sport, too, with a rod such as that I have described than with a longer and more fatiguing and unwieldy weapon ...

It should be borne in mind as a mechanical axiom in this matter of the length of rod, that exactly in proportion as you gain in casting power by the increased leverage, so (the motive force being equal) do you lose in the propelling power by which only the leverage can be utilised – the practical deduction from which proposition is that every man has a length of rod exactly proportioned to his physical strength – a rod out of which, that is, he can get the maximum of casting force compatible with sustained muscular effort – and that it should be his object to ascertain what that length is. Bearing in mind the mechanical argument, I am disposed to think that a shorter and more powerful rod might in many cases be substituted with advantage for a longer and lighter weapon, and this principle has been carried out with success by Farlow in a 13 ft. 6 in. green-heart salmon rod they make according to my instructions. With this rod I get plenty of power and excellent casting; in fact there is little really appreciable difference in these respects between this and the steel-centre spliced bamboo built for me by Hardy, except when casting against a strong head wind.

However, as I have said, these are matters of individual taste, and must be left to the appreciation of individual salmon fishers. Till we have our fly-rods made entirely of steel – an improvement which I take it is only a question of time (unless, indeed, as a reviewer suggests, an objection be made on the score of carrying about a 'lightning conductor!') – one or other of the salmon rods above described will probably be found as perfect a weapon as any fly-fisher need desire. With a slightly shorter top either makes an excellent rod for heavy lake trolling, spinning for salmon, etc ...

The split cane with steel core makes a handy powerful trouting rod for heavy work. The length of mine is ten feet seven inches when put together, and the weight ten ounces. It has three joints and ferrules. I can cast about twenty-two yards with it on a still day on level ground; and the combination and 'correction' of stiffness and swishiness leave, to my mind, nothing to be desired.

I find no advantage in a single-handed rod much over ten feet, as it generally results, in my experience, in both hands being sooner or later called into requisition. If the size of the water demands a larger rod, then I should advise a double-handed rod at once. Such a rod should not exceed thirteen feet, nor weigh more than from 16 to 18 oz.

Ladies' rods can hardly be too light for real pleasure, as not only their wrists are weaker and their muscles softer than ours, but they have seldom acquired the knowledge of using what physical powers they do possess to the best advantage. This is half the battle, as anyone knows who has tried to lift a trunk that some diminutive porter, perhaps, has just been carrying about in a light and airy fashion as if it were a mere feather-weight. Eight feet and a half, or so, is ample for a lady's single-handed fly rod, and such a rod should not exceed eight ounces in weight. These are the measurements of a spliced rod belonging to a lady of my acquaintance; which is as serviceable and handy a little 'tandem lasher' as a trout can wish to be coaxed with. It was made by Mr. Jas. Ogden, of Cheltenham, whose 8 ½ and 10 feet spliced rods – *of greenheart, N.B., not blue Mahoe* – are excellent. With one of these latter rods I have killed, during several years past, I hesitate to say how many stone weight of brown and white trout – some of them up to 4 lbs. – and it is still as sound in every respect as the day I first put it together. It has had to take its chance with all sorts of rough work – boat and bank – but not even a ring is bent. This last is owing to the form of ring with which it is fitted.

The cut shows the form of this ring, now called the 'snake' ring, to which I have to some extent, it might be said, 'stood god-father.' At any rate, since prominent attention was first called to it in 'Modern Improvements in Fishing Tackle and Fish Hooks,' it seems to have become more or less the 'fashion' with tackle makers, and, therefore, it may be presumed, with their customers, A, B, C, and D are facsimiles of snake rings – which should be eight in all – suited to my pattern of 13 ft. 6 in. salmon rod. For trout rods of all kinds the rings should be both smaller and of lighter wire. The form of the ring gives it these undeniable advantages over the old pattern, whether upright or movable: it can hardly get bent; it cannot practically get broken; it cannot stick in the rod bag.

In thus describing my four favourite fly-rods, I have indicated in the most practical manner I can the description of rod which has appeared to afford, on the whole, the best combination of qualities for the different descriptions of fly fishing.

Before taking leave, however, of the subject of rods and rod fastenings, I should be omitting a most important item if I failed to direct attention to the various improved methods of uniting and fixing the rod joints.

Until the Fisheries Exhibition either called forth, or called into public notice, these inventions, joint fastenings may be said, so far as any general adoption of them is concerned, to have been comprised in three categories. The first, the ordinary ferrule joint, in which one joint slips into the other – and it

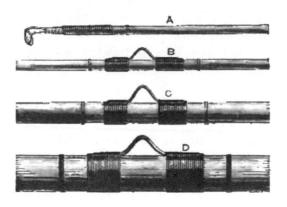

Fly-rods: A, B, C, D.

may be added, out of it again with considerable regularity at inauspicious moments; secondly, the spliced joint; and, thirdly, the screw fastening, peculiar, so far as I am aware, to the rods turned out by some Irish makers.

I have one of the last named still in my possession made for me by Martin Kelly, of Dublin, I am afraid to say how many, but certainly fifteen or twenty years ago, which has seen some service in its day and is still fit to take the field. I therefore speak of this fastening with respect. It had its drawbacks, however. Perhaps owing to the necessity of the case, or perhaps to the incomplete application of mechanical knowledge, or a little of both, the ferrules which were attached to the tipper joint and slipped down from above and had an awkward habit of breaking at the point where they were attached by a screw or rivet to the upper joint. Consequently, I need not say that since I have become its owner that single-handed three-joint trout rod of about eleven feet, has paid several enforced visits to Dublin for purposes of reparation.

The only drawback that I see to this fastening is that, should either the fine outer, or 'doubled,' ferrule get dinted, or damaged in any way, the joint will, of course, absolutely fail to close. In order to make such a contingency impossible there ought to be plugs for both halves of the joint.

A still simpler jointure, and one, I should say, in every way most admirable and efficient, is Bernard's Lock joint, in which the upper ferrule, furnished with a projecting 'rim,' is simply slipped down into its place and turned under a 'catch' (attached to the lower ferrule) till the rod rings are in line, by which process the joints are effectually locked. This jointure is also 'waterproof.'

Farlow, who exhibited at the Fisheries Exhibition a joint on a completely different principle – a screw 'nut' locking the inner and outer ferrules – has since registered another lock-fast jointing, on a new and, as it would appear, much improved plan, viz. that of a movable band, etc ...

Lastly we have Messrs. Hardy Brothers' 'patent lock-fast'

Fly-rod attachment.

joint, which is thoroughly sound and serviceable, and also waterproof.

The spiral wire on the outside ferrule gives some additional strength where most required, and Messrs, Hardy's system of brazing an additional short ferrule, the same size as the outside ferrule, on the top of the inside one, is a decided advantage, as it strengthens the joint just at the point where so many breakages occur, and is superior to the plan sometimes adopted of putting the inside ferrule on flush with the wood.

Amongst these several rod fastenings the fly-fisher can easily choose for himself. Any one of them will be found in practice immeasurably more convenient than the old-fashioned unfixed double ferrule or even, perhaps, for the ordinary run of fly-fishers, than the spliced joint, though the latter gives the most perfect play to the rod when once adjusted.

If, by the way, the rod joint should become stuck in the ferrule, the best and, indeed, the only means that I know of for separating it, is to turn it slowly in the flame of a candle at the 'sticking point,' when the swelling of the outside ferrule produced by the heat will generally enable a separation to be effected without damage to anything beyond the rod varnish. A little grease rubbed on to the ends of the joints before starting will, especially if the joint be not 'double brazed' – i.e. covered with brass as to the lowest part of the plug – often anticipate 'lesions' of this kind, and prevention is better than cure.

LANDING NETS

Quitting now the subject of rods, reels, lines, and hooks – the apparatus, that is, destined for hooking and playing a fish – the next and by no means unimportant question is how to land him.

For all fish of the trout and salmon species up to three or four pounds in weight a net will be found the most convenient and serviceable implement for this purpose – the province of the gaff coming in only in the case of larger and heavier fish. I will not here enter into the vexed questions of net or gaff on salmon rivers, although there is no doubt that nets can be made large enough and strong enough to 'bag' the largest salmon that ever took a fly, and to do all the work of the gaff, and do it effectually, whilst at the same time probably saving the lives of many gravid or unclean fish which ought to be returned to the water – saving also, when the fisherman is a conscientious observer of the salmon laws, a considerable amount of time and temper.

Putting this question aside, however, the use of the landing net, as I have observed, is practically confined to fish under about 'salmon size,' the gaff, on the score of portability, possessing a decided advantage in the case of heavier weights. Turning, therefore, to the subject of nets adapted for the purpose indicated, we find that the stimulus given to angling inventions by the Fisheries Exhibition has not left us without some distinct advance in this direction also.

The portability of nets, as well as of gaffs, is of primary importance to the trout fisher, who constantly does his work without an attendant. This is one sort of portability. Another is the portability of the net, not as considered with reference to the fly-fisher's shoulder or pocket, but in regard to his rod case or portmanteau. A net that does not 'compress' or fold up in some form or other is a most unmanageable and inconvenient addition to a traveller's impedimenta, and numerous inventions have accordingly been made to supply this demand. Hoopshaped nets, both of steel and whalebone, which stretch out at full length and thus form, when not in use, an appendage that can be readily strapped on to, or carried in the rod case, are amongst the ingenious dodges which the inventive talent of tackle-makers or their patrons have called into existence. A less modern invention was the steel hoop in three joints, which, when out of work, could be folded up with the net around it into a shape and compass not much unlike that of the fish itself. This net, however, has the disadvantage of being heavy, and unsuited to the second great requirement in the matter of portability – so far as the fly- fisher or worm-fisher is concerned – or, in fact, in the case of anyone who fishes without an attendant – namely, that he should be able to carry his own net, and that in a form and in a position where it will be most out of the way when not required, and most ready at hand when wanted.

This position is undoubtedly under, or just behind, the left arm or shoulder of the fisherman. Here it would oshould hang clear of all embarrassments caused by the creel or fish carrier, and ready, of course, to be taken hold of by the right hand, when, at the proper moment, the rod is transferred to the left.

Without occupying space by discussing tbe merits and demerits of various nets, bandies, and net carriers wbicb do not fulfil these requirements, let me proceed at once to describe a combination which does so. I call it a 'combination' because the net is the invention of Messrs Hardy brothers, and the handle and carrier that of Messers Williams, Great Queen Street, Lincoln's Inn.

The net, as will be seen by the engraving (fig 1) of two side pieces, made of flexible wood, and these when stretched to their proper dimensions, and so held by the brass socket into which the right-hand side slips, are kept at the regulated distance by a cord stretched between the two upper points. The net itself – as all nets should be, in order both to keep them from getting rotten, saturated with water, or entangling the tackle – is made of fine oiled, that is, 'dressed' silk. It will be readily seen that the shape of this net favours its being carried in the position I have indicated, namely, under and behind the left arm –   for which purpose, however, it is necessary that it should be limited in size, the limit being

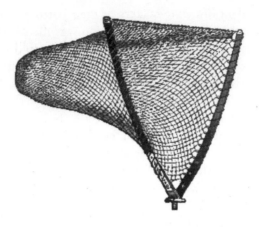

Fig. 1.

about 14½ inches between the projecting arms. But this allows ample space for netting a fish up to 2 or 3 lbs. – or, at a pinch, even more. The net engraved has a width of 1 foot, and is suitable for lighter fishing.

The handle, with the net and suspending cord complete, are shown in the engraving (figs. 2 and 3), where also the other dimensions of the net are given. A represents the net; B, the top connection; C, the net-screw working in ferrule E on net handle; D is a loose movable metal band held by the projecting rim, F (in later models moved up to C), out of which it slips easily; and G is the exterior or lower half of the handle, into which the upper half telescopes. Weight of handle and net figured, fourteen ounces. Should the net show the least sign of being top-heavy when suspended, the addition of a small piece of lead at the bottom of the handle will adjust the equilibrium.

The advantage of a net of this sort – or some other pattern answering the same purpose – especially when wading in the middle of a stream, either when fly fishing or worm-fishing, can hardly be over-estimated. The Hardy-Williams net-handle takes also a gaff suitable for light work.

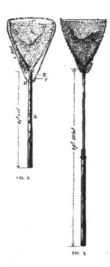

Fig. 2. & Fig. 3.

A very convenient net for trout-fishing, especially with the worm, when the fisherman can bring his fish close up to him, and does not want to disturb the stream by frequently getting out on the bank. Best length, 2 ft 6 in.; ring, 10 to 12 in. diameter; weight, 6 or 7 oz. This is a larger implement – 5 ft long open – and a very convenient net for any sort of bank-fishing. The 'suspension' is from the hook, passed over the creel-strap, and the 'disengagement,' as well as the movement for extending and bringing it into action, are exceedingly rapid. The length when closed is 2 ft 7 in. Both the foregoing nets are non-collapsing.

In taking a fish out of this or any other net the best plan. I find, is to grasp the fish first in the net; then administer the coup de grace and extract the hook. In boat-fishing this will save much time, and usually when it is most wanted.

In cases of heavy fish a more powerful and solid gaff handle than that fitted to the 'combination' net is desirable. This, of course, presents no difficulty when, as is usually the case, the salmon fisher is accompanied by an attendant who carries both the weapons and spoils of war. A hollow bamboo, 5 or 6 feet long – or say 6 inches longer than the rod joints, so as to carry a spare top – makes a comparatively light and at the same time thoroughly efficient handle. The 'flaw' in it is that the screwed-in gaff is given to turning in its socket, a performance as often as not accompanied by the loss of the fish. To remedy this I got Farlow to drive a steel rivet right through both gaff- ferrule and the screw of the gaff itself, the pointed end passing through and screwing into the opposite side (only). This, of course, makes any turning or twisting of the gaff impossible, whilst it is readily unscrewed whenever the gaff has to be taken off.

Should it happen that 'Donald is too late,' or that the salmon fisher has to depend on himself for gaffing his fish, a largish gaff with a handle only a few inches long, and a knob at the end, that he can slip into his coat pocket, will be found most convenient. Some time is, of course, required in killing a fish under such conditions, as he must be brought within arm's length of the fisherman who has only got his left hand with which to 'show him the butt,' as the expression is; but that it is a perfectly practicable performance I can testify, having done it over and over again myself, sometimes in the case of very heavy fish. Indeed, even when I have had an attendant carrying the ordinary long-handled gaff, I have frequently preferred gaffing the fish with it myself rather than run the risk of the clumsy treatment which it is too likely to receive at his unskillful or unpracticed hands.

It is curious how difficult it is to become a really first-rate gaffer. Indeed it seems to be an accomplishment as a rule entirely beyond the reach of the uneducated, or half-educated, man. I fail at this moment to recall more than two or three instances – notable ones, I admit – of a gillie or keeper being really an adept in the art, and not once, but constantly I have, I fear, disgusted my professional 'fisherman' attendant by either gaffing my fish myself with the right hand, whilst the rod was held with the left, or summoning to my assistance the trusty friend and companion of many a red-letter day's salmon and pike fishing to whose steady nerve and skilful hand I owe not one but scores of fish that would never otherwise have been brought to bank...

On a very rocky bit of the upper part of the Usk where we – Mr. Edwin Darvall and myself – have killed some hundreds, if not indeed thousands, of *salmonidae*, the gaffing business was the despair of my friend's faithful henchman, Timothy – as it is written of him:

> The wily Tim with dextrous gaff
> Tries hard to cut the line in half;

and I am afraid he has many a time thirsted for my blood when his master has insisted upon my depriving him of his 'wand of office' at the critical juncture. On one occasion the wily Tim not only succeeded in thus cutting the line whilst failing to gaff the fish, but also, by what Artemus Ward would call a 'dextrous movement,' managed to bring the gaff point into contact with the flank of his master's favourite bull-dog. Between the imminent peril to his legs on the one side and to his head on the other, the faithful Tim's chances of getting off with a whole skin were at that moment not worth a pin's purchase; but Fate came to his assistance – the gaff turned in the handle, thus releasing its astonished and howling victim, and his master's gathering wrath found vent in a peal of irrepressible laughter. 'Pongo,' however, who I was delighted to meet a few days ago as broad and as 'bull-doggy' as ever, will bear the gaff mark till his dying day.

Gaffing in really rapid torrents is a matter of considerable physical as well as artistic difficulty, and the choice is frequently between Scylla on the one hand and Charybdis on the other. It is often necessary to gaff 'when you can,' to snatch a passing stroke, that is, in the middle of an intervening shallow, or to take a mean advantage of the glimpse of a back fin as it is carried past in a whirl of foam by its still struggling, though retreating owner. In trying these impromptu conclusions, however, the victory is not always with the gaff. Repeatedly, I have seen – and I may say felt! – the bearer of the gaff dragged head over heels into the stream by the vigorous efforts of a salmon which he was endeavouring to gaff before it was, to use angling vernacular, half-killed. Many similar catastrophes I have seen averted only by an ignominious let-go of the gaff, and it has more than once happened to me personally to be saved from a ducking by the gaff handle or hook or both giving way.

I well remember a tussle of this sort when fishing the Usk, two or three years ago, below Pantysgallog Bridge. I had hooked a heavy fish under the fall – at this spot a series of 'rushes' over sharp gradients – and he at once headed straight up-stream for the heaviest of them, half-foam half-water. Here he 'sulked,' and nothing I could do would move him. The keeper was invisible, but I managed to get hold of the gaff from the bank where it lay, and then by some slight exercise of agility secured a foothold on a flattish rock right over where my friend was taking it easy. Throwing back the rod over my left shoulder, and tightening the strain on the fish as much as possible, I contrived with the right hand by sheer muscle to force the gaff down to the bottom, right under where he was lying – a depth perhaps of two and a half or three feet. A lucky stroke upwards did the rest at the first attempt. I shall never forget the rush that fish gave. For an instant or two it was 'pull devil, pull baker.' But, with the weight of water on him, four hands instead of one might have failed to haul him out. In the present case, it was perfectly evident that he on the contrary would haul me in. I felt I could not hold on another moment, and yet could not bring myself to let go; when suddenly the gaff twisted, I imagine, in the socket, cutting the line as it came away, and leaving me to struggle my way back to terra firma as best I could. A long, deep, still pool, some two or three hundred yards long, stretched away below the fall, and down the bank of this I wended my way towards the next cast, in a sufficiently un-amiable frame of mind. Suddenly my eye was caught by something that looked like a huge bar of gold wavering slowly with the current about mid-stream. I guessed in a moment that it was my late antagonist who, poor fellow, had gotten his death as well as his liberty. With an impromptu grappling tackle I succeeded after a few attempts in hooking and bringing him to bank. He was not quite dead, however, but still made a feeble fight, and was game to the last; like Hotspur:

> ... in bloody state Rend'ring faint quittance,
> wearied and out-breath'd.

Another, somewhat ludicrous, incident of this sort occurs to my memory, although the successful party in the encounter was, I believe, on this occasion a pike. I say I 'believe,' because the whole of his body except his tail fin was deeply embedded in weeds from which it would have been impossible to extricate him by any legitimate method.

It was on the Hampshire Avon at Summerley, the beautiful seat of Lord Normanton, to whose courtesy I have been indebted for many a charming day's pike fishing, that the in cident in question occurred. My trusty friend and alter ego, Mr Darvall, and myself, with Lord Normanton's fisherman, Tizard, were paddling our way slowly down stream in one of the small Avon punts, when we suddenly caught sight of this tail, 'broad as the baldrick of an earl,' gently undulating in an opening in the water lilies. The fish was evidently a huge one; the chance of tempting him to be caught *secundum artem* was *nil*; Tizard earnestly assured me his master was most anxious to have a large pike for the table – and so – I yielded to the tempter ... The boat glides noiselessly down to the unconscious *esox*, and now the gaff is steadily but surely stretched over the spot where leviathan's shoulder is likely to be, giving him an imaginary length of about four feet ... *Whish!* There was a rapid 'stroke,' a plunge, and with a rush sufficient to have upset a whale boat the stricken monster dashed for the bottom of the river, at that point at least twenty feet deep.

It was an exciting moment. I found myself being pulled

incontinently over the boat's side, which was taking in water freely, and clutched at the nearest available support, which happened to be the seat of the keeper's corduroy nether garments. It came bodily away in my grasp ... at this juncture nothing, as I believe, could have saved the boat from capsizing, if the gaff, yielding to the excessive strain, had not first twisted in the socket and then straightened out – thus, of course, releasing the enemy, who, though deep struck, may, I would fain hope, have yet survived the indefensible attack made upon him, *contra bonos mores*, and lived on to attain a still greater age and a yet vaster breadth of tail.

Tizard, the keeper, was the only one who did not laugh heartily; but on a hint that we should contribute to his next tailor's bill his countenance resumed its wonted serenity. Some of us on the occasion had certainly, however, a narrow escape of being drowned ... and the verdict of all good pike fishers would doubtless have been – 'and serve them right.'

While I am on the subject of my poaching experiences let me make a clean breast of it and relate how, when a young man, reading at a tutor's on the banks of the Thames, my finer perceptions were on one occasion blunted, and my better feelings done violence to, by the sight of a splendid specimen of *Esox lucius* in one of the stew ponds of Mr Williams, of Temple, the then member for Great Marlow. That morning I had seen him (the pike) lying basking, and in the afternoon (I can hardly tell to this day how it could have happened) I found myself, for some unexplained reason, standing by the side of the aforesaid stew pond, and wondering whether anyone would see through the surrounding withy beds, topped by a notice board threatening legal pains and penalties against trespassers? What is still more inexplicable, I carried in my hand an extra long sort of walking stick – or, shall I say it at once? *hop pole* – and in my pocket a coil of what certainly bore an external resemblance to copper wire. A couple of feet of this wire had somehow got on to the end of the hop pole, whence it dangled in such a manner as almost to deceive the eye into the notion that it was not altogether unlike the abomination commonly known amongst certain persons of impaired moral perception as a noose or 'sniggle'...

Hop pole in hand, I bent carefully over the water and reconnoitred the position of my friend *Esox* – merely in order, of course, the better to admire his majestic proportions, as he supported his huge body on his ventral *pinnae*, and 'feathered' the water with his pectoral and caudal fins.

'A delicate monster, truly,' I observed, 'quite an ichthyological study.' And simultaneously an uninitiated spectator might have imagined that the appearance of the noose aforesaid passed gently but quickly over his head and shoulders...There was a curious sudden commotion in the water; and at the same moment a rustling in the withies behind – and then a well-known voice (being, in fact, that of Mr. Williams' head water bailiff and fisherman) was heard, in accents the sarcastic tones of which I shall never forget, observing:

'Well, Mr Pennell, this 'ere be a pretty go!'

'Confound you,' said I, furious with conflicting emotions, 'you've made me lose him – a twenty-pounder if he was an ounce!'...

'Well, what is to be done, sir?' was the next remark.

By this time my wrath had cooled down a little and I instinctively felt in my waistcoat pocket. It was empty.

'Unluckily, Edwards,' I said, 'I have left my purse behind.'

'Oh! Never mind, sir,' was the reply, 'everyone knows your credit's good at the Bell!'

'How sad and mad and bad it was'! I should like to quote – if only to 'keep myself in countenance' the confsessions of Mr Thomas Westwood (poet, and author of 'Bibliotheca Piscatoria'), which he makes in one of his charming angling idylls, the 'Lay of the Lea'. Not that I would 'Drag his frailties from their dread abode,' But merely that, as he is an old friend of mine, I should like to do my best to give his confessions the publicity that I know he would desire for them!

Bobbing 'neath the bushes,
Crouched among the rushes,
On the rights of Crown and State I'm, alas! Encroaching,
What of that? I know
My creel will soon o'erflow,
If a certain Cerberus do not spoil my poaching.

The 'certain Cerberus' being, in fact, the Government water
bailiff employed to look after the well-known Enfield Powder
Mills. Still I must say Mr Westwood's crime was of a far less
heinous complexion that mine. He only fished, fairly, where –
well 'where he didn't ought to' whilst I... but let me drop the
veil over these sad examples of human depravity, and come
back to gaffing.

The 'queerest fish' that it ever happened to me – to gaff,
I was going to say, but I remember that on this occasion it
chanced to be to net – was a wild duck. Spinning one day for
pike on Loch Lochy I saw the duck – an overgrown 'flapper'
– swimming not thirty yards from the boat The idea occurred
to me to try and cast over him, and after a few attempts I had
the pleasure of seeing the bait settle gracefully across his neck.
A 'gentle stroak,' as Nobbes calls it, and the next moment he
dived, and, 'playing' like a veritable fish, never came to the
top again till I had him at the side of the boat and passed the
landing net under him. An hour afterwards he was roasting
before a drift-wood fire on a spit of arbutus; and washed down
with a glass of genuine 'Long John' he made a most excellent
lunch. 'These to his memory!'

It is wonderful what an appetite the air of a Highland
Loch gives – a thing most excellent when one has the
wherewithal to satisfy it; but I often think it must be 'hard
lines' on the Gaelic tramps and gipsies – if there are any so
far north of the country of 'Meg Merrilies' (Galloway). I
once had myself the experience of a supperless tramp with
a friend in these 'high latitudes,' and the recollection has
by no means that 'enchantment' which 'distance' – we had

covered some thirty miles of ground more or less – ought proverbially to lend. When it is getting dark and a man has distinctly lost his way in a country where there are no roads, and no visible population, it is the wisest plan to yield as gracefully as may be to the 'inevitable;' and if he cannot, like Mark Tapley, be 'jolly under circumstances,' at least to do the best he can for his bodily comfort, without waiting till he has taken the last mile out of himself, and left his physique too much exhausted to contend on fair terms with damp grass and night dews.

Acting on this view, we utilised our 'last mile' in 'prospecting' – and eventually made ourselves a fairly comfortable shakedown of heather under the shelter of an overhanging rock – *sub tegmine* fern-i. But now we began to feel the air effect upon our appetites, and to remember that we had been on the go since breakfast and had eaten nothing. We were in fact starving! A raw turnip would have been a godsend, and a dish of potatoes a wild delirium. But there was nothing for it, so we put on whatever extra in the way of garments we had in our knapsacks and turned in fasting. What my friend's dreams were about I cannot say, but mine ran on lakes teeming with fat luscious trout which came up to be caught of their own accord, and then, to save trouble, jumped spontaneously into the frying pan. Assuredly these visions must have been prophetic; for though we fondly imagined we had camped on a plateau of bare and unbroken moorland, when morning dawned the scene had been transformed as by magic,

> And on a sudden, lo! the level lake,
> And the long glories' of the rising sun!

The sight of water – and water doubtless containing trout – gave, as Ingoldsby says, 'a new turn to the whole affair.' I fortunately had my fly rod with me, so I left my friend to make a fire as best he could and

... stepping down By zigzag paths, and juts of pointed rock
Came on the shining levels of the lake.

Without stopping, like the bold Sir Bedivere, till 'both my eyes were dazzled,' I soon put together my rod and adjusted a cast of flies. Never before did I fish with such energy; never did I watch for a rise with such breathless attention! The first fish I hooked was a mere 'troutling' – little bigger than a gudgeon – who would at other times have been incontinently returned to the water; but circumstances being as they were I played and landed him and deposited him on the bank with as much care as if he had been a five-pounder. He was two mouthfuls at any rate. A friendly breeze, however, shortly afterwards sprang up, and with the 'long ripple washing in the reeds' a satisfactory repast was soon provided...

Later on we discovered a farmhouse hard by the lake shore, and finding that the trout fishing in the Laggan and neighbouring Spean-water was excellent – we arranged to put up for a week with its hospitable inmates, and enjoyed really first-rate sport, more than once being literally unable to carry home our spoils. I revisited the spot some years later, but whether I had incautiously betrayed the whereabouts of our 'happy hunting grounds,' and they had been invaded by tourists, or whether the trout thought they had done enough for me on my first visit, I cannot say, but the fishing was indifferent, not to say decidedly poor.

But where am I wandering to? I started at gaffing salmon, and I find myself now describing the catching and eating of half a dozen troutlings, whose united ounces would not have outweighed a Devonshire peel... Let me for the sake of consistency finish where I began, and end this part of my notes on Tackle with a few practical hints on the subject of Gaffs and How to Gaff a Fish. To the novice, at any rate, they may not be altogether useless.

The skilful use of the gaff, besides demanding special qualities, can only be acquired in perfection by actual practice, and circumstances 'beyond one's control' are constantly occurring which of necessity make their own laws, and the best-considered system inapplicable. The following are, however, a few axioms that can be safely formulated as general guides.

1. Never thrust your gaff forward until you are prepared to strike, and never make any half-attempts. These feints generally scare the fish and not unfrequently cut the line.
2. Under ordinary circumstances do not attempt to gaff a fish that is more than a foot below the surface, or until he is pretty fairly spent. The best position is when he is 'broadside on,' but often, of course, you must gaff whenever you can.
3. The 'proper' place to gaff is between the head and the back fin.
4. The critical moment having arrived, rapidly, but at the same time steadily, extend your gaff over and beyond the back of the fish, bringing it gently down upon it as it were. Then a short sharp jerk from the wrist and elbow will drive in the gaff without prematurely frightening the fish or endangering the tackle.

After landing the fish, whether by net or gaff, the next point is to carry him.

If the catch be a good one, especially of salmon, it is practically out of the question for the fisherman to carry them himself from place to place and fish at the same time. '*Necessitas non habet legs*,' as a friend of mine once dog-latinised it and these conditions are, of course, also a law unto themselves.

In trout fishing, or where the spoils are not likely to be weighty, the fly-fisher, and still more the worm-fisher, will probably very often have to carry his fish himself. For this purpose bags and baskets 'many and great' are sold at the tackle shops, but that they are most of them defective in some points in which they might have been perfected, goes without saying. In fact, as regards the bags (which for ordinary purposes I always use myself), I have found them mostly to suffer the disability of coming to pieces – if not the first time they had a good catch to carry, at any rate, after, say, a few days or weeks of real hard wear and tear; others, again, let the slime and drippings ooze through. After trying various patterns, including one of my own, figured in the first edition, I am disposed to think that for combined strength and simplicity, and taking one day's fishing with another, nothing beats, or perhaps equals, the 'Freke bag,' as it is called, which is, or should be, made double.

That is, there are two bags, in fact, buttoned together at the side edges: one bag, of strong waterproof cloth, fitted with a flap, and the other – the inner one – with the mouth left open, so to speak, although kept practically closed when carried by the combined action of its own weight and that of the shoulder-straps passing through two metal rings at the top. One of the bags can be used for carrying fish, the other for tackle, lunch, etc...; or, at a pinch, both may be used for fish. The bag without the covering flap is moreover so constructed that if an unexpectedly large fish be caught its head and tail will project through the openings left at the top of the sides.

The 'Usk' basket, made by Farlow, which is carried over the shoulder of the attendant by means of a stout handle, some two feet long, resting on a leather shoulder-pad, is the best special arrangement I have met with for the purpose. A basket of this form 32 inches long by about 15 deep will carry half a dozen moderate-sized salmon or pike comfortably – the comfort including that of the attendant, on whose shoulders the mechanical adjustment of the crutch or handle, having a soft leather shoulder-pad under it, makes it sit as lightly as possible.

In deciding upon the question of basket or bag I personally prefer the latter in every respect but one – when you have caught nothing it exposes the nakedness of the land!

WADERS AND WADING BOOTS

Following up the subject of the fly-fisher's equipment, let me strongly advocate the use of waterproof boots, stockings, or trousers whenever wading is really necessary. When it is not indispensable several self-evident advantages are presented by fishing from *terra firma*. But by getting wet and remaining so are engendered many of the after ills that flesh is heir to, in the shape of rheumatisms, neuralgias, varicose veins and what not, which when 'wild youth's past,' are apt to remind the veteran of his early indiscretions. I formerly suffered a small martyrdom myself from lumbago – the result of 'fairy follies' in the wading line when I was still in my teens, and used to look forward to a sort of amphibious existence for eight or ten hours as 'half the fun.' To have unfrolicked such fun I would since have given something considerable... Ergo, don't make a practice of going into the water without waders.

In the matter of material for waterproof boots, etc., there is a plethora of choice, and 'scope and verge' enough for the most fastidious. It matters little, really, whether the waders be of waterproof cloth or leather, or felt or leather India-rubber coated, so that they keep the legs dry and have plenty of nails. Of 'felt soles' I have had no practical experience; but I know that a scientific distribution of sharp-cornered nails will add greatly to the security of the foothold in deep and swift water.

One further hint: the higher the trousers come up the better. Neither the ordinary wading trousers, nor stockings, however (nor their equivalent in leather boots), fulfill adequately a need which I have constantly experienced myself, and which I suppose, therefore, other fishermen have also felt: namely, a nether garment, that one can 'paddle about with' in wet weather, wet grass, and (if occasion requires) do a little extempore wading in, without encumbering one's movements with the ordinary waders or boots, which, whatever their other merits, are a serious hindrance to locomotion, and, in the case of the less robust (owing to their weight), a tax on the physique which is almost prohibitive. In Hampshire, for instance, where 'water-meadows', periodically inundated, form the usual river borderings, a pretty constant state of dampitude is likely to be the condition of the lower extremities of the 'unwaterproofed' pike-fisher or fly-fisher. Then there are the 'drawns', or shallow watercourses – sometimes dry, but more often 'flooded', – and draining into the main stream, where to cross, unfurnished with something in the shape of waders, is, of course, to insure a ducking at least to the knee, and to 'turn the flanks' of which by a succession of strategic movements to the front and rear involves much waste of time. Bearing in mind the caveat I have already entered in the earlier pages of this chapter against the cultivation of damp legs, on the ground of stored-up rheumatisms, etc..., I lately had made for myself a sort of 'half' waders, not so cumbersome nor quite so long as the ordinary wading stockings or boots, but long enough to make me independent of watery impediments so far as flooded meadows and irrigation conduits are concerned, and which at the same time are so light and comparatively cool as to be no hindrance to locomotion. These aids to the amphibious have been christened 'over-knee waders,' and, as their name expresses, they come well up five or six inches above the knee, below which again they fasten with a buckle-strap.

By this arrangement I get rid of those inconvenient appendages, waist or shoulder straps, by which the ordinary wader is suspended, at the same time reducing the weight and transferring the point of suspension to its more natural situation below the knee.

The 'leg-part' of the over-knee waders is of fine, but at the same time perfectly waterproof, material – like that of ordinary wading stockings, but very much lighter – and this is continued at the foot under light buff leather boots, kept in position by a strap across the instep. The 'sum tottle of the whole,' as Mr Hume used to say, is that whereas a similar pair of ordinary wading stockings and boots (coming up only an inch or two higher) weigh between five and six pounds – more often nearer six than five – the over-knee waders are, for a man of six feet, barely over three pounds – not much more than one half, and little, if at all, in excess of the weight of an ordinary pair of shooting boots. There are many anglers, not quite so young as they used to be, to whom the weight of the orthodox waders is almost prohibitive; and there are many others who, though like myself, quite up to 'carrying weight' when really necessary, object to doing so when no real necessity exists. And all this holds good just as much in the case' of the Trout-fisher as the Pike-fisher. Perhaps, indeed, even more; inasmuch as, whilst the enforced wadings of the one are more or less exceptional and intermittent, those of the other are the normal conditions of his sport.

I often think that the question of 'weight-carrying' in the matter of dress and equipment generally is less studied than it ought to be by sportsmen. A man will give fifty guineas more for a pair of Purdey guns, because they weigh perhaps a few ounces less than a pair by some other maker – with, as he believes, an equal chance of safety to his head – and he knows by experience how those few ounces will 'tell' towards the end of a long day's tramp over a grouse moor. In all this he is, so far as avoirdupois is concerned, perfectly right – but why does he not go a step further and devote a little attention to the weight of the other portions of his equipment? Why, for instance, will he allow his boot maker to put nearly a pound more into his shooting boots than is really necessary? As I have said, the weight of the latter is usually not far short of three pounds, whereas, two pounds is nearer the weight that is really necessary, if the bootmaker is anything of an artist in his business. By using one very thick and solid piece of leather for the sole, and thinner leather than usual above the foot (where thickness is not needed except by those with weak ankles), I get my shooting boots down to the weight indicated, without any sacrifice that I have ever been able to discover either on the score of 'water-proofness' or durability – but then my boot maker, Moykopf, of the Burlington Arcade, is an artist.

As all waterproof garments are liable to become more or less damp from repressed perspiration, they should invariably be dried after use, as well to prevent the linings, and, indeed, the rubber itself, becoming rotten, as for purposes of health and comfort. The best way of drying is to fill the legs and feet of the boots, stockings, or trousers, with warm bran, oats, or barley, which should be shaken out as soon as it begins to cool (if this precaution is not attended to the moisture which has been absorbed begins at once to re-evaporate). When the waders have been emptied of their drying contents they should be turned inside out and hung up, foot upwards. In the case of the combined rubber and leather boots noticed, this (of course) cannot be accomplished, and many fishermen keep the 'feet-part' always filled with carefully dried grain or sawdust or on boot-trees, with the object of swelling or keeping them in shape, and to avoid shrinking.

Whenever waders are used, thick warm woollen stockings, and leggings also if possible, should be worn inside. I used always to wear and recommend for this and other sporting purposes the all-wool garments made by the well-known Jaeger Company, but my patience has recently given way before the combined inconveniences of excessive shrinking – which I suppose in their otherwise excellent manufacture is inevitable – and the inconvenient forms in which they seem determined to thrust an essentially good idea down the public throat. Shirts doubled over the chest rather than (if anywhere) over the back, and buttoning up at the side instead of in the front – woollen neck-bands which contract into 'chokative' dimensions the first time they are washed – and so on; until one feels at last inclined to start a rival company, and call it the 'Jaeger system stripped of fads and made possible for ordinary mortals!'

As, however, I still feel under obligation to Dr. Jaeger for his capital idea – from which, all drawbacks notwithstanding, I have derived much advantage – I tried instead what could be done in my own small way for my personal comfort, by persuading another firm – Messrs Harborrow, of Cockspur Street – to take up the manufacture of 'Jaeger shirts,' and so forth, on principles free from the inconveniences alluded to. The very slight admixture of cotton in the 'webbing' of the material, which they use at my suggestion, is practically preventative of shrinking, and makes on the whole, I think, a more agreeable and equally healthy garment, whilst, as I say, I can now get my fishing and shooting dress in a form which gives me the advantages of the Jaeger system without its eccentricities.

A propos, I cannot imagine why some more simple and convenient style of dress has not long ago been adopted by 'lady fishers,' as well as by anglers of the sterner sex. Many ladies who now would never dream of approaching the river bank (nearer than the towing path) for fear of spoiling their dresses or wetting their shoes, would if suitably 'appareled' find as keen an interest and enjoyment in the sport as we do, and might even become enthusiastic votaries of the gentle art. How charming it would be when we sally forth after breakfast to lake or stream, to have the companionship of some 'sweet girl graduate,' who, with hair either golden or otherwise, would by her graceful companionship double the pleasures of success! There would be no slovenly casting, no calling to halt for pipes or liquor when fish were on the rise then.

Fight on, brave knights! Bright eyes behold your deeds, written of the 'free and easy passages of arms.

There are indeed already not a few angling champions of the gentler sex who now enter the lists, especially as fly-fishers, and amongst whom the fair daughters of a well-known noble Duke have acquired enviable fame.

We are not all, however, so lucky as to have a salmon river at our door, and I have often thought, watching some modern Dame Juliana punt fishing under the dip of a Thames chestnut tree in August, or later in the autumn sending her spinning bait skimming into the foam below Hurley weir, how much of pleasure, now lost to most of us, is gained by the man whose wife takes heartily to fishing or hunting or whatever other field sport he is devoted to. In this way she becomes not only his helpmate at home, but his 'chum' and true comrade when on his rambles by flood and field, or, rifle in hand, mounting the 'imminent deadly breach' which is shortly to witness the campaign against chamois or red deer.

Not that shooting is a sport by any means so naturally fitted to women as fishing. Their figure makes the handling of the gunstock always rather awkward, and the recoil is sometimes apt – unless very light charges are used – to be dangerous. But to fishing there is no drawback, unless, indeed, it be the petticoats with which some thick-ankled leader of fashion in bygone times has managed to cramp and disfigure one of the prettiest parts of the human form. No skirts will vex the tameless ankles of our women of the future. Already there, is a marked and healthy improvement visible in the length of the dress, and women need no longer draggle about behind them a ridiculous and often muddy train, which if it does not do duty for a road-sweeper cannot certainly be shown to subserve any other useful purpose.

The influence of dress has been recognised by many philosophers as exercising a powerful effect in moulding the national character, and I am quite satisfied that if English men and women, and those living in town as well as in the country, were to adopt a dress allowing greater freedom and play to the limbs and muscles, and (so far as men are concerned) would discard, once and for all, chimneypot hats, frock coats, leg bags – I use the term literally, not in a slangy sense – and the other paraphernalia of the bandbox, there would be a marked advance in the manliness and 'robustness' of the race.

Women who shoot or fish should never hesitate to wear a dress suitable for the purpose; long skirts are not only constantly in the way, but often prove a source of real danger to the wearer. The same remark holds still more true in regard to long riding habits, and if the readers of these lines had seen as many accidents, and hair-breadth escapes from accidents, in the hunting field, as I have, owing to long skirts, they would join in the outcry which ought, in the name of common sense, to be raised against them. However, I am glad to see that there is some improvement of late years in this respect also.

In arranging a lady's fishing dress, next to the short skirts thick boots more or less waterproof are the most important item, having regard both to protection and comfort; but this is precisely the point on which the male adviser finds the greatest difficulty in procuring a favourable hearing for his views. Simply on the score of 'prettiness' it cannot be said that a stout double-soled shooting or fishing boot is as killing as a Queen Anne slipper, Louis Quatorze shoe, or a pair of dainty *bottines*, expressly designed to set off and emphasise the delicate arch of the instep, whilst displaying the foot and ankle in a position which, if not quite natural, is at least exceedingly picturesque.

> The flower she touched on, dipp'd and rose,
> And turned to look again.

But, my dear lady readers – if I should be so favoured as to have any – do not let it be forgotten that there is 'a beauty of fitness,' and that where really rough work has to be done 'ease before elegance,' and, it might be added, 'health before both,' is a golden maxim.

The following hints for dress, which have been kindly given me by a lady who has had large practical experience with both rod and gun, may possibly be found of service:

Short skirt of linsey wolsey made as simple as possible – in fact, a kind of 'housemaid's dress.' Norfolk jacket made of all-wool material. A comfortable toque (the close-fitting toque does not catch the wind). It is best to have the costume of one colour, say a nice heather mixture or whitish grey. I advise 'linsey' for the skirt, as it is everlasting in wear, and the 'all-wool' for the Norfolk jacket, being warmer and more healthy.

Now for the most important item: boots. They should fit perfectly, and be made of porpoise hide, with honest broad soles and plenty of room for the toes, and flat heels – in their proper place, not under the arch of the instep. The boots should lace in the same way that men's shooting boots do, and be made to come well up the leg (so that gaiters can be dispensed with). Length of skirt an inch or so above the ankle.

This dress is suitable for either fishing or shooting. If worn for the latter over a 'clayey' country, a few inches of light waterproof on the bottom of the skirt are advisable. Some ladies wear gaiters, but I think if the boots are made high enough they are not necessary. Woollen under-garments should be worn, from stockings upwards.

For 'waterproofing' all cloth and woollen materials – I do not say making them actually waterproof, but sufficiently so to keep the under-garments practically dry – I can recommend the following receipt, given me by R. Atkinson, Esq., of Temple Sowerby:

> Dissolve sugar of lead and alum in rain water, one ounce of each to a quart of water. When settled down, draw off the clear (this is most easily done with a syphon), saturate the woollen article in it (I generally leave it in twenty-four hours), and dry in the open air. From my own experience I have found a coat thus treated to be quite waterproof. For a few days there is an unpleasant smell, but it soon wears off. I infinitely prefer such protection from rain to any macintosh or other india-rubber manufacture.

FISHING ETCETERAS

I might under this heading fill a chapter, if not a volume; as taking the term in its broadest sense, fishing 'etceteras' might be made to embrace the entire contents of a tackle shop, less the half-dozen prominent items of the fisherman's equipment which I have already noticed. But I must leave these minutiae to take care of themselves, as questions of 'space' – represented in a concrete form by Messrs Longman – warn me to bring this chapter to a close.

In doing so, however, I would briefly refer to a few items which may be of use to the fly-fisher.

The first is a fishing knife – an almost indispensable addition to a satisfactory outfit for the river-side; containing in a small compass, scissors, knife, and 'disgorger blade' – three implements which are liable to be called into requisition at every turn.

The second 'etcetera' is rather a bulky one, being in fact a fishing boat! 'As such boats made of inflatable India-rubber can now be obtained at several waterproof manufactories, and at a reasonable price, and as the comfort of one of them on many fishing expeditions, especially in lake districts, is simply not to be exaggerated, I think fishermen travelling *en luxe* will be wise to make a portable boat part of their equipment.

They are made to hold 'any number' of people, and even a boat of the smallest size is steady enough for all the purposes of the fly-fisher.

2

Salmon Fishing with the Fly Also a Few Notes an Fly fishing for Sea Trout

MAJOR JOHN P. TRAHERN

It is with great pleasure, although with considerable diffidence, that I accede to a request, made in very complimentary terms by Mr Cholmondeley-Pennell, that I should write an account of my experience in salmon fishing; and I am induced to do so in the hope that it may be instructive to gentlemen who are inexperienced in the art, and also to a certain extent interesting to the angling public.

There are certain well-known and established facts connected with salmon fishing that need no mention on my part, and I will endeavour to confine myself, as far as I can, to the relation of that which I know of my own knowledge. During an experience of over thirty years, in England, Scotland, Ireland, and Norway, I have had most favourable opportunities of studying the habits of the salmon and the art of fishing for him, and, if any information I am able to give should prove useful to my brother fishermen, I shall be amply repaid for my trouble.

All the knowledge we possess of the habits of the salmon has been acquired during that period of his life which he passes in fresh water. We know nothing of his habits during his sojourn in the sea, except that at certain seasons of the year he feels his way along the coast until instinct teaches him he has found the estuary of the river he has been bred in, and he then makes his way up it. From this time until, in the natural course of events, he returns to the sea, we have many opportunities of studying his habits, and we get to know certain facts, from which we draw our own conclusions. We start theories without end, some of which, after a short argument, will be found utterly baseless; but others seem more plausible, and have a certain amount of evidence to support them, such as may make it reasonable to assume that we have arrived at something like a near approximation to the truth.

We know a salmon enters fresh water at certain seasons of the year for the purpose of propagating his species, that sooner or later he makes his way to the locality where instinct points out to him he is to deposit his spawn, and that on his journey upwards he will occasionally take whatever bait is offered him by the angler. When the time comes he deposits his spawn, after which he gradually makes his way down the river and re-enters the sea. The sea is his native element, and I think it must be taken for granted that he feeds voraciously during his sojourn there: intact, he must do so, otherwise he could not grow so rapidly or attain such condition in the short time it is known he has to stay there. Nature has provided him with a formidable set of teeth, and it may be presumed he makes the best use of them.

When he first enters fresh water he is in his prime, and in the full glory of his strength. Doubtless instinct teaches him not to leave the salt water before he has attained this condition that he may be able to surmount the difficulties he will have to encounter before he can reach his spawning ground. A half-conditioned, ill-fed fish could not accomplish this: his strength would be exhausted before half the journey was completed, and he would probably be no more seen. A fish in this condition is seldom caught by nets in fresh water or on the sea-coast.

There is great difference of opinion as to whether or not a salmon feeds in fresh water. In my opinion there is positive evidence that he does; otherwise, why does he take flies, live and artificial bait, worms, and shrimps? Is it to be supposed for a moment that if he takes these he will not take any other food fresh water affords him? It is true he deteriorates in condition from the date of his migration from the sea: but this may be accounted for by the fact that the food the river affords is not of that fattening nature which he gets in the sea, and Nature evidently did not intend he should remain in the same prime condition in fresh water as when he entered it. He has to undergo certain changes before he is in a fit state to spawn, and, if he remained in the same prime condition as when he entered the river, this would be impossible.

It is well known that a newly run salmon will take a fly or bait sooner than one which has been a longer time in fresh water, and I could quote many instances to prove this. A few years ago I was fishing in the north of Norway, where there was a large pool under a fall which was impassable for salmon. The fish congregated in this pool in vast numbers, but I seldom killed one in it that had not sea lice on him. (The presence of sea lice is a certain sign of a new-run salmon: these parasites die after being twenty-four hours in fresh water.) I also remember, when fishing in the Galway river, in Ireland, in the spring months, where from twenty to thirty salmon were killed daily with rod and line, nine out of ten had sea lice on them. The fish congregated in the stream below the weir in thousands, and, although they had only been a short time in fresh water, they did not seem to care much about feeding.

To account for this satisfactorily is impossible, but it may be reasonable to assume that for the first few hours after a salmon has left salt water, where he has been in the habit of feeding voraciously, his appetite does not leave him: but eventually the absence of the food he has been accustomed to will make him sulky and disinclined to feed. He is in such good condition that he can afford to abstain for a while; but he will sooner or later be obliged to feed to maintain his strength, in order to enable him to reach his spawning ground. It is not to be supposed he can exist on water, and we know that at times he takes a fly or bait greedily, particularly after a 'fresh,' when he shifts his quarters up stream. He will then take the first fly he sees; but when once he is lodged it is generally difficult to get a rise out of him.

There is a certain time of year when salmon are less inclined to feed than at any other period – this is generally from about the middle of July to the middle of September. The temperature of the water and of the atmosphere is then higher than at any other time, and this has doubtless a great effect on the appetite of a salmon. I have found this to be the case upon almost every river I have fished. It matters little whether the fish are fresh-run or stale, they are indifferent to taking food, and it is quite exceptional to get a good day's sport during those months. They begin again, however, to take at the latter end of September and up to the time of the close season; but these are mostly gravid fish, and hardly worth the trouble of fishing for.

After a salmon has spawned he is at his lowest ebb – thin, emaciated, and unsightly to behold. He then gradually makes his way to the sea, but, as it is necessary to recruit his strength before he finally leaves fresh water, Nature seems to have provided him with ample means for so doing at this particular season, as on his downward journey he is accompanied by millions of the fry of his own species, and it is supposed he makes such havoc amongst them that it has been in contemplation to alter the salmon laws, making it legal to take spent salmon after a certain date. I have seen spent salmon in such a condition that it has been difficult to distinguish them from newly run fish.

It is commonly believed, because nothing has ever been found in the stomach of a salmon, that he does not feed. A friend of mine, who takes the greatest interest in this subject, told me that, when he was fishing in Norway some years ago, he cut open every fish he caught (thirty in number), and did not find anything inside any of the salmon, but three of the grilse were gorged with insects, which he thought were daddy-longlegs.

This is the only instance I ever met with of food being found in the stomach of a salmon; it is, of course, an exception: but if any evidence were wanting, this of itself proves that salmon will feed, though how to account for the absence of food in their stomachs is a puzzle. I have often noticed, fishing with natural bait, when a salmon is landed the bait is torn from the hooks and sent up the line a foot or more. Does not this show that a salmon has marvelous power of ejecting its food? Is it not probable that, when he gets into trouble, either by being hooked, or netted, he will disgorge the contents of his stomach? A trout that is full of food will, we all know, do so after he is landed – and why not the salmon? My friend who told me he found food inside the grilse also said that several Norwegian net fishermen informed him that, after their nets were drawn in they generally found a number of half- digested fish amongst the salmon thus caught. He also said he had heard the same story at Newcastle-upon-Tyne. If these fishermen spoke the truth, it goes a long way in support of my theory.

The absence of food in a salmon's stomach has been accounted for in one other way. A salmon may have such powers of digestion that whatever food he consumes disappears almost at once; but against this supposition there is the fact of what my friend found inside three grilse. As it is certain grilse are only salmon in youth, this theory must fall to the ground, and I am inclined to think the former explanation is the correct one.

A spring salmon will not travel as fast as a summer salmon. The rate at which salmon travel is dependent upon the state of the weather and the temperature of the water. Should there be a hard winter, lasting, as it often does, well into the spring, hardly a fish will have found his way to the upper waters; but should there have been an open winter, with good travelling water and no obstruction, the upper reaches will be fairly stocked by the time the fishing season commences. Of course there are exceptions, and, however mild the spring may be in some rivers – for instance, the Wye and the Usk in Monmouthshire and Brecknockshire – spring fish will not travel above a certain distance, and the upper waters do not get stocked until well on in the season. In Scotland the temperature of the water in the early spring is always very low, and obstructions in the Scotch Rivers stop the fish running, so that they will not pass these until the weather gets warmer and the temperature of the water higher.

On the Helmsdale and Shin, in Scotland, are falls over which salmon can easily pass, but they will never do so until the month of April, and it is known almost to a day when they will make their appearance in the stream above these falls. That salmon are very susceptible to cold is quite certain; although they are fresh out of the sea, and in their primest condition, and will take a fly or bait greedily, yet they will not lodge in a rapid stream in the early part of the spring, but are always found in easy water, just where one would expect to find a spent fish; and it is not until well on in the spring that they will lodge in rapid water.

The climate of Ireland is milder than that of any other part of the United Kingdom. The temperature of the water is consequently much higher than in either England or Scotland, and many newly run salmon will be found in early spring in the upper waters of Irish rivers where obstructions exist. The majority of them, however, seem to object to face an obstruction until about the month of April, when the weather gets warmer.

A lake is a great attraction to a salmon. If there is no obstruction between lake and sea, a spring salmon will, on leaving the salt water, make straight for the lake without halting. This is particularly the case in Irish rivers, where the temperature of the water is generally high for the time of year.

Autumn salmon are different in their habits from spring and summer fish. For some unknown reason they remain in the sea until they are full of spawn, and then, not being able, on that account, to surmount the difficulties which a spring or summer salmon is capable of, are seldom found above a certain distance from the sea. Their journey up is also a very slow one, and I have always noticed this peculiarity in the habits of an autumn salmon.

In many of our rivers the heaviest salmon of the season, in splendid condition and in appearance like spring salmon, run during the winter months. The run commences in the autumn, when now and then one is caught, but the great run takes place in December, and I often think it is a pity we are prohibited by law from fishing for them.

If the rivers that are frequented by these fish were closed from October 1 to December 15, and angling only allowed after the latter date, there would be far less harm done than by allowing angling during October and November, when almost every fish hooked is gravid.

By December 15 every gravid fish will have left the pools for the spawning beds, and the catches will be occupied only by those heavy, fresh-run winter salmon. No doubt there are objections to allowing angling during the winter months, but it is a pity we should lose the sport these splendid fish would afford. It is true they can be caught when the season opens in the spring, but by that time they get 'foxey' and have lost condition, and are only fit for kippering; as it is, they do an immense amount of mischief among the smolts in their downward journey to the sea, and we should be far better without them.

Having introduced the salmon to the notice of my readers, I will now endeavour to describe the best way to catch him, and, as it is the most important part of a salmon fisherman's gear, I will commence my remarks with:

THE ROD

I have tried all sorts and sizes of rods, by various makers, but the one I am now using, and have used for many years, is to my mind perfection. It is a greenheart in three splices, made by Farlow, and, if a rod is to be judged by its powers of casting, it should be a good one. It is the one with which I won the first prize at the Fishing Tournament at Hendon, in July 1884, for the longest overhead cast, with a cast of forty-five yards one inch. To cast a long line, a rod requires great lifting power, and my rod possesses this quality to a great extent, although, at the same time, it is not heavy enough to tire one in a hard day's fishing. I am at a loss how to describe it, but its virtue lies in an equal distribution of strength, in proportion, from the butt to the point.

A heavy butt with no spring to it, and with a weak top, is of little use for casting purposes, beyond a certain distance. The spring should be felt, to a certain extent, to the bottom of the butt when casting and I consider a rod which does not possess this quality of little or no value. Castle Connell rods are made on this principle, but, in my opinion, they are too top-heavy. If they had a little less weight at the top and more in the butt, I think they would be pleasanter to fish with and would lose nothing in power. They will doubtless cast as long a line as rods of other descriptions, but, owing to their being so thin at the butt and so top-heavy, it often happens that, when throwing a long line in a gale of wind, they are apt to smash just above the reel. I fished with these rods for years, but for this reason I discarded them. They are, however, very powerful rods, and well suited to the Shannon, where the fish run very heavy and a powerful rod is required; and, as all fishing is done out of a boat on that liver, long casting is unnecessary.

Every rod requires a line to suit it; and it will be as well to bear in mind when making a choice of one that a rod with a weak, whippy top is not suitable for casting thick lines and a stiff or more powerful rod is not adapted for casting a thin line. The best wood for a rod is green or brown heart. It is very light and pleasant to fish with: the only drawback is that rods made of it will sometimes smash at a moment's notice without any apparent cause.

I have sent my favourite rod to Farlow's, and, should anyone wish to try one made on the same lines, he will be able to obtain it at that establishment. In choosing a rod, a novice will walk as it were blindfolded into a fishing-tackle maker's shop, and generally order the biggest rod he can get, and of a caliber which will tire him in half an hour. A big rod seems to be a necessity to him, and a gentle hint from an older angler that the rod is rather too heavy is not often taken in good part. It is only by bitter experience that he will find out his mistake. If fishing-tackle manufacturers would but 'take stock' of their customers, and recommend the beginner to choose a rod which will be found suitable to his strength, it would be no loss to them, and would save a great deal of disappointment. It would, moreover, start the novice in the right road to success; whereas, if he begins fishing with a big rod that is over his strength, he will have probably to toil and labour for weeks before he can make a decent cast, which he might have succeeded in accomplishing in a day or two if he had taken a friend's advice.

A seventeen-foot rod is quite long enough for any ordinary casting for salmon, provided it is of sufficient power. A sixteen- foot rod is long enough for peel or grilse fishing, or even for salmon, when the water is low and where fine tackle and small flies are required. Anyone who has read the reports of the Casting Tournaments at Hendon, will see what marvelous casts were made with sixteen-foot rods: but they must be made of good stuff, with plenty of lifting power. Fishermen of any experience will of course select a rod to suit their own fancy, but I strongly recommend the novice to make his first effort with a rod under his strength, and, above all things, to avoid using one with a weak, whippy top.

The art of rod-making has been brought to great perfection in America; the split-cane rods are marvelous works of art, and are being much used in this country; but they are very expensive, and, as I cannot discover any particular advantage they possess over our old-fashioned English-made rod, I prefer to use the latter.

THE REEL AND LINE

It is a great mistake to fish with a big, heavy reel, as every ounce of needless weight in reel or rod will tell against the angler in a hard day's fishing, as surely as it does upon a racehorse when running a race. A man who thinks it necessary to fish with a big rod generally uses a big reel to match, with as much line as it will hold, very often needlessly thick. To make a clean cast the line must be used to suit the rod. When fishing with a powerful rod a moderately thick line is required, a thin line, as I have before remarked, being of no use. A reel four inches in diameter, with a drum of if inch in width, will hold thirty or forty yards of thick line for casting purposes, and 100 to 120 yards of thin back line – in all about 140 yards, which is long enough for any of our rivers. The majority of fishermen use a thick line, of the same thickness from end to end; but, as I think it may be taken for granted that forty yards only, at the outside, are required for casting purposes, nothing is gained by the remainder of the line being of the same thickness.

I will endeavour to show that there is a great disadvantage in using a continuous thick line, and that there is a good deal to be gained by using a line made as I have described. When fishing with a continuous thick line, should a salmon take a long run when hooked in a rapid stream, the pressure of the water upon the line is so great that, unless the casting line is of unusual strength, there is great risk of its getting broken. On the other hand, fishing with a thin back line, the resistance to the water in a like case is so much less, in proportion, that the chance of bringing the fish to bank is far greater and the risk of a break reduced to a minimum. Another advantage in using a thin back line is that the reel of the aforenamed dimensions will hold a far greater length of line. The line I recommend, say thirty or forty yards, is tapered at both ends, and moderately thick in the middle. The advantage of having this line spliced to a back line is that when one end is worn from casting it can be cut off, the worn end respliced to the back line, and the other end brought into use. Anyone who has not fished with these tapering lines will be surprised at the ease with which they can be cast, and their superiority will be found out when fishing on a windy day. Some say it is best to use a light line upon such an occasion, because it cuts through the wind better than a heavy line, but in my opinion a light one is utterly useless for casting purposes upon a windy day, and the heavier the line the easier it is to cast.

Thicker lines are required for spring and autumn fishing, when large flies and strong tackle are used, but in the summer time, when the peel commence to run and small flies are used, light springy rods and light lines are preferable to the heavy salmon rod, and far more pleasant to fish with. The mouth of a fresh-run peel or grilse is very tender, and the strain likely to be put on the line when the fish is hooked will, if a heavy salmon rod is used, be very apt to tear the hook out. Very little strain is required to fix the barb of the hook, and when fishing for peel the fish should be very lightly handled; easy- running reels should be used when fishing for either salmon or peel, but most particularly so when fishing for the latter.

The tapering lines I have mentioned can be obtained of any length or thickness to suit the angler's fancy, dressed or undressed. I prefer to buy them undressed and dress them myself. An undressed line will last quite as long as a dressed one, and be quite as pleasant to cast, but care should be taken to dry it each day after fishing. I have an undressed line that I have used for two whole seasons, and it is now as sound as the day I bought it. This is more than I can say of most dressed lines sold by fishing-tackle makers, which will seldom stand more than one season's work.

In selecting a dressed line care should be taken to ascertain it is not hollow. A hollow can easily be detected by cutting off the end of the line with a pair of sharp scissors. My objection to a hollow line is this: that should there be a flaw or bruise the water will gradually find its way into the hollow, run down the whole length of the line, and as owing to the outer coating being waterproof the line cannot be dried, it will therefore quickly become rotten. I have seen many lines that have been used only two or three days become quite rotten, which I am convinced has been from no other cause than the one I have mentioned. A hollow line may be easily known, as it is round; a solid plaited line is square.

[See also preliminary chapters on 'Tackle.']

DRESSING LINES

The following recipe for dressing lines I can safely recommend. Mix equal parts of raw linseed oil and best copal varnish, boiling until the mixture singes a feather (this should be done out of doors, owing to the inflammable nature of the solution). When cold put the line in to soak. A week will be enough for a solid plaited line, but if the line is hollow it should remain in much longer so as to allow time for the solution to fill up the hollow. When thoroughly saturated, a fine day should be taken advantage of, and the line put out to dry in the open air, stretched at its full length, fastened at both ends to two wooden posts, all the superfluous dressing being carefully removed with the hand or a bit of cloth, It should not remain out, in its first stage of drying, in the rain, as a very few drops will spoil it, and the dressing will come off; but when the outer coating is tolerably dry, which will be in about a week in warm weather, wet will not affect it, although it will be advisable not to leave it out in the rain at any time if it can be avoided.

In about a fortnight after it has been out the line should be re-dipped in the solution, and the operation of stretching and removing the superfluous dressing repeated. This will be found sufficient, and nothing will remain but to allow it to dry.

A line should not be used for at least six months after being dressed. It may be hung up indoors, but it will be advisable whenever the weather is favourable to put it in the open air.

The best months for performing the operation of dressing are June, July, August, and September, the temperature being higher during those months than at any other time of the year. Dressed lines can be dried in a very short time by mixing 'dryers' with the solution, but there is the greatest objection to their use. The object of the wholesale manufacturer, owing to the great demand, is to get the operation performed as soon as possible, and therefore dryers are required; but the consequence is, although lines dressed in a solution in which dryers have been used look like perfection in the fishing-tackle maker's shop, it will often be found after they have been used a very short time they will 'knuckle,' when they may just as well be thrown into the fire. There is no mistaking a 'knuckled' line, and nothing can be more unsightly. Instead of being the beautiful even-looking coil that came out of the fishing-tackle maker's shop, about every two inches or so, where the line has passed through the rings of the rod, the varnish comes off in dust, and a small white ring appears, giving the line the appearance of the knuckles of the finger.

I have seen many of the best American dressed lines 'knuckle' in a very short time and become quite unfit for use. After paying a good price for a line, nothing to my mind can be more annoying or disappointing, and if this were to happen in a far-off country where there were no fishing-tackle makers' shops, for instance in Norway or Canada, the consequences might be very serious. This evil can, however, be avoided by dressing lines in my fashion, and these I will guarantee to last for years if taken care of and dried every day after fishing. I would not trust the-best looking dressed line that ever came out of a fishing-tackle maker's shop; but the wholesale manufacturers are to blame for this, and not the fishing-tackle makers, who as a rule do the best they can to supply the best article for their customers. I would recommend anyone who has time to spare to dress his own lines, but without dryers; or, if he has not any time to spare, to use them undressed. An undressed line will get saturated with water after the first cast, and this supplying the place of the dressing, the line will be found quite heavy enough to make the longest cast required. The only objection, and it is but a very trivial one, to the use of undressed lines, is that should it be desired to add to the length of a cast by pulling out a yard or so of line before the cast is made, when this is let go it is very apt in its wet state to get twisted around the butt of the rod, which will defeat the object.

CASTING LINES

The selection of a suitable casting line (i.e. the gut line that connects the reel line with the fly) requires great judgment and care on the part of the angler. If the water should be high or stained after a fresh, the strongest lines may be used, and finer ones in proportion as the water gets lower and clearer.

During the early spring months salmon are keener to rise at the fly than at any other time of the year, they will take larger flies than later in the season, and do not seem to care what the casting line is made of; but during the later spring and summer months, when the water is very lew and clear, they are more particular, and very fine casting lines and flies, not much bigger than trout flies, must be used. To land a big salmon in low water with a light rod and fine tackle is a feat any salmon fisher may be proud of.

Treble-twisted or plaited gut casting lines are generally considered the strongest, but these are not to be trusted. Some of them will doubtless last a long time, but many are made up of inferior cast-off gut which is difficult to detect in the piece, and would not stand a week's work. It is also difficult to twist gut so evenly that when a fish is being played, an equal strain shall be made to bear on each strand. Lines made of two strands of carefully selected round salmon gut of equal thickness, untwisted, are much stronger than most of the treble gut casting lines that are generally used, but great care must be taken in making these lines, as when the links are knotted together it will be found that, nine times out of ten, one of the strands will be longer than the other, consequently the shorter strand would have to bear the whole strain when a fish is being played, and the other strand would be useless.

This can be avoided if the following directions are attended to: after the strands that are to compose the line have been selected, and have been allowed to soak in cold water for some hours, take the two that are to form the first link, and having made the loop that is to connect this with the reel line, whip the strands tightly together (this need not be done closely) with well-waxed silk, from the knot where the loop has been made down to nearly the ends of the strands. Knot to the next link and remove the whipping, when it will be found that the strands will lie evenly together and any strain that is put on will be equally shared by both. Commence whipping from the last knot made in the manner above mentioned, and continue until the casting line is complete. I myself never use anything but single gut, unless fishing in big rivers, but I make up my own lines and take great care to use only the strongest gut.

Not long ago I discovered what I thought was a new method of fastening strands of gut together without knots, but I have since found that the invention was not a new one, and that my plan had been adopted years ago by Mr. Cholmondeley-Pennell, and described in his book *The Modern Practical Angler*. His principle and mine are identical, although somewhat differently carried out. The result however, is that in both cases the fastening together of the gut in a casting line is the strongest part of it.

On testing a line so constructed with strands of ordinary salmon gut, dry, it broke at a strain of 15 lbs. in the middle of one of the links and not at the fastening.

Another line of apparently the same strength, the links of which were fastened together by knots in the ordinary way, broke at a knot at a strain of 7 lbs. A third, again, made of two strands of the strongest picked gut, untwisted, without knots, pulled the index of my steelyard down to 20 lbs. without breaking. I am certain it would have stood a strain of several pounds more, but

I was content with such a result, and I feel satisfied that such a line would hold the biggest salmon that was ever caught by rod and line, and a break would be almost impossible.

There is nothing more disappointing or trying to the temper than to get a line broken owing to using bad tackle. The man from whom the gut is bought is pronounced to be a swindler, and never to be patronised again, but in the majority of cases carelessness on the part of the angler lies at the root of the evil, and it is not fair to lay the blame on the man who sells the gut, which varies in quality so much that it is quite a chance to get a good hank of it. Good 'made-up' single-gut casting lines can be bought at any of the leading fishing-tackle makers establishments, but the greatest care should be taken in the choice of one. If there is but one link in the cast of uneven thickness it will be better to put it aside. A cast may be to all appearance perfect, but if the thin end of one of the links is knotted to another which is thicker, there the weak part of the cast will be, and it will be very apt to break at that point. The same care must be taken in making up one's own casting line. Each link should be of even thickness throughout the whole length of the line, and round without a flaw or a scratch. A flat strand, or one which is coarse-looking, should never be used.

If every reasonable care is taken in the selection of a casting line and a fish breaks it, as will occasionally happen to the best of us, the angler has the satisfaction of knowing he has done his utmost to avoid such a catastrophe, and will feel the disappointment far less than if he were conscious a fish was lost through his own carelessness. When a casting line gets worn and ragged, which will probably be the case after two or three months' use, it will be advisable not to trust it. Some of the links may be sound, and may be used in making up another cast, but I would rather not trust them, as it is like mending an old garment with new cloth.

All casting lines should be tested every morning before going out fishing, and also looked over several times during the day. Knots which are often made in casting in foul wind should be taken out whenever they appear, for, if allowed to remain, there is great risk of a break even with the strongest line. If they cannot be taken out, the link in which they occur should be cut out of the cast and replaced by a new one. The most severe test a casting line can be subjected to is to take an end in each hand and give it a sudden jerk. A line must be very strong to stand this, and unless it is intended to go in for big salmon, when the strongest line is required, such a severe test is unnecessary. In testing a line it is generally thought that if it will stand a strong pull it is sound. This is not to be trusted, and it should be subjected to an additional test as follows:

Hold the line by the forefinger and thumb of each hand about an inch on either side of each knot in succession; imagine for a moment that the line is a bit of stick or slate pencil, and proceed as if you were trying to break it. If the gut is worn at any of the knots it will knuckle at that point, and it should be cut off and a new knot made; although it might stand a strong pull, a sudden jerk would generally break it. If the line does not knuckle at any of the knots it may be assumed that it is sound.

Some fishermen prefer a tapered line, which they say will make a neater cast than one of a continuous thickness. This may be very well when fishing in low clear water in summer time, when fine tackle and fine casting are required, but in spring or autumn, or when fishing in a big water, where it is necessary to use the strongest tackle, I should prefer, at the risk of making an occasional clumsy cast, to use a casting line of the same strength and thickness throughout. A tapered line is weakest at the end where the fly is attached to it, and as a line should be as strong, if not stronger, at this point than any other, owing to the connecting knot getting the hardest work, I think a tapered casting line is objectionable, and I will engage to cast quite as neat a line with one of a continuous thickness.

It is not generally known that gut will quickly rot when exposed to a bright hot sun. But this is so. Casting lines, therefore, should not be wound round the hat, but put away when not in use; hanks of gut are best preserved in wash-leather.

It is a common belief that by staining gut it is less easily seen by the fish, but I think this is very doubtful, and I prefer to use it in its natural state.

I have entered into minute details upon this subject, as I think it of great importance. Rod, line, flies, etc., may be perfection in every other respect; but should there be one weak point in the casting line, the angler may just as well be fishing with rotten thread, and it is absolutely necessary to insure success that he should take such precautions as I have advised.

FLIES

There is more difference of opinion about salmon flies than upon any other subject connected with salmon fishing. Some people assert that it is necessary to use different patterns of flies for every month during the fishing season; others, that certain patterns are suitable only for certain rivers, and that it is useless to fish with any others. Another theory is that certain shades of colour must be used on certain days. Every fisherman one meets has his own ideas upon this subject. I have mine, and whether they are right or wrong I will endeavour to explain them. I think it is reasonable to assume that a salmon can discern the colours of a fly; but will the theorists, who believe that it is necessary to fish with certain patterns of flies in each month of the fishing season, tell me that a feeding fish will refuse a fly which is offered him, say during the month of April, because it is not said to be the pattern of that particular month? There is not a particle of evidence in support of such a theory, and it is not worth one moment's argument. That certain patterns of flies must be used on different rivers is a more plausible theory, and if the word 'colour' had been substituted for 'pattern' I should be quite of the same opinion. Some rivers are very clear; others more or less stained with bog water, and from other causes; and for this reason flies which are suitable for clear water will not suit peaty or stained water, and local anglers, having found out flies that will kill on their rivers, establish standard patterns, and will use nothing else.

Experience has, however, taught me that if due regard is paid to colour; any other pattern will kill just as well. Local professionals are a very prejudiced class of people as regards salmon fishing, and, if they can help it, will never allow a stranger they are attending to fish with any other than local patterns of flies. If he persists in doing so, and does not know the river, he will as likely as not be put to fish where he will get no sport, and it generally ends by his leaving the flies he has brought with him behind at his fishing quarters and filling up his book with local patterns. If he has sport with these flies, which is very likely to be the case, whatever opinions he may have had before he came, when he goes away he will probably have become impressed with the belief that no other flies were suitable to the river he has fished, and no amount of argument will convince him to the contrary. No doubt that is the reason why so many anglers become converts to this theory.

It may be presumptuous on my part to say I differ from them; but I have had so many proofs they are mistaken in coming to such a conclusion that I do not hesitate to say so. I have fished a great number of rivers all over the United Kingdom and elsewhere, and I have generally, when not fishing my own waiter, used local patterns, as it is as well not to fall out with one's attendant, who has it so much in his power to make or mar sport. These flies have generally proved to be killers; but whenever I have had an attendant who did not understand much about flies, I have always used my own favourite patterns, and have found them just as killing as the local ones.

When I fished the river Wye some years ago, the favourite local fly was made up of a dirty yellow rough body, blue cock's hackle, and the wring of a feather from a bittern's neck. Now all the modern patterns are used, the favourite fly in the spring being the 'canary.' What a contrast!

A friend of mine (a Lee, co. Cork, fisherman) told me not long ago that the fish were beginning to take the Jock Scott in that river; but the greatest revolution as regards local patterns has been on the river Usk, in Monmouthshire. Formerly the favourite fly used there was made of a dirty yellow body, blue or red cock's hackle, and brown wing. Now, that fly is quite out of date, and the favourite fly – I suppose it may be called a fly – is the 'Usk grub.' Its body is made of tinsel chenille, cock-y-bonddu hackle in joints, and it is certainly a killing fly. Other flies of modern patterns are used, but this is the favourite. This fly was first introduced in the Usk by Mr G. M. Kelson.

A gentleman considered to be the best fisherman on the Usk, who has fished that river all his life, uses nothing but bodies of flies without wings, made of various colours of seal's fur and mohair, with hackles to match. He never puts on wings, as he says there is no necessity for them, and yet he catches as many fish as anyone else, and often scores when others draw a blank. Two years ago I went with my friend Colonel R— to fish the Shannon at Killaloe, in the month of April. The river was high at the time, and the gaudy Shannon flies were being used. We had just come from the Blackwater, and had no flies excepting those we had been fishing with on that river. Our boatman had no Shannon flies to spare us, so we were obliged to fish with the Blackwater flies, but were told no Shannon salmon would look at them. The result was – whether it was luck or not – the Blackwater flies beat the Shannon flies, much to the astonishment of our boatman, who accounted for it by saying that the fish were tired of seeing gaudy Shannon flies and wanted a change. Almost every salmon we caught, however, had sea lice upon him, and the fish which were said to be tired of seeing the Shannon flies were in all probability in the sea at the time. I often ask myself the question whether it is the salmon or the angler that has changed his fancy. I am inclined to think it is the latter.

I think I have adduced sufficient evidence to prove that the salmon is not so very particular as to the pattern of fly, and it is my belief he will take a fly of any pattern when he is in the humour, provided it is of a proper size. Size has more to do with success than all the patterns of flies ever invented. Even if a fly is of the right colour too 'big' a salmon will not take it. He may rise at it, and probably get 'rugged' and will then be seen no more. The choice of a fly of suitable size is a very important matter, but I will allude to this hereafter.

I now come to the question of certain shades and colours being more suitable than others upon certain days. I have no doubt a salmon will occasionally prefer a fly of a certain colour to any other, although I do not admit he would refuse to take a fly of another colour, when he is in the humour, if it were offered to him. I remember upon one occasion watching a cross-line at work upon the Blackwater, when I noticed one fly take fish after fish, all the others, eleven in number, failing to rise one. I cannot think this was accidental; probably the appearance of the fly, under a peculiar condition of light, was the attraction. Whether the fish would have taken any of the other flies if that particular pattern had not been upon the cross-line I cannot say, but I am inclined to think, from what I know of their habits, they would have done so.

If it is taken for granted that a salmon prefers a fly of one colour to another upon certain days, the difficulty is to find out the right colour, and I think a great deal of time would be wasted in the endeavour to do so. All we can do is to select the fly we fancy will take, and if it is of the right size, and if any fish are on the move, we are not often disappointed. There are certain facts, however, which, to a certain extent, may guide us in the choice of a fly. I have tried the experiment of holding up flies of different colours against the sky, putting myself in the position a salmon would occupy with regard to each fly as it was held up. The result was that, with a bright blue sky as a background, I could see every colour fairly well, with the exception of light blue and a jay hackle, which I could not distinguish. With an overcast sky as a background, and a clear atmosphere, I could see all the colours much plainer, and more distinctly in proportion as the background was darker. If I held up the fly in a room, I could distinguish the colour of almost every fibre in the fly, but when it was dark a white fly was seen plainer than any other colour.

There were certain conditions of sky and atmosphere, however, when I was puzzled to distinguish the colours. If the sky was not wholly overcast, and there was a great glare caused by the sun shining through the broken clouds during the summer months, and on a dull heavy day, with a dark murky atmosphere, I could not tell one colour from another, but I could tell whether it was dark or light. In all states of the background I could distinguish black and red better than any other colour, and if it is taken for granted that a salmon can see a fly as we do, when it is held up to the light in the manner I have explained, it may assist us in the choice of a fly as regards colour.

In clear water, on a bright day, a fly composed of red or black, being decided colours and easiest seen, might scare a salmon when coming near it, or just about to take it; therefore it may be advisable to use a fly of a neutral or any light colour on a bright day. Upon a dark day, particularly if there is a wind, or should the water be stained after a fresh, as black and red are more distinctly seen, the more likely are they to attract a salmon's attention than a neutral colour, and in such a case I should say that a fly with a black or dark body would be most suitable. It must, however, at best be only guess-work. Large, gaudy flies, such as are used on the Shannon, are not suitable for ordinary-sized rivers, and are only good for fishing in deep rapids of big rivers, where they are more likely to attract the attention of fish than flies of more sombre or neutral colour.

In a deep and rapid stream a black or red fly, of a proper size, will be more likely to attract a salmon's attention than any other colour. Whether he would take a fly body, hackle, and wings all black, I am not prepared to say, but I have taken numbers of salmon with a red fly, and find this colour do well in a big water, particularly if stained after a fresh. Although big, gaudy flies are only suitable for big rivers, I see no reason why they should not kill as well as any other pattern upon smaller rivers, provided they are made of a suitable size. I have said success greatly depends upon the size of the fly used, and to judge the proper size is a most important part in the art of salmon fishing. On arriving at a river's bank the angler should carefully examine the pool he is about to fish, so as to ascertain the colour and depth of the stream, and whether it is rapid or smooth running. If it is deep and rapid, or stained after a fresh, a large-sized-fly should be used, and a smaller one in proportion as the stream is clear or shallow. The state of the sky must also be taken into consideration. In spring and autumn salmon will take much bigger flies than in the summer time. A fly that would be called big in summer will appear almost a midge in comparison to the smallest flies generally used in early spring or autumn. If the water, however, should be very low, even in spring, it will be necessary to use a very small fly, according to the size of the water. It is impossible to lay down any hard-and-fast rule for selecting a suitable fly. The art of doing so is only acquired by long experience, and the best of us are often at our wits' end to know what fly to select.

When a man is seen constantly changing his fly it is certain that sport is bad, and fish not on the move. It is possible, but very improbable, that a change of fly will change the humour of the fish. I have myself changed flies hundreds of times, but have never known it to answer when fish are sulky; a change, however, after a fish has risen is very often successful. It is a common saying that fish get tired of the sight of flies, and become shy by being much fished over; but if my experience can be taken as evidence, I rather incline to the opinion that it is the fisherman who gets tired of throwing his fly over the fish, rather than the fish that get tired of seeing it.

I was fishing in the Lyngdal, in the south of Norway, with my friend T. F.— the water was very low, and we could see from rocks overhanging every salmon in the pools. At the bottom of a pool celebrated for fish taking the fly, we saw four salmon lying close together. The pool was, I should say, ten feet deep. I scrambled down the rocks to where I could cast my fly over them. My friend stood above watching my proceedings. After about six or seven casts over the fish, he said, 'When your fly was in a particular position, one of the salmon seemed to get uneasy and shifted his position a trifle.' This happened two or three times, until at last the fish could not stand it any longer, and took my fly, but I had the bad luck to lose him after a hard fight.

Upon another occasion, when a little farther down the river, I was standing upon a rock watching my friend fish, where I could see everything which was going on. The water was high but very clear, and nearly a dozen times running I saw a fish rising to the fly whenever it came to a particular part of the stream, but he did not attempt to take it, and did not approach nearer to it than at least a foot. The sun was shining on the pool at the time, and thinking it was of no use trying any more until sunset, we waited until the sun had disappeared behind the hills. Afterwards, the very first cast my friend made he hooked the fish and landed him.

These are the only two occasions on which I have had the chance of knowing what has taken place below the surface of the water while a pool was being fished over, but after what I saw I cannot quite believe a fish gets scared by seeing too many flies. I have no doubt many a fish which we know nothing about comes 'shy' at a fly in the manner I have stated. We leave the pool we have perhaps fished the whole day blank in disgust, yet it often happens another fisherman takes possession of it, and hooks a fish before we are out of sight. What can be more aggravating than this? Yet there are few of us who have not had our tempers thus tried.

Fly tying is a very important part of the art of salmon fishing, and doubtless to be able to tie one's own flies enhances the pleasure of the sport. I have heard it said that a man cannot rank as a first class fisherman unless he can do so; but I think this is hardly fair. Many people's fingers are 'all thumbs,' and they could not tie a fly in a year of Sundays, as the saying goes other salmon fishers are professional men, and have no time to spare from their duties. These may be first-rate fishermen, although not able to tie a fly, and would loudly protest against being placed in a secondary position on this account. It might just as well be said that to rank in the first class a fisherman should be able to make his own rods and reels, yet there is not one in a thousand that can do so. Fly tying is a most interesting, and I might almost say exciting occupation, and many a dull rainy day, during the winter months especially, may be thus pleasantly, and as far as salmon-fishing matters are concerned profitably, passed. Doubtless a man will feel much prouder when he has landed a fish with a fly of his own making, than with one he had bought, and I would recommend every fisherman who has the time to spare to try his hand at it.

In selecting bought flies care should be taken to ascertain that they are firmly tied. A fly that is to all appearance perfect, may when used a short time come to pieces, and it will probably be found that this is in consequence of no varnish having been applied when finishing off at the head. It is necessary this should be used to make the wings sit firmly and keep their position. This can always be tested in the following manner. Hold the bend of the hook between the forefinger and thumb of the left hand, and the head, where the wing is attached, in those of the right hand. If the wing is firmly put on it cannot be moved, but if the fly is badly tied the wing can be shifted with ease right and left at an angle to its proper position, in which case it should be discarded. Bought flies are generally made with too much feather in the wing; this is a great mistake, especially in the case of a mixed wing. If the wing is too heavy the fly cannot work properly; every fibre of a mixed wing should be separate in the water, and, if the angler does his work properly, made to assume a natural and lifelike appearance. The loop also of a fly should be carefully examined. It should be made of stout single or treble gut, and on no account of thin gut. I prefer making loops of two pieces of single gut to treble gut, as I think the latter is more apt to fray the casting line where it is fastened to it. Loops should always be tested by giving them a strong pull.

It should be borne in mind by the maker of a fly, be he professional or amateur, that not the least important part of his work is to securely fasten the loop to the shank of the hook. If this is neglected all the precaution the angler may have taken will have been in vain. Before a fly is used the temper of the hook should be tested by holding the shank between the forefinger and thumb, and having inserted the point in a piece of soft wood, giving it a moderately hard pull. A hook that will stand this test may be trusted.

HOOKS

There are many different shapes of hooks, each of which has its advocates, but I have not yet come to any conclusion as to which is best to use.

Opinions are often formed according as the fish take badly or well. Supposing a man to have fished for a week with a Limerick bend, when salmon were rising badly, and he lost a large proportion of the fish he hooked, he would condemn the Limerick hook and try another description of bend, say a sproat; with this he might fish all the succeeding week when salmon were taking well, and lose hardly a fish. He would then adopt the sproat and say there was no hook like it, and he would fish with it until he again came across fish that were rising badly, when the sproat in its turn would be condemned and perhaps the Limerick again adopted. He would thus go on changing from year to year, never being able to give a decisive opinion as to which is best to use; and that is precisely my case. If, however, I have a preference for one shape over another, I would take the Limerick, as I think a fly looks better when dressed in this shape than in any other.

With regard to patterns of flies, my favourite is the Jock Scott, and if I were told that I was only allowed to fish with one pattern that is the one I should choose; but in any case, with half a dozen flies in addition of different sizes and colours, I should be quite content to go on a fishing expedition and would engage to hold my own. Many salmon fishers, however, prefer a larger selection, and the following list of some of the most popular standard patterns may perhaps assist them in making their choice.

The selection has been made to embrace flies which are all more or less general – suitable, that is, to the generality of rivers – rather than those having a comparatively restricted range, however popular and successful they may be in particular localities.

The 'descriptions' of and remarks about all but a few of the last flies are by Mr George M. Kelson, who has made the question of salmon flies and their dressing a special study.

[Messrs Foster, Ashbourne, have patented a tinsel of platinum – 'silver' of course – which it is claimed will neither tarnish nor corrode. The 'Sunbeam,' they call it. The experiments I have tried seem, thus far, to bear out their statements. – H. C.-P.]

THE JOCK SCOTT

Tag: Silver twist and light yellow silk.

Tail: A topping and Indian crow. Butt: Black herl.

Body: In two equal sections, the first light yellow 7 silk ribbed with fine silver tinsel; above and below are placed three or more toucan's according to size of hook, extending slightly beyond the butt and followed with three or more turns of black herl. The second half black silk with a natural black hackle down it and ribbed with silver lace and silver tinsel. Throat: Gallina.

The 'Jock Scott'.

Wings: Two strips of black turkey with white tips, below; two strips of bustard, and grey mallard, with strands of golden pheasant tail, peacock (sword feather), red macaw, and blue and yellow dyed swan over; having two strips of mallard and a topping above.

Sides: Jungle fowl. Cheeks: Chatterer, Horns: Blue macaw. Head: Black herl.

No one will dispute that Jock Scott, when dressed correctly, is the most remarkable of all our standard patterns, and therefore entitled to the precedence it has been here accorded. It is probably the best known fly that 'swims' throughout the length and breadth of the three kingdoms, and indeed it would hardly be an exaggeration of language to say that this splendid specimen of artificial entomology has won an almost superstitious veneration amongst salmon anglers.

Whether used in rushing streams or rapids, or in still, sluggish, oily pools, its appearance seems to be equally attractive and its success assured. It was invented by the late Lord John Scott's water bailiff some forty-two years ago.

THE 'DURHAM RANGER'

Tag: Silver twist and light yellow silk.
    Tail: A topping and Indian crow.
    Butt: Black herl.

The 'Durham Ranger'.

Body: Two turns of orange silk, two turns dark orange seal's fur; the rest, which is about half, black seal's fur.

Ribbed: Silver lace and silver tinsel.

Hackle: From orange seal's fur, a white coch-y-bonddu dyed orange.

Throat: Light blue hackle.

Wings: Four golden pheasant tippets overlapping, as illustrated, and enveloping two projecting jungle fowl back to back; and a topping.

Cheeks: Chatterer.

Horns: Blue macaw.

Head: Black Berlin wool.

The Durham Ranger owes its origin to Janies Wright, the famous fly dresser of Sprowston, near Kelso; and its name to the circumstance of its being first successfully tried, some twenty years ago, on the Sprowston water by a party of gentlemen from Durham, to whom it was let at the time.

This was the christening of the Durham Ranger, one of the very best of bright flies, and one that in open pools and bright weather, no matter what the river, rarely fails if not mounted too large. Indeed, as a rule in regard to flies generally, I have often noticed that failure, particularly with gaudy patterns, is due to the fly being disproportionately large or small.

THE 'CHILDERS'

Tag: Silver twist and light blue silk.

Tail: A topping with strands of red macaw, powdered blue macaw, and pintail.

Butt: Black herb

Body: Two turns of light yellow silk continuing with light yellow seal's fur, leaving one-fifth at the shoulder for scarlet seal's fur.

Ribbed: Silver lace and silver tinsel.

Hackle: A white furnace hackle dyed light yellow.

Throat: A scarlet hackle and light widgeon.

The 'Childers'.

Wings: Golden pheasant tippet and tail, turkey, silver pheasant, pintail, summer duck, bustard, powdered blue macaw, parrot, red macaw, and gallina, with two strips of mallard above and a topping.

Horns: Blue macaw.

Cheeks: Chatterer.

Head: Black herb. This fly is art old favourite, having been introduced about the year 1850. Dressed large or small it kills well in any part of the three kingdoms. Originally Colonel Childers, who was the inventor, 'formulated' this fly without a topping, but there is some justification for the addition of one, as, to use his own words, he 'always put one when he could get it.' The black 'list' down the centre of the hackle has a very telling effect in the water.

It is as well to note that 'turkey,' unless when otherwise indicated, means the brown mottled feather.

THE 'BUTCHER'

Tag: Silver twist and dark yellow silk.

Tail: A topping, teal, and powdered blue macaw. Butt: Black herb.

Body: In four equal divisions – beginning with light red-claret, and continuing with light blue, dark red-claret, and dark blue seal's furs.

The 'Butcher'.

Ribbed: Silver tinsel (preceded on large hooks by silver lace).
Hackle: Natural black, from light red-claret seal's fur.
Throat: Yellow hackle and gallina.
Wings: One tippet feather, and a breast feather from the golden pheasant, back to back, tied edgeways as illustrated, the points of the breast feather extending to the length of the wing. Both well covered on the side with slight strips of teal, golden pheasant tail, gallina, bustard, and peacock wing; with strands of parrot and swan dyed yellow, and with two strips of mallard at top.
Horns: Blue macaw. Cheeks: Chatterer. Head: Black herl. Measured by the standard of antiquity the Butcher is entitled to the first place in our list of standard flies. Its claim to seniority would probably be admitted by a jury of fly fishers *nemine contradicente*. I can trace it back to the first fountain head. In its infancy it went by the name of Moon's Fly, and was the invention of Mr Jewhurst, of Tunbridge, Kent. About the year 1838 it was re-christened at Blacker's establishment, from which date it became a popular favourite, and no standard pattern has undergone less change of toilette whilst still retaining its high reputation everywhere.

It is very much more effective when the outer wing-coverings are arranged to 'veil' the tippet and breast feather, so as not to form a confused mass at the top, as is the case with carelessly dressed specimens.

THE 'POPHAM'

Tag: Gold twist.

    Tail: A topping and Indian crow.

    Butt: Black herl.

    Body: In three equal sections butted with black herl. The first dark red orange silk, ribbed with fine gold tinsel having Indian crow above and below, as illustrated; the second, or middle joint, yellow silk with similar ribbing and crow's feathers as before; the third light blue silk and silver ribbing, with the Indian crow repeated.

    Hackle: At the throat only, jay.

    Wings: Tippet, teal, gallina, golden pheasant tail, parrot, light brown mottled turkey, bustard, red macaw, yellow macaw (swan dyed yellow instead of yellow macaw for large sizes), with two strips of mallard above, and a topping.

    Cheeks: Chatterer.

    Horns: Blue macaw.

    Head: Black herl.

This fly retains, and – if a prophecy be admissible – will continue to retain, its high reputation on many of our best salmon rivers. The combinations in the body are, in my opinion, absolutely free from blemish, and reflect great credit upon the inventor, a dexterous and persevering fisherman who has given his name to the fly, and who is further known as the winner of the Derby in Wild Dayrell's year. Another variety was

The 'Popham'.

introduced by the late Mr. John George Children, of Halstead Place, but the original here given is not only considered better, but is certainly more popular.. The great mistake generally made is in overlaying the body with too many Indian crowds feathers.

'THUNDER AND LIGHTNING'

Tag: Gold twist and yellow silk.
  Tail: A topping.
  Butt: Black herl.
  Body: Black silk.
  Ribbed: Gold tinsel.
  Hackle: From first turn of tinsel, orange.
  Throat: Jay.
  Wings: Mallard, in strips with a topping.
  Sides: Jungle fowl.
  Horns: Blue macaw.
  Hecui: Black herl.
This – another creation of the redoubtable James Wright – is, in my estimation, as a dear-water fly, the best that he has ever invented. It is a well-recognised fact that salmon 'take' better just as the water is beginning to rise after rain, and in such conditions – without detracting in any way from its merits under other circumstances – I know of no fly that can be recommended in preference. It is not, however, a pattern that I should select

'Thunder and Lightning'.

when a river is at all inclined to be muddy; but in heavy rains and boisterous weather it is the one of all others entitled to a patient trial. In fact, to perpetrate a mild joke, 'Thunder and Lightning' is the natural accompaniment of a storm.

THE 'SILVER GREY'

Tag: Silver twist and yellow silk.

Tail: A topping, unbarred summer duck, and two strands of blue macaw.

Butt: Black herb

Body: Silver tinsel (flat) ribbed with silver tinsel (oval).

Hackle: From first turn of ribs, a silver-white coch-y-bonddu.

Throat: Light widgeon.

Wings: Silver pheasant, bustard, golden pheasant tail, pintail, powdered blue macaw, gallina, swan dyed yellow; two strips mallard above, and a topping.

Sides: Jungle fowl.

Horns: Blue macaw.

Head: Black Berlin wool.

The Silver Grey, another of the Sprouston list, also by James Wright, is a very old and well-established pattern.

I have cast this fly for years with considerable success in all kinds of pools and corners, and it seems to be equally effective either in bright or dull weather, in open or shaded places. In rivers

The 'Silver Grey'.

where the fish are proverbially sulky it is a great favourite, and I have one or two instances recorded of its success in out of the way districts 'where no fishers abide.' The Silver Grey makes a capital change with the Lion – the two most valued silver-bodied flies in general use. Many anglers are shy of tinselled bodies, but either of these patterns can be safely recommended, and, the question as to size being correctly estimated, exceptional sport is frequently obtained with them.

THE 'LION'

Tag: Silver twist and light yellow silk.

Tail: A topping.

Butt: Black herl.

Body: Silver tinsel (flat) ribbed with silver tinsel (oval). One fifth part being left at the shoulder for dark scarlet seal's fur.

Hackle: Natural black, three parts down the body.

Throat: Gallina.

Wings: Commencing with a few fibres of tippet, sword feather of the golden pheasant, and peacock herl. Yellow macaw, red macaw, bustard, golden pheasant tail, teal, gallina; with two strips of mallard above, and a topping.

Sides: Jungle fowl.

Horns: Blue macaw.

Head: Black Berlin wool.

The 'Lion'.

The Lion, as already mentioned, is another exceptionally good silver- tinselled pattern. Some of our most distinguished fly-fishers adduce an imposing array of facts and arguments in its favour, and whatever local opinions may be, anglers will do wisely to give it a trial. When the water is slightly stained, it is, perhaps, a little more attractive than the Silver Grey, and may be used with advantage one size smaller, speaking comparatively, the materials in the dressing being more conspicuous. In the event, however, of one or tsvo downright refusals, the Jungle – which cannot be too black and white as a rule – should be nipped entirely off. The Lion is another invention of James Wright.

THE CAPTAIN

Tag: Silver twist and light blue silk.

Tail: A topping and chatterer.

Body: Two turns oflight orange silk, two turns dark orange seal's fur, two turns dark red-claret seal's fur, and finish with dark blue seal's fur.

Ribbed: Silver tinsel.

Hackle: A white coch-y-bonddu dyed light red-claret, from the orange silk.

Throat: Blue hackle and gallina.

Wings: Pintail, teal, gallina, peacock wing, Amherst pheasant, bustard, and golden pheasant tail; swan dyed light

The 'Captain'.

orange, dark orange, dark claret, and dark blue; with two strips mallard above, and a topping.

Sides: Jungle fowl.

Horns: Blue macaw.

Head: Black herb

The Captain is one of my own patterns, and was introduced by Bernard, of Church Place, Piccadilly, with another of mine called the Champion, many years ago. But it has long since adopted the name of the Poinder in Scotland, and is perhaps better known there by that erroneous appellation.

It is rather difficult to recommend this fly without appearing to blow my own trumpet; at the same time I shall probably be justified in saying that as a general pattern it holds its own everywhere. I have had good sport with it dressed in all sizes and very rarely meet with disappointment, especially as a change when the Durham Ranger, for example, has moved a fish. It should be dressed very small for lakes or shallow' streams.

THE 'BLACK JAY'

Tag: Silver twist and dark yellow silk.

Tail: A topping.

Butt: Black herl.

Body: Two turns black silk; the rest black seal's fur.

Ribbed: Silver tinsel, preceded by silver lace for large patterns.

Hackle: Natural black from silk.

Throat: Jay.

Wings: Tippet, scarlet ibis and gallina; golden pheasant tail, bustard, teal, black cockatoo's tail, and swan dyed green and dark yellow; with two strips mallard above.

Horns: Blue macaw.

Head: Black herl.

A complete contrast to the preceding series is the Black Jay, a pattern for the introduction of which I am also responsible,

The 'Black Jay'.

and which has been in general use for more than a quarter of a century, though invented long before that. Unlike the rest of the 'jays' it will be found most useful in dark water, and although it kills well dressed small, it shows perhaps a more marked superiority when tied on very large hooks. I then generally add jungle to the wings and a topping.

There are numerous imitations of this fly, all varying trivially in minor details; but I think the formula here given will be found satisfactory upon hooks up to an inch and a quarter in length, without any alteration or addition.

THE 'CLARET JAY'

Tag: Silver twist and light yellow silk.
   Tail: A topping, scarlet ibis, and gallina.
   Butt: Black herb
   Body: Two turns light red-claret silk, the rest claret seal's fur.
   Ribbed: Silver tinsel.
   Hackle: Claret.
   Throat: Jay.
   Wings: Teal, tippet, and florican; light mottled turkey, parrot, golden pheasant tail, gallina, and dark bustard; swan dyed light yellow, yellow-green (or powdered blue), yellow and claret; with two strips mallard above.
   Sides: Yellow macaw and ibis, in married strips.

The 'Claret Jay'.

Horns: Blue macaw.

Head. Black herb

The Claret Jay is the best known and most popular of the 'jay set.' In rivers where medium-sized flies are used the 'Claret,' as it is generally termed, kills as well as anything. There is one variety of it that may be mentioned having yellow seal's fur instead of light red-claret silk on the body, but the description given is that of the original dressing.

These three sombre patterns – the Black and Claret Jays and the Dirty Orange – are more suitable for medium sized rivers, and although they are rarely tied on very large hooks, there are plenty of flats, streams, nooks, and corners in our largest rivers where I am satisfied they could be tried with considerable success on hooks up to, say, No. 2.

THE 'DIRTY ORANGE'

Tag: Gold twist and light blue silk.

Tail: A topping and tippet.

Butt: Black herb

Body: Two turns light orange silk; the rest light dirty orange seal's fur.

Ribbed: Gold tinsel.

Hackle: Light dirty orange from silk.

Throat: Jay.

The 'Dirty Orange'.

Wings: Ginger turkey, gallina, and strands of breast feather of golden pheasant; bustard, peacock herl, golden pheasant tail and strands of black turkey with white tips; red macaw, swan dyed dirty orange and dark blue, with two strips of mallard above.

Sides: Summer duck.

Horns: Blue macaw.

Head: Blue herl.

Another of the Jays, and also a popular favourite, is the Dirty Orange. Salmon fishers, and novices more especially, are often so eager to try every imaginable novelty that makes its appearance in the way of flies that they are unconsciously apt to neglect the more quietly dressed but well-established patterns. So far as appearance goes, there are doubtless many patterns more taking, but I have included this and the two preceding flies in my standard list advisedly, believing that in the long run they will be found to justify the selection.

THE 'FIERY BROWN'

Tag: Gold twist and light orange silk.

Tail: A topping.

Body: Fiery brown seal's fur.

Ribbed: Gold tinsel.

Hackle: From first turn of tinsel, fiery brown.

Wings: Tippet strands between broad strips of mallard.

The 'Fiery Brown'.

Homs: Blue macaw.

Head: Black herl.

N.B. – There is also another variety by the inventor (Michael Rogan), having a blue hackle alongside the fiery brown hackle down the body.

The Fiery Brown, facetiously termed 'The All Ireland Fly,' is gradually becoming more popular elsewhere, and many a victory won in 'despite of fate' maybe credited to this singularly attractive yet plain-looking pattern. Indeed, however unpropitiously the campaign may appear to be going, Michael Rogan's ingenious offspring will very likely retrieve the situation, whether the *champ de baltaille* be in the north or south, in pool, stream, or rapid. Rogan's mode of dyeing the seal's fur and hackles is most successful, and far superior to all others for securing the fierce flame-like tint desired.

The Fiery Brown is another fly that seems to answer best when dressed on medium-sized hooks, though I have never tried it, or even seen it tied very large.

THE 'SPRING GRUB'

Tag: Silver twist and light blue silk.

Tail: Scarlet ibis and blue macaw in married strips.

Body: In two sections having three hackles as illustrated: in the place of the butt.

The 'Spring Grub'.

Butt: A furnace hackle dyed orange. The first half of the body yellow silk ribbed with black chenille.

In the centre is placed a natural blue hackle. The second half of the body black silk ribbed with silver tinsel, and the shoulder, or head hackles, a natural coch-y-bonddu, and a gallina dyed dark orange.

This is one of my earliest of the scorpion tribe, and belongs to a numerous collection of wingless flies which are coming more and more into fashion. There are times when fish require a good deal of coaxing, and on many days they will rise in pool after pool merely, as it were, for the sake of inquisitiveness. Upon these occasions especially I make it a rule to tone down the colours by mixing them with deeper shades, and dress then and there a fly of this description, if, that is, I do not happen to have a suitable one by me. The pattern here given I have often found a good change with Excelsior, Jock Scott, etc. I have found these wingless 'nondescripts' kill well wherever I have fished, and every standard fly should, I believe, be partially imitated in a similar fashion.

The 'Spring grub' completes the list of general standard flies, with one or other of which, from the beginning to the end of the season, and in any part of the United Kingdom, salmon are to be killed if at all.

CASTING

I have so far given all the information I can think of that may be of use as a guide to the selection of the principal requisites for an outfit for salmon fishing. There are, however, several other articles to make it complete, such as fly books, tin boxes, etc.; but these do not require any mention in detail, and, as they will not make or mar sport, the choice of them may be safely left to the angler's fancy.

The first thing a beginner has to learn is, how to cast overhand, and he should commence work with a short line, say from ten to fifteen yards. When he can make a tolerable cast with this length, he may gradually lengthen the line; and if he perseveres and works upon a sound principle, and has provided himself with a rod suitable to his powers of casting, he will gradually become master of it, and be able, with tolerable ease, to cast a line of twenty or twenty-five yards, which is as far as will be required for general purposes.

To make a clean cast overhand, it should be borne in mind it is necessary that the line be lifted out of the water to the very end to where the fly is attached; and that it should be thrown to its fullest extent in the backward cast (that is, behind the angler's back) prior to the forward cast being made. If this be neglected, the fly will as often as not be cracked off, and the line sent out in a slovenly corkscrew fashion, or else both line and fly will fall in a heap together in the water, the disadvantages of which will be explained later on.

To make a cast in a workmanlike manner the line should be sent clean out, down, and across stream at an angle of not less than 450 (see D E, fig. 1). As soon as the fly touches the water, the rod, supposing the angler to be standing at a, should be held in the position A D at an angle of about 45° downstream from a line taken from where the angler stands straight across to the opposite bank, and it should remain in that position until the fly has reached midstream, G, after which the point should gradually follow the direction of the fly, H, until the cast is completed, A B K, which will bring the rod into a favourable position, AB, to make a fresh cast; the dotted line, EFGHK, marks the course of the fly from beginning to end of the cast. The advantage of making the fly work in the manner I have explained is that every fibre of the wing and hackle will be in their right position; it will assume a natural, lifelike appearance; and, owing to the slow rate and direction it is travelling, every fish in the pool will have a fair chance of discerning its colour; and if he rises, he will be more likely to be well hooked than by any other method.

If the stream is of even rapidity from bank to bank, it will be a comparatively easy matter to make the fly work in the manner I have explained; but should the stream run more rapidly at the middle than at the sides, which is generally the case, a 'belly' in the line must necessarily be made as soon as the line touches the water. If this is allowed to remain, the fly cannot work as it ought to, which will be explained in the diagram, fig. 2. AB represents the rod, supposed to be in angler's hands standing at ABC, the line cast, as it should be, down and across stream, B D represents the belly made in the

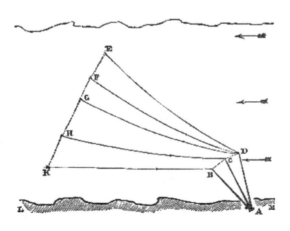

Fig. 1.

line, which will increase, DEFGH, until the cast is completed at I, K the point of the rod meanwhile being shifted from b to l The disadvantages of a fly working in the manner I have shown when a fish rises, are, I think, obvious; and I will explain this more fully in describing a straight-across cast.

There is a way of taking the belly out of a line, which was taught me by an old fisherman when fishing the Kirkcudbrightshire Dee in my younger days. I dare say many of my readers will recollect old Jemmy Gordon, professional salmon fisherman at Kirkcudbright, who was called the 'Emperor,' and right well he deserved the title, for he knew more about salmon fishing than any professional I have ever met, and I acquired a store of knowledge from him that I have found useful ever since. He is dead and gone now, and the like of him I shall never see again. It was Jemmy that pointed out to me the evil of allowing a belly to remain in my line, and who taught me how to rectify it.

To accomplish it is a knack which can only be acquired by practice, but I think it of such importance that I will endeavour, by the aid of the diagram, fig. 3, to explain how it is done.

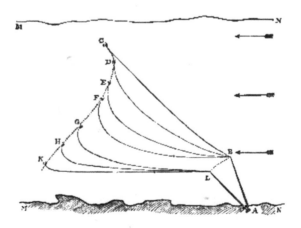

Fig. 2.

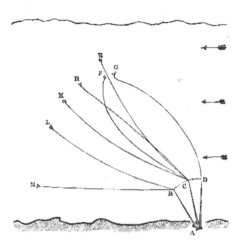

Fig. 3.

AC represents the rod and CE the line – as first cast, in correct position, CF represents the belly, almost instantly made. Eye making a back-handed upward cast, the belly, CF, the outward curve of which is facing downstream, is changed in its direction to DG; the outward curve facing up stream, the position of the rod being shifted from C to D the action of the stream will then straighten the line, which will gradually get into the position CH, the position of the rod being shifted back to AC; the fly will then work gradually across stream, the rod following the direction of the fly until the cast is completed at A B M. Few fishermen I have watched fishing take the trouble to take the belly out of their line, and are content to let the fly work in the same position as it was cast; but if they would look at it in the light I see it, I feel convinced they would be of my opinion.

Many experienced fishermen advocate casting straight across stream, and assert that by adopting this method many more fish are risen than by any other; they may be right, but I much doubt it, and maintain that, even should more fish be risen by the straight-across method, more fish are killed by casting down and across.

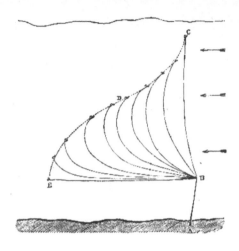

Fig. 4.

A reference to diagram, fig. 4, will show how a fly works cast straight across stream, ABC, from the time the fly touches the water at c to when the cast is completed, ABE. The course of the fly is represented by the dotted line CDE; the position of the rod cannot be altered, as it would make matters worse. It will be seen that the fly is travelling from first to last head foremost downstream, the cross action of the stream on the fly will put all its feathers out of gear, the fish in the pool will get but a momentary sight of it, and will have no time to discern its colour, and if they rise at it, by the time they reach the surface of the water the fly will be a yard behind them down stream, and the disappointment thus caused will be apt to scare them to such a degree that they will not rise again.

That fish are thus caught I do not deny, but I maintain that many more are caught by adopting the down and across cast.

Figs. 5 and 6 are diagrams representing the two slovenly casts I have before alluded to. In both diagrams BC shows where the fly should be cast, and b d where it should not be cast; in fig. 5 the line assumes the shape of a corkscrew, and in fig. 6 it is thrown all of a heap in the water, and it will be seen that the fly cannot be got to work properly until it has reached mid-stream, BE, thus losing the chance of catching the rising fish in half the pool.

I am aware it will be impossible for anyone to follow my directions to the letter, particularly, as is often the case, if there is a foul wind all that can be done is to adhere to them as nearly as circumstances will permit, and to endeavour always to cast the fly in such a manner that the fish can see it before he sees the casting line. I believe the principle is a sound one, and will guarantee no one is misled by adopting it. I should have mentioned that the fly should begin to 'fish' directly it touches the water, and to insure this a foot may be taken in with the hand through the rings when the forward cast is made, which

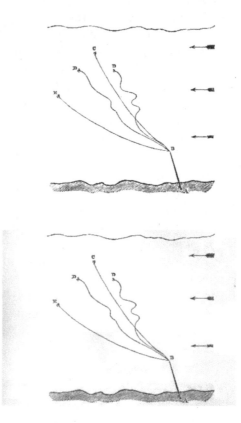

Fig. 5.

Fig. 6.

will have the effect of straightening the line in case it has become slack, when the fly will begin to work at once.

When a beginner has perfected himself in overhand casting he may then begin his lessons in casting underhand, which it is quite necessary he should learn, as he will find himself occasionally having to fish streams where if he cannot make an underhand cast he may as well go home. Of all the various undercasts, the one as practised on the Spey is the most pleasant and satisfactory to make, and, as fat as I can judge, a longer line can be got out with it than with any other. It is generally believed this cast can only be accomplished when wading, but if anyone knows how to do it, it can be done with quite as great ease and to as great perfection, when standing on the bank; but in the latter case it requires a sharp stream to be running evenly close into the bank which is being fished from. Until very recently I found could when wading. One of the longest underhand casts I ever made was when fishing from a bank in that position, and I have found it so useful that I recommend those who may not know it to give it a trial.

To make a Spey cast successfully, the line should be allowed to be carried well down the stream, straight and tight to its fullest extent, the point of the rod following the direction of the fly and held very low. Before making the cast the whole line should be lifted clear of the water. If it is allowed to drag under the surface of the water the cast cannot be made. A rod with a powerful top must be used, and one which has great lifting power. The Spey fishermen, who I think are the finest underhand casters in the world, use rods made especially for the purpose. The upper portion, instead of being straight, is made in a curve, and, when fishing, the curve faces the stream, which gives a rod made in this fashion a greater lifting power than an ordinary one, but I have always found I could make as good a cast with the latter. I have made these few remarks upon the 'Spey cast' as it is my favourite, although I find other methods useful at times. To learn how to cast underhand can only be acquired by practice, and in the course of an angler's experience he will have every opportunity of becoming proficient in this branch of the art.

HOW TO WORK A FLY

There are differences of opinion as to how a fly should be worked. Some fishermen shake their rod so as to make it saw the water, as it were, but this method adds greatly to the fatigue of fishing, and is, moreover, in my opinion, labour in vain. I watched upon one occasion a man working his rod in this fashion. He had out a pretty long line, and when his fly came round close to the bank where I was standing I could see what the effect was. I was rather surprised to see there was no motion given to the fly more than that which was caused by the action of the stream. The fact was the action of the point of the rod did not affect the line at the distance at which the fly was working. I have no doubt that when fishing with a short length of line, shaking the point of the rod would give the desired motion to the fly, although I maintain that in a stream it is quite unnecessary to work a fly at all, the action of the water being quite sufficient to give it a lifelike appearance.

I learnt a lesson when fishing with a cross line where flies are sometimes almost stationary, and I feel certain anyone who has seen the glorious rises which salmon make at flies on a cross line would never think it necessary to work or shake his fly.

The method of working the fly in this fashion is generally adopted by all professionals and many amateurs on the Irish rivers, and a stranger who does not conform to their ideas in this, as well as in the choice of flies, is put down as a 'duffer.' The first time I wetted my line in the Shannon I worked the fly in my own way, hardly moving the point of the rod The man in the stern of the boat watched me for a few minutes with disgust written on his face; at last he sprang up, and before I knew what he was about, snatched the rod out of my hand, saying, 'This is the way we fish in the Shannon, your honour,' and then began to show me the see-saw method. I was rather taken aback, as I fancied I knew how to do it before the man was born. However, I had my own way, had very good sport, and heard no more about it from my friend in the stern of the boat.

The most deadly method of fishing is to hold the point of the rod well down, letting the fly sink as deep as possible. If the fly is worked at all it should be in dead sluggish water, and then only by a very slow 'up-and-down' motion of the top of the rod.

But there is no accounting for the wray a salmon will sometimes take a fly.

A short time ago, when fishing the Usk, a friend of mine put down his rod on the bank to go and talk to his wife. The fly was left in the water, and when he returned he found to his surprise a fish was on, and after an exciting struggle he landed him; he had been fishing that pool for hours before this happened.

HOW TO FISH A POOL

The proper way to fish a pool is to commence at the head, moving down stream about one yard, or step, before each fresh cast, always taking care the old cast is completed before the downward step is made. This is of greater importance than might perhaps appear, for if the new cast is made first and the downward step taken afterwards, it will make all the difference in the working of the fly.

The latter will have to travel all of a heap for yards before it begins to fish, the disadvantages ol which I have already stated. I have seen many salmon fishermen having taken a downward step and made their cast, take one or two more steps forward, without being apparently aware of it. This is one instance of the bad habits a young fisherman may get into, and which he may never be able to break himself of. These are small things in themselves, but, nevertheless, are apt to mar his sport to a degree he is quite unaware of.

When a fish rises to a fly, it is best to wait about thirty seconds before throwing over him again, and the angler should remain stationary and shorten his line a yard or so, by pulling it through the rings of the rod, and not by winding it up with the reel. He should then commence throwing over the fish again with the shortened line, letting out the slack until the exact length is cast which rose the fish. If he does not rise him again, a smaller fly may be tried of the same pattern, and, if needs be, one of another pattern. If this should prove unsuccessful, the fish may be left alone for a quarter of an hour or twenty minutes, the angler continuing to fish the pool down and returning to try his luck again in about that time. He should first, however, in case he is fishing from a bank, make a mark with his heel on the spot where he stood when the fish rose, or, if wading, take some bearings by which he may recover the place where he was standing. He should then try the fly that rose the fish in the first instance, and if he is not successful after one change, he may leave the fish for good.

If, when fishing a pool, several fish rise, but the majority of them are only pricked and not hooked, it may be taken for granted the fly is too large, and the pool should be fished over again with a smaller one. It may be that the colour of the fly is not suitable to the state of the sky, or that it is too easily seen, and has made the fish somewhat shy. If this should be the opinion of the angler, he can change his fly for one of another colour. This is, however, all guess-work, and nothing but long experience will be able to give any aid under such circumstances.

STRIKING A RISING SALMON

There are different methods adopted for striking a salmon. A great many experienced anglers advocate striking or hitting a rising fish 'from the winch,' without the line being touched. Others say it is necessary to strike with the line held tight between hand and rod. Others, that if the line be held tight between hand

and rod, a fish will hook himself without striking; and this latter is decidedly my way of thinking, and I am convinced that striking is a mistake. The question of striking or not striking is of the greatest importance, and I will therefore endeavour to explain the pros and cons of each system.

Striking from the winch has many advocates. The advantage claimed for it is that, with a properly constructed reel, a salmon can be hooked before the reel plate revolves, but that it will revolve before the fish turns. This may be so, but I cannot understand how the point of the hook, particularly if it is a big one, can be forced over the barb unless the line is held tight, or the winch a very stiff one, a very- unpleasant thing to use, and involving the utmost danger in playing a lightly hooked fish. My belief is, that in the case of any salmon struck from the winch, in whose mouth a hook has been found fixed over the barb, the result is due to the pulling and dragging he gets when being played, and which must, sooner or later, have this effect. If an easy running reel be used, which is in my opinion the proper one, the reel plate will revolve the moment the line is tightened in a fish, and, if the line be not held tight, the barb cannot get fixed, unless the hook is a very small one. These remarks are equally applicable to single and to double hooks.

Long before the question as to the advantage of striking from the winch when using double hooks was discussed in the sporting press, I had given the double-hook plan an extended trial, but I lost so many fish with them, that I gave them up. I did not strike from the winch, and I am told by advocates of this system that my not doing so was the cause of my want of success. They may be right, but I cannot agree with them, and I am convinced that striking a fish, in any form, is a mistake.

Many fishermen advocate striking with the line held tight; this is accomplished by a sudden upward jerk of the point of the rod the moment the fish is seen to rise, or that it is felt that he has taken the fly; this is in my opinion the worst possible method, and a very risky one, although it is the one generally adopted. I think the habit has been acquired in consequence of the majority of salmon fishermen having fished for trout in their younger days, before they were allowed to handle a salmon rod.

Fishing for trout and grayling and fishing for salmon are two very different arts; the former are far quicker than a salmon in their action when rising to a fly, and require great dexterity to hook them, but even they do not require to be what is called 'struck' at in the sense that is meant in striking a salmon; and a slight turn of the wrist, which may be called a strike if it pleases anyone to do so, is all that is required to fix the barb of a trout fly. If the rod was suddenly jerked up, as when striking a salmon, the chances are, with a heavy trout, the casting line would break, and perhaps the rod into the bargain. I am inclined to the belief that striking from the winch would suit trout fishing better than salmon fishing.

The evil arising from striking at a rising fish with the line held tight, is that there is great risk, owing to the sudden jerk of the rod, of either smashing the top or leaving the fly in the fish's mouth, or should the fly be suddenly snatched away from him in the act of rising, the disappointment would most likely scare him to such a degree that he would not rise a second time. I have been told that it is necessary to strike at a salmon in order to prevent him from ejecting the fly; I have already stated my opinion regarding the power of a salmon of ejecting his food. It is only natural he should do so on finding that it was not natural food, but I have myself seen many salmon come at my fly with open mouth, and in such cases striking at him would be most likely to defeat the object in view, and the chances of hooking him would be far greater if he were allowed time to close his mouth on the fly.

It is highly probable that whether he is struck at or not, he often succeeds in ejecting a fly without being touched, having found out the trick that has been played upon him, and it is for this reason that many salmon which have been risen, cannot be tempted to rise a second time. What is desired when a salmon rises is to fix the barb of the hook, and to effect this the surest and safest way, in my opinion, is by adopting the following method: When a fish rises at the fly the rod must be held steady in the same position as before the fish rose; if he has taken the fly he will hook himself by his own weight on his downward course after the rise, and he will soon let you know it. Nothing more is required to fix the barb of the hook unless the fly used is of a large size, when, to make certain of doing so, it may be advisable to give one or two steady 'pulls', the force of which must be left to the angler's discretion; if the barb is not then fixed it will be in consequence of the point of the hook coming into contact with a bone, when striking or pulling would be of no avail.

If, after a salmon has risen it is found he has not taken the fly, the rod should still be held in the same position, and the fly allowed to work as if nothing had happened. By adopting this plan there will be a far greater chance of his rising a second time than if the fly had been snatched away from him; and I have often seen fish that have risen at my fly and not taken it, follow it and make two or three rises at it before the cast is completed, but I do not often remember to have caught a fish following the fly in this fashion. I think it is a sure sign that the fly is too big, and I should much prefer his going back to his corner after the first rise, and giving me a chance of changing my fly. I have also observed that a fish that follows the fly will seldom be seen again. He finds himself before he is aware of it in shallow water, and the chances are he gets scared; this is the only drawback (if it can be called so) that I can suggest to my plan of hooking a rising salmon, and I will now leave it to my readers to form their own opinion on this very important question.

PLAYING A SALMON

Of all the delights of an angler's experience, there is nothing to compare with that of 'rising' and hooking a salmon.

The rise of a big salmon to your fly is electrifying in its effect. There is a moment of intense uncertainty and suspense as he disappears after having risen, and you are awaiting the result... He has missed it! Your face is as pale as death, and you sit down unable to stand from sheer excitement. You have to wait a minute or two before you make another cast. All cares and troubles, all thoughts of everything and everybody, even of the wife of your bosom, are cast to the winds during those glorious moments of uncertainty; your whole soul is bound up for the time being with the silvery monster you have roused from his stronghold.

Perhaps the idea comes across you that your fly is too big, and with trembling hands you change it for a smaller one. Watch in hand, with an impatient longing to be at him again, you wait till the allotted time has elapsed. 'Time is up,' and you rise to again try your luck. You may be an old hand, and no outward sign will betray the beating of your heart, as you proceed to cast over your fish with the same unerring precision as before, as if apparently nothing had happened, and you were only commencing to fish the pool. Or perhaps the excitement will be too much for you, and trembling from head to foot – scarcely able to hold your rod – you will make your cast, but how you will never remember. With eager eyes starting almost out of their sockets, you watch the progress of your fly as it comes nearer and nearer to where you rose your fish. 'He should come now', is your mental ejaculation, and quick almost as the thought a swirl or perhaps a scarcely perceptible wave in the water will betray the presence of your prey.

One more moment of intense uncertainty and suspense; you feel a slight pull, then your line tightens, your fly of your own making, in which you took such pride, has done it; 'you are in him!'

A thrill of exultation and joy runs through your veins as those magic words escape your lips...The foregoing description, however uneloquent, may give those who have never experienced it a faint idea of what every lover of the sport feels on rising and hooking a salmon.

Anglers I have heard of who even consider that when once they have hooked their fish, the sport is over, and hand the rod to their attendant to play and land the fish; but I prefer as long an acquaintance with my salmon as he will vouchsafe me, and nothing would ever induce me to give up the rod to anyone to play a fish if I could avoid it; besides, there is the finish to look forward to. The few moments of uncertainty just before the fish is being gaffed or landed – particularly if he should be a heavy one, perhaps the biggest you have ever hooked – are most exciting; and the fishermen who forego this part of the performance, lose, I cannot but think, a good deal of the pleasure of the sport There is also a great risk in handing over the rod to an attendant; in the act of doing so, the line must necessarily get slack, and, should the point of the hook be only skin deep in the fish, as is often the case, ten to one that the angler and fish will part company. Is there a salmon fisherman of any experience who has not often seen his fly drop out of a fish's mouth, the moment he was gaffed or landed, when the point of his rod was lowered and the line slackened? It might probably not occur to him to ask himself the reason why the fly had dropped out; but if it did, the fact would tell its own tale, and he would be made aware that if for one moment he had given the fish a slack line, he would never have been brought to bank.

If a fish is well hooked, no harm can come by the rod changing hands; the angler has often to scramble up a steep bank when playing his fish, in order to enable him to follow him, should he have taken a run up or down stream, in which case he will have to hand his rod over for the time being to his attendant; but, as it is impossible to tell whether a fish is firmly hooked or not, the rod should never change hands if it can be avoided. To keep a tight line from first to last is a golden rule that should be always borne in mind by every salmon fisherman when playing his fish. He should hold the point of his rod well up, and keep it opposite to him if he can. Should the fish take a run, ending with a leap in the air, he must instantly lower the point of his rod, which ought to defeat this effort to rid himself of the fly – the object doubtless intended.

In lowering the point of the rod, a slack line must necessarily be given; but it is a case of kill or cure: if he is well hooked, he will be brought to bank; if lightly hooked, the chances are against it. It is the 'glorious uncertainty that adds to the pleasure and excitement of the sport. If it was a certainty, there would be none.

In playing a salmon, the amount of strain necessary to be put on the line must be left to the judgment of the angler, and should be proportionate to the strength of his tackle. It is not generally known what amount of strain a rod can put on. I may therefore mention that, in trying the experiment with a very powerful rod, all I could do was to pull four pounds on my steelyard, which, at first sight, seems very little; and, if a salmon remained stationary when being played, and the angler were merely pulling dead against him, with a fairly strong casting line, I do not think he could break it, do what he could, unless he gave it a sudden jerk; but, the moment the salmon began to move and pull as well as the angler, a double strain would be put on the line, and it would probably break, unless of unusual strength.

The foregoing may be of some use as a guide to the amount of strain to be used in playing a fish. If skilfully handled, he will generally be brought to the gaff in from five minutes to half an hour from the time he is hooked. It is not often he will take longer to kill, unless he is hooked foul, when he may keep on for hours.

If there is plenty of room, and no danger of being broken owing to sunken rocks, roots of trees, snags, etc., it will be as well to put only a moderate strain on the line, and to let the fish run out as he feels inclined; but there are occasions when it is necessary to hold on at any cost, and not to give an inch of line if it can be avoided. It is astonishing how easily a fish can be cowed in this manner. On a river in the south of Norway that I was fishing with a friend there was a narrow rapid stream, in which salmon congregated in large numbers, waiting to take the falls just above, where it was a certainty to rise or hook a fish. We fished from a high rock overhanging the stream, and there was only one place where a fish could be landed, which was a backwater, about the size of a large dinner table, on the side we fished from. Directly a fish was hooked, it was a case of pull baker, pull devil, and we tried to haul him into this bit of slack water; and, if we once succeeded in getting him there, he seemed to lose heart, and gave in at once. I dare say I shall not be believed; but the average time we took to kill any fish we landed in this pool was about four minutes. A fish over fifteen pounds would generally beat us, for, do all we could, we could not pull him into the slack water. If once he got into the rapid below, down he went, and, not being able to follow him, he invariably broke us. We had to resort to these tactics in most of the other pools in the river we were fishing, but this was the most difficult of all to land a fish in. These are, of course, exceptions to the orthodox methods of playing a fish; but they show what can be done with good single gut, which was what we used.

If a heavy fish is hooked, and makes a run down stream, then suddenly takes up again, it will test the qualities of the strongest casting line; the strain on the belly of the line thus made will in all probability, if the line used is a continuous thick one, be fatal; and it is under such circumstances that the advantage of using a thin back line will be found out and appreciated, the strain on the thin line being so much less in proportion. If, however, any line stands such a test, there is still great danger: for, should the fish take it into his head to come down stream again, the line cannot be reeled in quickly enough, and the slack will get fast in any stones, rocks, or snags that may be at the bottom of the river. If the angler is playing the fish from the bank, he will have little hope of saving it under such circumstances; but, should he be fishing out of a boat, the chances are far greater against him, as he cannot follow the fish, and is utterly powerless to help himself; all he can do is to get in the slack line as fast as he can, and, this being a very slow process, reeling in with the rod in hand, the best thing he can do is to put down the rod in the boat, pull in the slack with both hands, and trust to luck to secure his fish.

When playing a salmon from the bank, should the fish prove more than ordinarily stubborn, and show no signs of giving in, it is a good plan, if it is practicable, to coax him up stream as far as is possible and then pull him down with a run; if this can be repeated two or three times, he will generally give in. There is another way of playing a fish that is stubborn: the rod is laid down on the bank, and the fish is hand-played, and, although it does not seem a very sportsmanlike method of proceeding, it is astonishing how quickly a fish will give in when thus treated. I have seen fish that have been played half an hour, showing no signs of giving in, landed in a couple of minutes by hand-playing them. This is a common practice on the Aberdeenshire Dee, particularly during the spring months, when the spent fish, which run to a large size, get recruited, give the angler a great deal of trouble, and waste a great deal of valuable time in bringing them to bank.

GAFFING AND LANDING A FISH

There is a great art in bringing a salmon to the gaff. It should never be attempted in very shallow water if it can be avoided. The gaffer should always keep a little below where he expects the fish will be brought towards the bank, and wherever he places himself he should remain stationary, in a stooping position, with the gaff ready for action. Should he move about the fish will probably get sight of him, and if he does the chances are he will make a run out into mid-stream, and will not allow himself to be brought within reach of the gaff until he is quite exhausted, fighting it out to the bitter end. What the angler has to do is to wait until the fish is quiet, and if he can get his nose above the water bring him in with a run to the gaffer, who will seize the opportunity, give one clip, and all is over with him.

On no account should he attempt to put the gaff in should the fish commence to struggle, but wait patiently until he is quiet again. A fish will often be brought within reach of the gafif over and over again, and just as the gaffer is about to strike him he commences to struggle. This is a trying time for the man who is playing him, but he must not, as is often the case, lose his temper and abuse the gaffer, for if the latter is of a nervous temperament he will probably make a bungle of the business, and the fish will reap the benefit. It may be taken for granted that the gaffer is as keen and as anxious as the angler to see the fish on the bank, and does his best to secure him for his own reputation's sake. Should he miss a chance and the fish get away, it is doubtless very annoying, but it is one of the disappointments the salmon fisher will have to put up with.

There are few men who can gaff a fish as it should be done. It requires great nerve and a great deal of practice. The Norwegians are the best gaffers I ever came across, with the exception of the Shannon men, whose dexterity is wonderful. To gaff a fish in deep rapid water is a more difficult thing than it appears to be, yet the Shannon men never miss a chance; they use a gaff made of well-seasoned hazel wood, that will give and take with the struggles of the fish, which run to an immense size.

A stiff handle to a gaff would be liable to break when gaffing one of these monsters in a rapid stream, besides being most unwieldy. An inexperienced gaffer will generally gaff a fish anywhere he can put his gaff in, but an experienced man will bide his time and gaff the fish somewhere below the back fin, which will balance him as nearly as possible, and prevent his flesh being torn in his struggles. In landing a fish with the net similar precautions must be taken; the man who has charge of the net should remain stationary where he thinks it probable the fish may be landed. The net should be held under water with a stone in it, which will keep the meshes in their place. The angler must run the fish in towards the net in the same manner that he would when the fish was to be gaffed. If the fish is quiet he will generally be able to run him in at once, but should never attempt to do so if he commences to struggle.

When the head and shoulders of the fish are well into the net, the netter should raise it sufficiently to get the whole of the body within its meshes; the hoop of the net should be then lowered, the farther end downward, and the handle at the same time raised – thus forming the net into a purse from which there is no escape. The fish can then be drawn into the bank, net and handle in the same position. On no account must the net be raised high out of the water; if it is attempted to land fish in such a fashion the weight of the fish will soon tell on the hoop of the net and make it unfit for use. It must never be attempted to net a fish tail first; he may be got into the net, but he has an awkward habit of using his tail, and would be out of it again before you were aware. When once, however, his head and shoulders are in over the hoop he cannot escape.

Many fishermen gaff their own fish, and will not on any account delegate this office to anyone else. To accept aid would deprive them of half their pleasure in fishing, and if they are of this opinion I think they are quite right; no doubt there is much excitement in gaffing one's own fish, but it requires great skill and practice to be able to do it artistically. There is, however, a certain amount of risk incurred, as when the line is wound up so short as it necessarily must be to enable the angler to reach his fish, if care is not taken to lower the point of the rod and slack the line the moment the gaff is in, the chances are the top will get smashed. This has happened to myself on several occasions, and the object being to get the fish safe on the bank, I prefer adopting the surer method of having my fish gaffed by my attendant.

If it can be ascertained for a certainty that a fish is firmly hooked, and there is a beach anywhere handy, he can be stranded without the use of gaff or net, but this must not be attempted until the fish is quite 'done' and has not a kick in him. The angler must wait until he can get his head above water, and he can then run him in high and dry without a struggle. If he cannot completely 'strand him thus, he can put down his rod and tail him; this is done by grasping him firmly just above his tail with the second finger and thumb. By this means he can be pulled out of the water without risk of escape, and carried to a place of safety; but it is only salmon that can be landed in this way;

the tails of all other fish, sea trout included, would slip through the fingers, and this is an infallible test should it be doubtful if the fish caught is a salmon or a sea trout.

Salmon fishing out of a boat in a lake should be carried on on the same principle as when fishing on the river bank, with the exception that a drop fly may be used in addition to the tail fly. A drop fly is often used on a river, but I think it is objectionable in consequence of the risk of its getting foul at the bottom.

MISCELLANEOUS

There is no accounting for the humour of a salmon. You do not know the minute he will take it into his head to rise; he will rise freely sometimes on the worst possible looking day for fishing, when no sport is expected. The appearance of a day is most deceptive. You may go out full of hope and certain in your own mind you are going to have great sport, and you will often go home blank without a rise; but although as a rule it is impossible to foretell in the morning what sort of fishing day it will turn out, there is an exception. If the wind is in the east with a blue hazy atmosphere it seems to affect the fish in some unaccountable way, and while it lasts a rise can rarely be got out of them. I have noticed this hundreds of times, often when the water was in splendid fishing order, and the river full of new run fish, but whatever quarter the wind blows from there is always a chance while the fly is in the water, and to insure success the angler must make up his mind to have many blank days. He must never tire of throwing his fly, and never be put out by failure.

The time of day when I have found salmon take best is between the hours of nine o'clock a.m. and one o'clock p.m., and from four to dusk in the evening. In early spring if there is no frost it will make little difference what hour one fishes, but in a hard frost it is not often a salmon will rise until the afternoon, and then only for a short time. In the latter part of the spring months, when the weather gets bright and hot, the earlier the angler is out the better, but if the sky is overcast I should prefer the hours I before mentioned for choice. I have frequently known early risers to have flogged all the pools over all the morning blank, and the man who appeared on the scene at nine or ten o'clock to get sport in those same pools. Salmon will often only rise at certain times of the day, and it is luck to come across them when in the humour. There is one time of the evening, however, when I should never despair of catching a fish if I had been blank all day.

The time is about a quarter of an hour after sunset, after a hot bright day in the spring months, when the glare is off the water. There was a pool on the Kilmurry water, on the Blackwater, county Cork, that hardly ever failed me under such circumstances; it was a sharp running water, as smooth as glass, and a very good rising pool at any hour of the day. When there was no wind, I used to commence fishing at sunset, but although I had fished the pool once, twice, or three times, I never could rise a fish until about a quarter of an hour afterwards. It was then a certainty, but the fish were only on the rise for about twenty minutes, and there was seldom time to catch more than one fish. This was the only pool they seemed to care about rising in at this hour, and the less wind there was the more certain I was to get a fish.

When fishing private water the angler can choose his own time for beginning operations, and will have the satisfaction of knowing that his fly will be the first one seen by the fish in the morning, but when fishing in club or open water those that go out late will be considerably handicapped, and will very often have to travel a long way to secure a pool.

A club or open water is a very good school for a beginner to commence his salmon-fishing education. Here he will find plenty of competitors, and he will have a far better chance of acquiring knowledge than if he were fishing in private water, with no one but perhaps an inexperienced prejudiced person as an attendant to advise him. In an open water he will come across old and experienced anglers who, although they cannot be expected to give him information that would mar their own sport, will be found as a rule ready to offer him good advice if he will take it; and he may soon learn the rudiments of the art. He will have many opportunities of losing his temper, and will find out that the best thing he can do is to keep it.

There is as much luck in salmon fishing as in any other pursuit we are engaged in, and the most experienced angler will often be beaten by the veriest tyro. It is very trying to the temper of a man who 'fancies himself,' and who is going to teach all the world how to fish, to go home blank. The man who is lucky has no feeling of pity for his neighbour who has been unsuccessful, and, if the truth is known, often chuckles at his discomfiture, even though he should be his bosom friend. Not long ago I was fishing some private water I had rented with a friend.

We used to meet at lunch to compare notes. One day when we met as usual, my friend produced five splendid new run fish, one of them over 20 lbs, and I had nothing to show. I could see that he had no pity for me, and that he was highly pleased with himself, and although I pretended that I rejoiced with him, I was in reality not at all happy and felt very small. This was bad enough, but when, on our separating to resume our sport after lunch, he said to me, 'Well, as you are not getting any sport perhaps you would like to read the newspaper (handing me one), instead of fishing this afternoon,' it was almost more than I could stand. However, I declined with thanks and said nothing more, but I hated him for half an hour most cordially, and vowed I would pay him out some day, and shortly afterwards I had an opportunity of doing so, for I produced eight spring fish one day at lunch time, my friend having only landed a kelt; but knowing what his feelings must be, I did not chaff him or offer him a newspaper to read. May my forbearance be chronicled by the recording angel! That day I killed eleven fish, averaging 10 lbs., the best day I ever had spring fishing.

I have seen many strange incidents during my salmon-fishing experience, but the cleverest thing I ever saw done was by the above-mentioned friend. He was fishing a pool in the Blackwater, co. Cork, a short distance above me. All of a sudden I heard shouting, and when I went to see what was the matter, I found that after a long play he had been broken by a big salmon, who took away his fly and about forty yards of his reel line. He had put on another casting line and fly and was fishing the same pool down again when he noticed a fish rising two or three times in a very eccentric manner, and the idea struck him that it was the same fish that had broken him trying to get rid of the fly and line.

He was a man of great resource and never at a loss what to do in any case of emergency, so he took off his fly, put on a triangle weighted with a good bit of lead, and casting this over the stream below where he saw the fish rise, and dragging it across, in a little time he succeeded in recovering his line, and the fish being quiet at the moment he was able to pass the end through the rings of his rod, and attach it to what was left on the reel. In a few minutes I had the pleasure of gaffing the fish; he was new run, and weighed 20 lbs. The pool he was fishing was a quarter of a mile long, and very broad, and it was a hundred to one against his recovering the line.

On looking round after I had gaffed the fish I missed my attendant, left in charge of my rod, who did not appear on the scene until sometime after the fun was over. The fact was he had taken advantage of my back being turned to go into the hut, which was close by, to eat my friend's attendant's share of a very good lunch we had brought with us for an expected visitor. He managed, however, to pick up a very good version of the story, for shortly after we heard all over the garrison of Fermoy how he had been the instigator and prime mover of the whole thing from beginning to end, including the gaffing of the fish.

And so I say farewell, and wish all my brother sportsmen our old greeting on the Conway – 'A tight line!'

John P. Traherne.

3

Fly Fishing for Trout and Grayling: Or 'Fine and Far Off'

It is a shallow as well as a dismal scheme of life which ignores or undervalues the importance of recreation. Never, I believe, was there an age in which it was more indispensable 'For weary body and for heavy soul.' We are living at high-pressure; business has become more engrossing and the pursuit of what is called pleasure more laborious. It is more than ever desirable to find occasional change of scene and occupation which shall be really refreshing; which shall at once recruit our bodily energies and give free play to faculties and feelings which are shelved during the daily routine of working life. Mere locomotion is not enough; our thoughts must be turned into new and pleasant channels, and we must seek places suited to new phases of agreeable activity. It is told of one of the most eminent of English conveyancers that when induced for his health's sake to visit the seaside, he carried with him, by way of light reading, 'Fearne on Contingent Remainders.' Sea air may have done something for him; but where was his recreation? His mind was kept running in the old groove.

It is of course true that what is recreation to one man might be mere weariness to another of different tastes and habits, who feels the strain of over-work in different functions of body or mind. A well-earned holiday may be employed in fifty different ways, each having its own fitness. But in comparing various recreations we may fairly give the palm to that which suits the greatest number of cases; that in which the largest proportion of intelligent men can find healthful bodily exercise combined with light yet interesting occupation for the mind. And I know none which satisfies these conditions more completely than angling. In its most refined form indeed – I need hardly add that I speak of fly fishing – it rises to the dignity of an elegant and ingenious art, combining in a singular degree the active and the contemplative, the practical and the scientific element.

I have had my fair share of other more violent, perhaps more exciting field sports, and am not insensible to their attractions. Happily, Piscator in these days need not wage a wordy conflict with Venator or Auceps, for the same men often excel in several branches of sport, and the friend whose opinion on the following pages of angling notes I shall value most highly is not only well known in the hunting field but singularly successful in the practice of falconry.

Instead of apprehending any lack of sympathy with the zeal for my favourite recreation which leads me to add yet another to the many contributions recently made to its literature, I rather fear that I shall be held to have done but scant justice to its varied attractions and resources…

But I will not open my case with an apology. An angler from boyhood – a fly fisher for more than fifty years, I will rather 'assume desert,' so far as to claim a favourable hearing for my experiences of an art which I can still practise with healthy enjoyment, and in despite of age, with a fair measure of success.

The very name of fly fishing carries back my fancy to many a pleasant hour – many a lovely scene. Once more afloat on the still bosom of a Highland loch, I watch with eagerness the dark line widening from its western shore, welcome herald of the breeze that will soon break up the 'mellow reflex' of the landscape around me, and refill the frame of the mirror, with 'rippled silver. The purple-robed, grey-headed hills seem closing' in upon me; high overhead sweeps the eagle, watchful, yet seemingly unterrified; and see, by the foot of yon burnie the roe has stolen forth to drink, from his-green couch amid the birches and brackens. Or, knee-deep in a ford of the Teme, where he lingers lovingly in many a circling sweep round the ivied cliffs and oak-clad slopes of Downton, I wave a potent, and in that well-proportioned stream, 'all-commanding wand' over the rough eddy, sentinelled with watchful trout, or where the quieter run deepens into the haunts of the grayling. Now I seem to hear the hoarse chiding of the Greta, as he chafes along his narrow bed, or the roar of 'old Conway's foaming flood' – now the gentle murmur of some English stream, rippling through sunny meads, is 'rife and perfect in my listening ear.'

The enjoyment of these local memories is heightened to anglers by association with the stirring details of what is always an interesting, often a most exciting sport. We remember where the monarch of the Test, long coy and recusant, was at length fascinated by the drop of the tiniest of midges over his very snout; and where, with our gillie's assistance, we contrived to land three lusty trout together, like the elfin in the ballad, 'a' dancing in a string.' We execrate the treacherous stake which had well-nigh robbed us of a good fish and a cast of flies at once, or bless the memory of the smooth sand bank, pleasant to weary feet, where we at last headed, turned, and wound in the salmon who had kept the lead for some three hundred yards down a rocky channel, among stones loose, sharp, and slippery – perilous at once to shins and tackle. How have we enjoyed the early breeze that crisped the stream on a summer morning; the well-earned rest on a mossy bank in the deep hush of noon, and the homeward stroll through the pensive calm of evening.

Independently of the fishes and insects with which the angler is more specially concerned – in themselves a little world of marvel and mystery – his avocation gives him no common opportunities for observing some of the most beautiful and curious forms of animal and vegetable life. Stealing along by the water's edge, his footfall lost in the murmur of the stream, or muffled by Nature's carpeting, he enters unsuspected the haunts of the shyest creatures. He sees the otter glide down from his cairn, or lift his sleek treacherous visage in the midst of the pool; he notes the general consternation of the *salmonidae* at the sinuous rush of the seal, whom hungry pursuit has tempted beyond the salt water; 'doe and roe and red deer good' slake their thirst in his sight; he surprises the blackcock's deserted mate and progeny in their moist dingle, the wild duck and her brood as they paddle through the sedges. Leaning back against the trunk of a willow, he sees the kingfisher, a living sapphire, shoot close to his dazzled eyes, or from her perch over his head drop on a sudden plumb into the river, and as suddenly emerge with her prey; or hidden in the shadow of an overhanging rock, he marks the water ouzel, glittering in a silver panoply of air bubbles, run briskly along the sandy bottom of the burn. Even the innocent gambols of the much-calumniated water rat, joyous after his guiltless feast of grass and water weeds, or the familiar wiles of the nesting peewit will find him not an unamused spectator.

If a botanist, he will pick his choicest ferns in the damp rocky hollows by the waterfall, his rarest lichens on the bare slopes above some Alpine tarn, his favourite orchises in the meadows watered by a well-peopled stream. He will rejoice in the delicate beauty of the pinguicula along some tiny moorland runnel, and admire the silver-fringed stars of the bog-bean beside deeper and blacker waters, where the quaking turf craves wary walking. Mr Balfour's utmost indulgence would hardly admit me to a degree in botany, yet it was with a glow of pleasure that I first found myself throat-deep in a bed of the *Osmunda regalis*, on the banks of the Leven, or gathered the 'pale and azure-pencilled' clusters of the wood-vetch by Greta-side, or discovered the fringed yellow water lily on Thames, gleaming like the floating lamp of a Hindoo votaress. If a geologist, the angler may ply his hammer and fill his note book along the very stream or tarn whence he fills his basket. If an artist, his rambles will acquaint him with every form of the picturesque, from the stern grandeur of Llyn Idwal to the tranquil beauties of Father Thames.

It is this many-sided character of the angler's art which has united so many suffrages in its favour, and has made it attractive to so many distinguished men of such dissimilar tastes and characters. It is this, finally, which has given to the art a literature of its own, abundant and various, in proportion to the number of its votaries and the diversity of their minds, and often highly enjoyable even by the uninitiated.

Writing as long ago as the year 1856 on a subject in which I then felt, as I still feel, the liveliest interest – that of the fly fisher and his library – I found a plea for my essay in the national taste. We were, I remarked, a nation of sportsmen, but the nation of anglers.

And now, after twenty-seven years, fresh from the attractions of the Fisheries Exhibition, I feel that what then was a truth is now almost a truism, and remount my favourite hobby in the full belief that in spite of the lapse of years he is not yet 'forgot.'

Both the art and the science of angling have made great progress in the interval; the education of our fish has advanced, and it is only an equal progress on the part of the fly fisher which can enable him to maintain his old mastery over the *salmonidae*. And if I venture to believe that I can still offer something worth a reader's notice on questions now better understood than ever, it is because I have retained my old taste for fly fishing in all its freshness, have pursued the sport on occasional leisure days both here and at the Antipodes, and have preserved a careful record both of successes and failures.

I take my motto from Charles Cotton,' whom even more than dear old Izaac Walton I regard as the father of modern fly fishing. In those bright Derbyshire streams which he loved so well and doubtless fished so skilfully, to fish 'fine and fair off' still gives the angler his best chance of success, and theie are few waters fairly worth fishing where it may not be practised with advantage. But at the outset of remarks which are nothing if not practical, I ought to observe that even in following Cotton's admirable rule there may be mistake or excess. The rule is, in fact, only one method of carrying out the great principle which underlies all success in fly fishing. Unless under exceptional conditions of weather, water or both, Piscator must above all things keep out of sight; must not allow Piscis to catch a glimpse of himself, his rod or the shadow of either; must show him, in fact, nothing but the fly which is to lure him to his own undoing.'

This principle, it may be said, is too obvious to be worth stating. Yet if generally admitted it is very insufficiently acted upon. Not long since I was chatting with a friend near Wansford Mill, on the well-known 'Driffield Beck.' He had been trying the lower water whilst I had fished down stream to meet him. The day was bright with little breeze, but the fish were feeding, and my brother angler's creel hung heavy at his back, while the lad who carried mine seemed nowise sorry to rest it on the bank. A third angler appeared on the scene. He was striding along close to the water's edge, down stream, making from time to time a long cast with a two-handed rod across the open beck. He really did not cast badly, though his tackle seemed rather coarse and his fly was of a size strange and alarming to Driffield trout of the present generation, whatever it might have been to their remote ancestry. But my friend and I were well aware that as he moved, there was *'fuga et ingens solitudo'* in front of him; that the fish were literally scudding in shoals from his obtrusive presence.

This was no doubt an extreme case, but the same error in kind, though less in degree, is constantly committed even by practised hands. I do not find crawling or crouching till within four or five yards of a 'shy' stream quite as easy as I did forty years ago, but I resort freely to each as my cast requires, and often withdraw completely from the bank to move again cautiously towards it without the risk of sending an alarm along the stream. Yet I can never fish a bright water on a bright day without saying to myself a dozen times, 'I might have had that fish, had I only kept better out of sight.'

There are of course many streams, mountain and moorland, where such cautious tactics are needless; but in the best English trouting counties – Hampshire, for instance, or the East Riding, Buckinghamshire, Salop or Devon – concealment is the first requisite for sport. In order to this, there are many details to be studied. In the first place, if the day be sunny, try as far as possible to look the sun in the face. To feel his warmth on your back and shoulders is doubtless far pleasanter than to be dazzled by his light, both direct and reflected from the water; but if you want a heavy basket you will disregard the inconvenience for the sake of remaining unseen. Beginning by a short cast under your own bank, you will gradually lengthen your throw till your stretcher drops in deep shade close under the opposite shore, and each fish successively covered will see your fly before any shadow from rod or line falls over him. If the wind as well as the sun be in your face, humour it as best you can by casting aslant, and working your rod horizontally instead of vertically, but unless it blows great guns, when the light from behind you will do little harm, persevere in defying both sun and wind. 'It's dogged as does it.' Secondly, avail yourself of every scrap of cover. On no account let a fish see your figure relieved against the sky. A big bush judiciously employed as a screen may enable you to do more with a short line than the best far-off casting could achieve without its shelter. The apparent stupidity of fish swimming high in a still sunny pool when thus approached under cover is often most amusing. I have seen large trout in the middle of a July day swim leisurely up to my fly and suck it in without the slightest misgiving. If bushes are wanting, a slight fringe of waterside plants and flowers – willow herb, loose strife, figwort and the like – often does good service by blurring the outline of your figure. Even the colour of your clothing is not unimportant. Black or white are on a bright day equally objectionable, especially for your hat. It should be remembered, too, that a screen is useful behind as well as in front of you. When there is barely footing between a high hedge and the water – I have a few such spots in my mind's eye – the fish will hardly be aware of your presence unless you exhibit some violent contrast of colour. But a far commoner illustration of my meaning may be found in the neighbourhood of mills and factories, where a dead wall lies near the margin of an inviting stream or pool. Move cautiously with your back close to the brickwork, and you often find to your surprise and satisfaction that while you see the trout on the feed, they fail to see you. Casting from such a position no doubt requires a peculiar knack; but that difficulty once overcome the game is all in your favour. The fish to whom you have thrown takes the fly in the most confiding manner, and till repeated experience has familiarised you with this result the whole affair seems almost uncanny – as though you had the fern seed and walked invisible. There will, of course, be great danger of betraying your presence when landing your fish, and I can only recommend you to keep as close to the friendly wall as you can till you have led your trout some way down the stream, and not to use the landing net till he has made his last rush.

There is another aid to concealment which I think is not generally recognised, but to which in certain waters (notably in Boston Beck in the East Riding) I have owed many a brace of heavy fish. Every angler has obtained some bold rises by casting somewhat heavily so as to break through the coating of foam – 'beggars' balm,' Walton calls it – which forms over eddies for some distance below a fall or strong rush of water. But in calm hot weather there often forms over the shoreward surface of still and somewhat shallow water a fine oily film, due partly to the sporules of water weeds, but mainly, I believe, to the floating ova and larvae of minute insects, which is only visible in particular lights, and yet very effectively dulls the quick sight of the trout. When you see a patch of inshore wrater dimmed by such a film, keep low within an easy cast and wait till you see not a distinct break or rise but a slight dimpling of the water caused by the suck of a fish. Drop a single fly a little above him, and his capture is almost a certainty. The value of this resource lies in its being most available in apparently hopeless days, when there is a strong sun and no breeze stirring.

Yet again, fish may often be taken, though at some risk to your tackle, when they are lying in small open spaces among

Teeds. Keep low – for on bright days this is a sine qua non – and if your fish be but a few inches below the surface the refraction will prevent his seeing you or your rod, and a long cast up stream or across will take him off his guard. But in such a case there must be no playing him; ere he has recovered the first shock of finding himself hooked he must be hurried down stream along the surface till you have him in open water, and can square accounts with him at your leisure. In this rough- and-ready process the hold, of course, may give way, and possibly the tackle. The latter disaster is, however, less frequent than at first sight would seem probable. The fish is taken by surprise, and has no time for organising an effectual resistance, while his forced march down stream quite upsets his ordinary habits. It is when you are fishing a loch on a breezeless day and are tempted to throw over a fish whose 'neb' you have seen quietly thrust up in a small opening among water lilies that the 'deadly breach' is most 'imminent,' and 'hair-breadth scapes' only attainable by the happiest combination of caution and audacity. There is no current to help you, and one turn round a tough stalk will lose you both fish and fly. Yet I can remember on a sultry July afternoon, then there was no other possibility of getting a rise, killing in Loch Kinder by this perilous cast four or five brace of pretty fish with the loss of but a single fly.

I am tempted here to give some instances from my own experience of success attained under difficulties by keeping out of sight in various ways.

There was a reach of the upper Itchin where I had more than once found the trout, though sizeable and fairly numerous, yet provokingly wary and suspicious. The bank on one side was absolutely bare and very low; on the other – the southern side – it was steep and moderately high, by no means favourable to 'keeping dark.' But parallel to the course of the river, and at nearly the same level, there ran an irrigation cut, some two feet deep with rather a muddy bottom, about five yards distant from the main stream. Into this one day I lowered myself – having long legs and wading boots to correspond – and worked the stream with a double-handed rod by long casts. I could only just see the opposite edge of the water, but was consoled for losing my view of the fish by knowing that the deprivation was reciprocal. The dodge completely succeeded. Though I felt the rises instead of seeing them I rarely failed to hook my fish and very seldom lost him when hooked. The difficulty lay in scrambling out of my ditch and rushing towards the river before my prisoner could bring me to grief by dashing under the near bank. In this way I did considerable execution on several occasions. I ought in frankness to admit that with more fishable water within easy reach many anglers would have thought the success hardly worth the pains it cost. This was certainly the opinion of a dear old friend and fellow-sportsman who witnessed my first sortie from the trench and landed my fish for me. He laughed till he cried at the figure I cut in scurrying towards the bank, and could never afterwards be induced to exhibit himself in the like undignified position.

I take my second instance from a lucky hit in loch fishing. Some thirty years ago I was afloat with two friends on Loch Treig, to the farther end of which we intended to fish our way. It was a hot forenoon in August, one of those tantalising days when,

> Instead of one unchanging breeze
> There blow a thousand little airs,

and I soon perceived that there was little profit in hunting the 'catspaws' which supplied the needful ripple – if you could only catch them. So I induced my friends to land me some three miles from the shepherd's hut at the end of the loch where we were to find our luncheon. I was equipped for wading, and had before me several reaches of fine gravel where the water deepened very gradually towards the 'brook' – that critical point, where, in this as in many other lakes, the shoreward shallow rapidly shelves away into water too deep for the fly. In fact it often happens that at this point a belt of water from ten to twenty yards in breadth contains all the best of the taking fish. Within this belt are mostly small fry, without it lies the deep, only fit for trolling. The water before me was smooth as glass, the bottom delightful for wading. Moving cautiously to make the warning wave which must precede me as small as possible, I advanced into the lake as far as I could, and as I did so became more and more aware that fish were moving just where the water deepened within a long cast of my two- handed rod. I threw but one fly, and that smaller than the size I usually preferred. Throwing as far as I could, I let my whole cast sink before giving any movement to the fly, and was repeatedly rewarded by finding that a trout had hooked himself a foot or so under water. Every now and then, however, the fly dropped so close before the nose of a feeding fish that he was fast on the instant. Briefly, when we met at our tryst (where I confess to have been half an hour late) my friends had three fish between them, whilst I had six-and-thirty. In this case it will be seen the secret of success lay in keeping low, so that the effect of refraction kept the unimmersed portion of the fly fisher's figure practically out of sight.

The question of fishing up or down stream is closely connected with this part of my subject. There is now so general a consent amongst anglers in favour of up-stream casting that it would seem superfluous to give the reasons which make it preferable in most cases. I am rather inclined to remind brother anglers that the rule must not be made absolute, and to point out some cases in which the opposite course should be adopted. And first, if in fishing up stream you would have a strong sun at your back, you will betray your presence less by making your beat downwards. This, however, must not involve the absurd blunder of hauling your flies 'against the current, thus making an unnatural ripple which cannot but alarm a trout of any experience.

In fishing down stream, begin if possible from a stand several yards distant from the margin, and throw lightly over the in-shore water a little above you, lengthening your cast by degrees till you have covered three-fourths of the width.

Then, and not till then, you may advance warily to the bank and try the deadly cast under the opposite shore. From first to last you must take care that the movement of your flies be natural; that they go down easily with the stream, with occasional slight checks from the wrist to mimic the struggles of a drowning insect and produce that play of legs and wings which is so irresistible to a hungry trout. Retire from the bank after working out your cast, and repeat the same process a dozen yards farther down. If you hook a good fish, let him fight up stream as long as he will, that you may avoid disturbing unfished water in bringing him to the net; but should he insist on a downward rush do your best to keep ahead of him, showing yourself no more than is absolutely necessary.

The portion of the stream which you are thus compelled to hurry by should be allowed a good spell of rest before you move up again to fish it. You must tread softly and cautiously. A heavy or hasty footfall will be felt by the fish under the near bank, who will rush out and spread alarm among their friends in mid-stream.

To return to the question of 'up' or 'down.' In a very rapid river, again, more, I think, is lost than gained by the up-stream cast The line is brought down so rapidly to the caster that it is hardly possible for him to keep it taut enough for the fish to hook itself, and 'striking' is practically out of the question.

Moreover, as the fly gives more hold to the water than the gut, and therefore moves faster, it is apt to be rolled back on the footlinks, and presented to the eye of the trout with most suspicious surroundings. Yet again, there are some places, and those often favourite haunts for fish, which must be fished down stream or not at all Let me give one example out of many. There was a small bye wash, some 120 yards long, leading down from the upper to the lower branch of a Hampshire stream; the near bank sedgy, the farther bank completely overhung with dwarf willows. It was scarce five feet wide, but mostly deep, and presenting in miniature every variety of stream and pool, but to throw on it was simply impossible, and I shall never forget the face of the old keeper when he saw me proceeding to fish it. He sat down and lit his pipe, expecting a quiet time till I returned to my right mind and the open river.

Beginning at the top of the streamlet, and keeping the point of my rod under the overarching boughs, I let my tail fly float down the water, varying its descending movement by wrist-play, while my dropper made dimples on the dark surface.

In half a minute I was shouting for old W– and the net. Luckily the fish chose to run up stream; a powerful rod and shortened line enabled me to keep him out of the willow roots, and he was easily netted in the hatch hole. A second capture followed very speedily, but the fish took down the watercourse, and I disturbed fifty yards of promising water in my struggles to keep him out of mischief. However, I managed to basket a third fish before I reached the junction with the main river. I tried the same unscientific but killing process on a dozen subsequent occasions, never taking more than three or less than two trout in that tangled thread of water. All these fish were dark-skinned, owing to their shady habitat, and all pretty nearly of a size, weighing from eleven to fourteen ounces, something doubtless in the conditions of the water making it a suitable feeding ground for middle-aged trout, though the cause of 'this thus-ness' I cannot pretend to explain.

I may add – to encourage the pursuit of fish under difficulties – that I do not remember to have lost more than one fish off the hook in all my battles up and down that dangerous reach. The rises were bold and sure, because the artificial fly was a stranger there – in fact I do not believe that anyone but myself had ever risked his tackle in such a spot. With an ordinary single-handed rod, however, success would have been impossible; I could neither have worked my flies nor controlled my fish. I used in those days a fourteen-foot double-handed rod of Eaton's, extra stiff and lengthened in defiance of all symmetry to suit a fad of my own. I fancied that the original hollow butt felt light and weak, and got the maker to shape me one nearly a foot longer and powerful enough to bear boring for a spare top. That rod, by the bye, is still forthcoming after forty-five years' hard work in many waters, and I wish its master were in equally good condition.

Thus far I seem to have proceeded without a due arrangement of my subject. I was tempted by my title to plunge as it were in inedias res, and to show the purpose and conditions of fine and far-off casting. But as fly fishing was my theme I might as well, perhaps, have begun with the fly, the lure to which above all others the true angler loves to resort. The mimic insect is in every way interesting. The variety of materials now employed in its structure exceeds in these days even the extensive range suggested by Gay in his elegant description. Bodies of quill or gutta-percha were doubtless unknown to him, and the endless shades of pig's down and mohair. The many forms of gold and silver twist or tinsel which seem to have so great an attraction for the *salmonidae* belong to a later date than his. And though he presses 'each gay bird' into his service, I doubt whether he would have known how to utilise the kingfisher's blue, the crest and hackles of the golden pheasant, or the killing plumage of the wood duck.

The Fisheries Exhibition brought out a wonderful display of artificial flies, English, Scotch, and Irish – I crave pardon of the judges for not having placed the Scotch flies first – of every size, build, and colour. Indeed, as I ranged from case to case trying to form my own estimate of comparative merits, I felt tempted to exclaim with Diogenes at the fair, 'What a multitude of things are here of which I have no need. Still the beauty, the delicacy, and in many cases the imitative skill of the work rendered the show very attractive.

Another source of interest in a well-tied fly, and notably in the very smallest, is its extraordinary strength and durability considering the materials employed. An angler must no doubt have tied many a score of flies for himself ere he can fully appreciate this excellence. In a case of flies set up for show it is assumed rather than proved to exist; but we may be sure that the exhibitor did not attain his reputation for such 'marvellous delicate ware' – as Queen Bess said of her first silk stockings

– without producing an article capable of resisting both the strain of a good fish fighting for his life, and the repeated grinding and chewing of tiny teeth.

To build a salmon fly strongly is comparatively easy. There is ample room and verge enough for the firmest lapping of the hook to the gut, and for the tying-on in due succession of the various materials which form the body, legs, and wings of the highly composite insect, while the loop at the head, which was almost unknown in my boyhood, gives the needful strength at the point where the friction is greatest. But when we look at a tiny olive-dun or quill-gnat, such as often plays havoc among the heavy trout of our best chalk streams, we may well marvel at the skill which has made a few turns of fine silk not only join hook to gut indissolubly, but bind minute portions of various material together in a firm and shapely whole.

A trout fly, be it remembered, needs above all things to be strong. Neatness and finish may often be dispensed with, if the colours be only right, but strength is indispensable. Without it, the more attractive the lure, the more grievous will be the angler's disappointment. The points which are naturally weakest in the fly ought to be especially looked to. Judging from my own experience, I should say that four fish are lost from the breaking or bending of the hook for one that escapes by the gut giving way. It is mainly with sneck-bend hooks that breakages occur, and these are apt to give way either just above the barb, or at the angle nearest to it. With regard to the number of flies to be used on a cast – a *vexata quaestio* amongst anglers – no really general rule can be laid down. In fishing a stream where the fish are large and the flies to be used small, it will often be found the best policy to use one fly only and that tied on a Limerick hook of the best make. Indeed, whatever the character of the stream, I prefer a hook of that class for my stretcher. It swims truer, and as it carries its point in the same vertical plane with the bend, seldom fails to hook your fish in the lower jaw. But on the other hand, there are many streams-in which a second and even a third fly will greatly assist your basket.

It is not merely that you may please the trout better by offering them a choice, though this is obviously true, and doubly so where the water often changes its character. The motion of a dropper cleverly worked, especially over an eddy, is essentially different from that of the tail fly, and imitates a phase of insect life with which fish are familiar, that in which the fly keeps dimpling the water in a series of short descents, probably dropping an egg every time it touches the stream. The nature of this motion is well recognised by the term 'bob fly' so often applied to the dropper, and the young angler will do well to study it carefully till practice makes him perfect.

If it wasna weel bobbit, we'll bob it again!

It is in this up-and-down play of the fly that the sneck-bend hook is so valuable, seldom failing to take hold somehow, somewhere. When it strikes on a bone, however good the temper, it is not unlikely to give way. But if care be taken to test each hook beforehand these mishaps will be very rare. If you have had a dozen flies dressed to your order, and cannot feel sure that the hooks have been carefully proved, tie one or two by fixing the point in a board and giving a strong pull on the gut.

Twice in my life I have come to utter grief by neglecting this precaution, the flies being in each case only too attractive, but the hooks almost rotten. In one case I lost seven fish in the course of an afternoon, which would, I honestly believe, have weighed very nearly two pounds apiece. The other case, though less disastrous, was even more remarkable, as I was using a medium-sized fly on a Scotch tarn where the trout ran small. I took above a hundred, which would hardly have averaged five ounces, though they were strong and red-fleshed. But the way in which they 'chewed up' one particular batch of flies which I had had tied especially for small rocky lochs was really extraordinary, It seemed as if they crushed the hooks in their mouths. Full a score of my favourites came home to me broken at the bend, and in many cases I had scarcely felt the rise, so that several fish must have had their wicked will of the defenceless fly.

As I have already said, my losses through the breaking of the gut have been comparatively few, and almost always distinctly due to my own fault. The point of greatest danger is of course close to the head of the tail fly, where a momentary check takes place in the free unfolding of the foot links, even when the cast is most carefully made. The friction at this weak point is naturally increased when a fish is being played, since if he is firmly hooked the gut is apt to be strained when forming an angle with the wire. In dressing a large or a medium-sized fly something may be done to obviate this mischief by a few turns of fine silk set with copal varnish round the gut just above the head of the fly. But in mere midges – and it is with these that the greatest execution is now done in our best trout streams – this precaution is impossible.

It only remains that the fly fisher look often and closely at this critical point in his tackle, especially when the trout rise boldly and the fun is fast and furious. It is a great bore, no doubt, to have to change a killing fly at the first symptoms of 'fraying;' but a far greater to put on a fresh one when the first has been carried off by a good fish.

The special danger here indicated is likely ere long to be a thing of the past. The eyed hook is now in the field, and when perfected will render what is now the weakest point in the delicate gut required for trout fishing practically secure against irregular friction. But thus far the 'eye' appears too clumsy for the tiny flies which most require it. Had I to design an eye suited to the smallest hooks, I should borrow a hint from the needle-maker, forming the orifice for the gut like that in a small gold-eyed needle, though rounder, and lining it with some soft metal. The lapping at the head of the fly would thus be quite inconspicuous, while the shank of the hook would keep a true line with the gut. For the present, however, the 'capital' danger must not be ignored.

Every knot, again, is a weak point in the cast; especially if tied in a hurry or not carefully soaked before use. A couple of spare collars which have lain in the slop basin during your breakfast may be carried round your hat with great advantage. Apart from an utter smash by bough or root – which is never impossible if you are in a hurry – it is often less troublesome to change the whole collar than to repair a trifling damage.

Having now dismissed the preliminary question of strength, I find myself face to face with the extensive and complicated subject of flies considered as lures; of the best flies for use, and the circumstances under which these or some of these will be found most useful.

To this subject no single essay can do justice, owing to the number of flies which have a recognised value only within a limited district. But in order to deal with it at all, one must first encounter that *quaestio vexatissima* – Whether artificial flies, generally speaking, are imitations of some particular insect, for which they are taken by the fish, or nondescripts (to borrow 'Ephemera's ' form of expression) which are seized only on account of their general appearance of life. The former position is generally maintained by English authors on fly fishing; the latter by brethren of the angle north of Tweed, or among the mountains of North Wales. Now, that the artificial fly should in general be an imitation, and on clear and often-fished waters a very close one, of some particular insect, I have no shadow of a doubt; nor do I believe that anyone who has fished in the Derwent, the Driffield water, the Teme, or the Itchin, will hesitate to agree with me.

Again and again have I found the 'March browns' supersede every other fly early in the season, when the natural insect, which I had imitated most carefully, floated on the water by thousands; nor do I doubt that at such times Mr Bainbridge's advice, to fish at once with three March browns slightly varied in tint and size, is most judicious. I have seen in like manner the little 'iron-blue' on a cold morning strong on the water, when I could not stir a fin with any other lure. The day warmed – a shower softened the wind – and the recent favourite was a useless appendage to my line; while a larger, gayer insect, visible on the water, warned me, not in vain, that the 'yellow dun' must now be taken into council. How often, again, in July and August, do the artificial fern fly and ant fly – killing through the sultry hours while the natural insects are also conspicuous – give place towards evening to that late-fluttering tempter the red- spinner, whom I have dropped on the water scarce distinguishable among his living likenesses!

The green-drake, again (better known perhaps as the 'May fly '), is a strong case in point. It is on the water little more than a fortnight, a large and 'ken-speckle' insect, and throughout that time it is very difficult, during the hours of its appearance, to induce a trout, in the streams where it is bred, to look at any artificial fly save a palpable imitation of this beautiful creature. To complete the argument, the same imitation is utterly useless on those English streams which do not produce the real insect.

Again, the experienced fly fisher will acknowledge the fact, that what the initiated call 'palmers' are taken, especially in swollen waters, in every river, and from the beginning to the end of the trouting season. Surely it is more than a mere coincidence that the rough caterpillar, or palmer worm, which these lures accurately resemble, should also be astir during full six months of the year, and be continually sent down the stream when a sudden rise of the water washes its margin?

To these examples, which I cited in favour of the 'imitative' theory nearly thirty years ago, I will add two or three more drawn from subsequent experience or overlooked at that time. There are certain flies tied in deliberate imitation of female insects carrying at their tails a ball of eggs to be dropped one by one in the water. I will instance two of these – the 'Grannom' or 'Greentail,' and the 'Governor.' The grannom – I speak now of the natural fly – is a reddish brown insect, not uncommon in the bushy reaches of many southern streams. It flies high, however, and so rarely touches the water that no artificial copy of it is in common use. But when the female fly develops her ova and is about to shed them she hovers close to the surface of the brook, with a green ball behind her, which may in more senses than one be said to wait upon her latter end. For as she drops egg after egg on the water, the eyes of hungry trout are soon attracted to her movements, and in some luckless moment of contact with the water she, with the portion of her rising family not yet launched on the world, disappears down a fish's gullet.

Now towards the end of April or beginning of May – for the breeding season of insects depends greatly on the weather – I often use the grannom fly, sometimes with signal success. But I have never done any good with it except during the few days when the female insect with her queer green appendage was actually visible on the water. The 'Governor' again – which should rather have been styled the 'Governess' – with its broad band of orange silk at the tail, represents another female fly generally seen on the water towards the end of July, conspicuous by a ripe cluster of orange-coloured eggs. Many practised anglers know nothing of this fly, but I have had the luck to use it occasionally when the natural insect was strong on the water, and it was taken in preference to anything else. I may add that the heaviest take of large trout which ever came to my knowledge – though, alas! I was not the captor – was made with this fly on the upper waters of Foston Beck, now in the hands of Colonel St. Quentin.

I might fairly rest my case on these two instances, in which the peculiarities of the natural insect during one brief phase of its existence are reproduced with such effect in the artificial fly. But I cannot pass by the 'local value' – to borrow an artist's phrase – of certain flies tied in imitation of insects unknown beyond a limited district. Every Devonshire man knows the virtues of the 'blue upright' – a dusky, smooth-bodied fly, varying from pale slate colour to a dead black. It holds, in fact, on Devonian streams much the same place as the murderous 'blue dun' with its downy body in a great majority of our English counties.

Now on my first introduction to a Devonshire stream I noticed great numbers of a slender, active insect which had no representative in my fly book, and which I felt sure I had never seen before. But a local artist soon supplied me with the imitation I wanted, and since that time I have killed more trout in Devon with the 'blue upright' than with any other fly, and have seen the natural insect on every stream I have fished in that land of brooks. Surely this is more than a mere coincidence.

All this is so obvious, that my readers may ask how anyone could ever propose to question it? Yet in defence of the Scottish 'nondescriptarians' it should be said that they can tell of experiences much at variance with those on which I have built my inference. I have fished in some forty Scotch lochs or tarns, rarely without fair success, sometimes with brilliant results; yet where the *Salmo fario* alone is in question; I have but half a dozen flies on my list for active service. Of these half-dozen two only, and those by no means the best, resemble any natural fly with which I am acquainted. I do not pretend to explain this fact, nor what mysterious harmony between a particular wing feather and a body of a particular colour renders their combination irresistible to the trout in so many lochs of the most dissimilar character. Still less can I tell why in one loch there is a standing furore for smooth silken bodies, in another for rough mohair and swine's down of the identical colours. Yet I have seen this deliberate preference for one or the other material proved beyond a doubt again and again

These and the like problems continually recur, and contribute to make fly fishing the intellectual amusement that many wise and observing men have found it. At the same time they warn us to beware of sweeping generalisations, and to gather our facts from a great variety of sources, ere we generalise at all. It is certainly curious that a dear relative, whom I 'coached' in the rudiments of fly fishing ere he became himself an authority on the subject, lays his qualified rejection of the 'imitative' theory at my door. I recommended to him my three favourite lake flies for use on a Scotch tour, and he found them so effective that he had them reproduced in various miniature forms for general use, and has certainly killed fish with them in waters where, from my own experience, I should have trusted to a very different cast. This, I admit, is curious; but it does not really affect the argument. To give it any logical weight we must beg the question of less or more; must assume that the system which was not tried would not have proved comparatively successful.

With this remark – which furnishes an answer to many fly fishers whose practice is better than their theory – I may dismiss this first of piscatorial cruces.

Having been for many years the willing victim of numerous applications for pattern flies on the part of friends, acquaintances, and even strangers bound for this or. that fishing district, and having in a great majority of cases received the thanks of those who consulted me for the success of my prescriptions, I may be forgiven if I claim to speak with such authority as is due to long experience on the subject of Trout Flies for lake and river. For lake trout I have found, as already stated, that a very few flies will answer every purpose, and I doubt very much whether three better patterns can be found than those recommended in the first edition of 'The Moor and the Loch.' With two of these I had been familiar before I read Mr. Colquhoun's work, my knowledge of the third – which has helped me to many a heavy basket – I owe entirely to his pages.

The flies required for our British rivers and brooks are far more various, and depend for their success on minuter details of colour and material. Nor can any amount of general experience make the fly fisher perfectly at home on a new river, though it will prevent his feeling quite strange. I have killed trout in 130 streams (to say nothing of 50 lakes); but still, on water which I visited for the first time, I should be glad to take a hint as to the style of fly to be used for the nonce from any intelligent 'local practitioner.'

The man of one stream, like the *homo unius libri* is a formidable person within a limited range. On the same principle constant readers of sporting papers may benefit greatly by the recorded experiences of brother anglers on particular rivers. And I would recommend fly fishers, who have sufficient leisure, to 'book' accurately not only their captures but a brief record of the flies which on each occasion served them best, in order to prevent the results of their own experience from eluding their remembrance. Such a record is not the formidable affair it might appear at first sight. Three minutes at the close of the day will answer every purpose. I have been a working man all my life, and have, I believe, at least an average memory; yet I do not regret the time which, after every angler's holiday enjoyed during something like half a century, I have given to brief entries such as the following:

> July 5. – Upper Ledditch. Warm day – light S.W. breeze. Red sand fly; orl fly (hackle) and dark coachman. Weight 10J lbs. Best fish 15 oz.

By keeping such records one guards against false impressions as to the season and the weather when a particular fly did execution on a given stream; impressions which will often lead us wrong in our choice.I shall not attempt any scientific classification of flies. But though I do not pretend to the character of an entomologist, it may be useful to beginners to remark that there are two great families of flies to which the fly fisher's imitations chiefly belong: (1) *Ephemerae*, (2) *Phryganeae*.

The *Ephemerae* include a great variety of species, from the May fly to the tiny Jenny Spinner. They have a long life in the water as larvae in the form of little green dragons, crawling about the roots of sedges and water weeds; and a very short one as perfect insects, having their 'little day of sunny bliss,' during which the sexes mingle and the females drop their ova on the stream.

Under certain conditions of the weather they 'hatch out' from the larva state in prodigious numbers, leaving their empty skins, like insect ghosts, on rushes, flags, or waterside grass. I was once witness at Bray Weir early in July to a singular phenomenon in the shape of a countless swarm of 'Yellow Sallies.' They gathered over the Thames shortly before dusk, and formed a dense yellow cloud extending some 150 yards in length, 30 in breadth, and 3 in depth; only a slight undulating movement in the mass, and the restless flashing up of scale fish from below to secure the stragglers who dropped out of the ranks, showing that what I saw was a prodigy of insect life and not an atmospheric phenomenon.

The artificial flies which represent the Ephemera are very various in size and colour; but they are all alike in attempting to represent by the most delicate feathers – for the most part mottled – the gauzy wings of the natural insect. They are also alike in having three 'wisps' behind – single strands of hair or feather – to imitate the delicate filaments at the tail of the natural fly, which seem designed to steady and regulate the up- and-down movements of the insect, especially in the act of dropping its eggs.

The feathers most used in dressing flies of this family are those of the wild drake (dark brown, pale grey, or dyed yellow); of the starling, landrail, snipe, and dotterel.

The *Phryganeae* are a less numerous family, nor, as far as my own observation goes, do they ever appear on the water in such amazing swarms. They often, however, muster pretty strong, and certain species are continually 'hatching out' during a great part of the year from the bundles of vegetable matter whence their name of 'faggot insects' is derived. The maggot-like larvae form for themselves cases for shelter or security in which they dwell for many months before they quit the water and take the air as flies. They carry their wings when crawling – which they do much more freely than the *Ephemerae* – not raised in pairs above the thorax, but folded pent-house fashion above the abdomen. The larvae are commonly known as 'caddis' or case worms, and the abodes they construct for themselves, partly by the use of their strong nippers and partly by the aid of some natural glue furnished by their own bodies, exhibit a curious and interesting variety. These 'cases' ascend by a graduated scale from the simplest to the most complicated forms.

First we have an inch of slender rush; then a more solid tenement formed from a piece of stick, in which the grub takes the place of the pith; then two leaves gummed together at the edges. Anon we find a fasciculus of tiny twigs, or a small clustered pillar of rush-rods, cut accurately to one length and curiously joined together. The most beautiful of all are cylindrical grottos, sometimes nearly two inches in length, formed of small fresh-water shells. A studious entomologist who was also a fly fisher might do worse than to make a collection of these ingenious dwellings and figure the 'imago' hatched from each. It would, I presume, be found that each class of dwelling belongs to a different species. I have found many kinds together in one spring ditch or sedgy backwater, so that there must have been a choice of material, though I cannot affirm that when I have dislodged the inmates for bait I have noticed any marked differences but those of size and colour.

It would be a curious experiment to transport a large number, say of the rush worms, to a stream where they would find no rushes, and then to observe whether, after the flies had hatched and bred, their progeny would disappear or would protect themselves by adopting some new building material.

But I am digressing. Let me return to my fly book, and say that the artificial flies representing the *Phryganeae* have mostly mottled brown or dusky wings, with dark legs and brown or yellowish bodies.

A third class of artificial flies – taking the term in its popular acceptation, without regarding the palpable misnomer – includes the palmers or rough caterpillars and the beetles. These may be usefully classed together, as they are formed of similar materials (the cock's hackle being generally dominant in both), and used in much the same states of the water. To these three distinct classes I would add for convenience a fourth or 'miscellaneous' class, comprising a great variety of insects not distinctively aquatic but occasionally attractive to trout and grayling.

I begin my list with the flies which I have found most useful all through the year on a great variety of waters; purposely limiting the number, in order that anglers who trust the results of my experience may, in the stocking of their fly books, avoid that *embarras de richesses* which will lead them to perplexity at the outset and useless changes in the course of a day's fishing. It should always be remembered that the fly is often blamed for the mood of the fish, and altered perhaps just when they are beginning to feed.

The Yellow Dun: This fly is good throughout the trout season, and is taken freely by grayling in August and September.

The Hare's Lug: This is the form of the blue dun with which I have done most execution through the year. In Wales, Scotland and the northern counties of England I prefer it to No. 1.

The Marlow Buzz, or Cockabundy (a corruption of 'Coch-y-bonddu'): This not only makes the best of droppers in rough mountain and moorland streams, where it is indispensable, but if tied very small and dark may be depended on in the clearest streams – those of Hampshire, for instance, or Derbyshire – especially when there are but few Ephemera on the water.

The Red Sand Fly: I have found this fly very killing from April to September in various rivers; more so, however, in the midland and northern than in the southern counties. There is a small ephemera closely resembling it in colour, for which no doubt it is often taken. It kills best when tied with a body yellower than the landrail wings.

The Black Gnat: This is generally considered a summer and autumn fly, and it is certainly most deadly just when the May fly has gone off. But if it be dressed, as I would have it, either with a dark wing or simply with black hackle and ostrich herl, it will take well in spring – passing doubtless for Walton's 'black hawthorn fly.'

The Partridge Hackle: This fly is rarely noticed by writers, but I have found it most useful throughout the season; especially as a drop fly. I tie it with a soft-stemmed, dark-mottled feather and an orange silk body; but I can hardly call it an imitation. It most resembles a large grey-winged gnat, like a miniature daddy-long-legs, which is often to be seen on waterside herbage; but it is certain that good trout take it freely in all weathers, whatever they take it for!

The Olive Dun: I have used this fly less than its excellence deserves; but I know that it is A 1 in the chalk streams in any but very cold weather, and believe that there are few English waters in which it will not take.

The Alder Fly: This fly kills well after the leaf is out especially where the alder grows freely. The body is always of peacock's herl – the legs should be of a dark dun hackle. When it is tied on a large hook it wants a dark mottled wing, for which I prefer a brown drake or night-jar feather.

The 'Dark' Coachman: As far as I know (but my study of books on Angling ceased some twenty-eight years ago) this is a hardly recognised fly; but it is very useful, especially in western counties, and where trout and grayling are found together. It is simply the ordinary coachman – much used on summer evenings – with a starling's feather substituted for the white wing commonly in use. It is deadly in brooks throughout the year.

Add to these flies a Red and a Black Palmer (the former ribbed with gold, the latter with silver twist), for use when the water is beginning to clear after a spate, and you will be 'armed and well prepared' under ordinary conditions in an immense majority of British streams. I speak with some confidence on this head, as for many years I noted the flies with which I killed on each angling holiday, and still continue to record any new experience. The eleven flies named above – adding the Red Spinner (whereof hereafter) to make up the dozen – have certainly been answerable for fully three-fourths of my captures in brook and river.

Let me now say a word of the flies which, unlike those numbered above, have but a short reign, though for a time they can hardly be dispensed with. Of the March Brown and the Green Drake, which at once suggest themselves under this head, so much has been written, and in such detail, that I might fairly say, in the words of the briefest epitaph I ever read, 'Silence is wisdom.' I do not profess to be an authority in either case as to the much-discussed niceties of feather or colour, and will merely remark that in my own experience I have found both insects work better as hackles than as wing flies, and prefer them tied a shade under the natural size.

The little 'Iron Blue' is a very killing fly on cool April mornings, and will take occasionally on cold days up to Midsummer.

The 'Jenny Spinner,' a still smaller and more delicate insect, appears at odd times on warm evenings, and will then kill in the lowest and clearest waters.

The Fern Fly I have found very taking, even at noon on sultry days in July and August; but rather in still pools than in streams, and only in the neighbourhood of bracken.

The Red Ant Fly comes in very late – generally in September, when emmet flights are commonest – and is therefore rather a grayling than a trout fly. This fly, as also the Fern Fly, is figured in the list of grayling flies. In spite of its peculiar form, I have found the 'Dark Coachman,' tied small, an effective substitute for it. But of all flies which are not 'permanent,' like Miss Nipper, but 'temporary,' commend me to the Red Spinner. In warm evenings, far into the dusk, I have found it the deadliest of lures from June to September. Its whirling flight and its colour make it conspicuous; but it figures in my evening cast whether I have seen it on the wing or not. Oddly enough, I killed my best fish with it in Tasmania. The fault of the ordinary imitations is that the bodies are of too crimson a tint. If you qualify the pure red, let it be with a little golden brown.

I might add to this list, but, after all, the real question for the practical angler is not so much how many flies he can utilise as how many he can safely dispense with. I have now only to notice a few important flies which have a purely local value, killing in one district, but being of little use beyond it. Lists of this kind are dry reading at the best, so to avoid tediousness I will name only three. The Blue Upright – mentioned already – is absolutely indispensable in Devonshire. It varies much in the tying as to size, build, and shade of colour; its one constant characteristic being the hard smooth body. For general use I prefer it without wings, tied with a black hackle, not too stiff, and a slate-coloured body.

The Silver Horns I have found very deadly in Salop and Herefordshire from the beginning of June. The natural insect is a small moth, glossy black; with very long black-and-white horns, easily imitated with a strand of a teal feather. It is very conspicuous on rank waterside herbage, and I rarely fail to use the imitation along sedgy reaches. Finally, there is the Derbyshire 'Bumble.' Of this queer fly I know nothing, save that I have killed with it, and have seen it successful in the hands of local anglers about Bakewell, Rowsley, etc. I have seen it tied with all manner of colours, but always with a fat body of smooth floss silk, ribbed with some bright short-stranded hackle. Its special oddity lies in its plumpness.

Seen in contrast with the ordinary Derbyshire flies – slender and almost midge-like things – it looks like Major Monsoon among a squad of light horse. What is it taken for? Not the veritable bumble, surely, which a trout rarely meddles with, and if in a whimsical mood he sucks it in, eschews without chewing. The 'great representative principle' seems quite at fault. Can it be meant for one of the local *Coleoptera*? Beetle – beadle – Bumble! A plausible derivation.

Having now given some general hints as to the best mode of fishing a stream, with some practical suggestions as to the choice of flies, I And that there is a good deal yet to be done ere the particular fish whom I have in my mind's eye takes up his proper quarters in the basket. My fly or flies are such as ought to kill – whether they will do so, or be wasted as good meat is by a bad cook, depends on the handling of my rod. I have yet to throw over the fish, to hook him, and to play him w hen hooked. I would say a word on each of these processes, and do not despair of advancing under each head something at once new and true. This would be scarcely possible had writers qualified their general rules by drawing the requisite distinctions.

We are told, for instance, to throw a perfectly straight line, that we may reach the farther and strike with the greater certainty, and I admit the general principle. But on a bright day and in a much-fished stream, such casting will not serve your turn, unless you aim at reaching an individual fish. Rather shake out your flies loosely, with a quivering motion of the rod, and let your links of gut drop lightly, in irregular undulations. The greenest trout, under such circumstances, takes alarm at a 'straight line' drawn across the surface of the water. Bear the same consideration in mind when working your flies down and across the stream.

Again, in throwing for a fish whose exact position you know, all the books tell you to cast two or three feet above him, and let the stream carry the fly down to the expectant trout – a good rule doubtless, for the general guidance of a tyro, but for the more advanced piscator, in sultry weather and bright shy waters, in place of 'feet' he may safely read 'inches.' It will not do then to let an old trout scan and study the insect approaching him. Drop the fly 'reet ower his neb,' as a young familiar of mine at Driffield used to phrase it, and ten to one, having no space for reflection, he will 'take the death' on the impulse of the moment.

Connected with the first dropping of the fly is the working of it on and in the wrater. Drawing it straight along, especially up stream, though common, is a ruinous error. In salmon fishing this is well known: the line is slackened at short intervals between the sweeping movements of the fly across and against the stream; and the lure is made lifelike and attractive by the alternate contraction and expansion of the fibres forming its wings and legs. Let your trout flies be played upon a similar principle, but more variously, and more down stream. Let the tail fly seem struggling in vain to resist the current which carries him down, and the near dropper dip enticingly as if in laying eggs. A tremulous motion of the wrist is sometimes most alluring. In the stillest waters, on a warm day, I have killed good fish by throwing far, and then suffering my whole cast to sink ere I moved my flies. Trout will take them thus sunk if they do not see the ripple of the line at the surface.

We will now suppose your fish to have risen – the next point is to hook him, if indeed your line is not so taut that you feel he has hooked himself. To do this you must 'strike,' as the common term is; which has been correctly, if not satisfactorily, explained as 'doing something with your wrist which it is not easy to describe.' Is this 'something' to be done quickly or slowly, sharply or gently? Not to distinguish too minutely, we would say, strike a salmon more slowly than a trout, a trout than a grayling, a lake fish than a river one, and, generally speaking, a large fish than a small one. As to the degree of force, a gentle twitch generally suffices – at all events; more is dangerous with any but very strong tackle.

Note especially, that in order to strike quick, you must strike gently. This requires illustration. Lay your fly rod on a long table, place a cork eighteen inches in front of the top; grasp it as in fly fishing, and strike hard, making the butt the pivot. The cork will be knocked off by the *forward* spring of the upper half of the rod before any backward action can take place, and thus much time will have been lost before the line can be in the smallest degree tightened. Remember, too, the great increase of risk to your tackle when the line is thus slackened before sustaining a severe jerk. Nine fish out of ten that are said to break the casting line are in fact lost by the eager violence of the striker, acting upon dry or ill-tied knots. I could say more on this subject did space permit. Thus much, however, as a parting precept Never be in a hurry, especially when you see a good fish rise. Take your time, as he will take his, and the result will not disappoint you.

Our fish is now hooked, and the next question is how to deal with him. Some of our angling friends call this 'working a fish,' some 'playing' – the former term, perhaps, having an objective, the other a subjective reference. Nevertheless, Halieus must sometimes work very hard, or Salmo will have the play all to himself. Two general principles may be laid down: first, the strain kept up on the fish should be the greatest attainable without overtaxing the strength of the tackle – which should be a known quantity – or the hold of the hook, which the most experienced angler cannot always calculate accurately; secondly, the direction of the butt should never make an obtuse angle with the line – in most cases a decidedly acute one.

As for 'showing a fish the butt,' it is very desirable in general. But if you do so when fishing with a single-handed trout rod in a deep stream with hollow banks, you only aid that inward rush of your fish which is but too likely to wreck your tackle. Never bring your fish to the surface till he is quite spent; he may break the hold, if not heavy enough to break your tackle. Don't go trouting without a landing net, whatever certain writers of the rough-and-ready school may say. And if you have an attendant, don't let him land your fish till you know that you can fully trust him.

Thus far I have dwelt wholly on what may be called the destructive side of the fly fishing question, and have tried to show how the accomplished professor of 'Fine and far off' may surmount obstacles and profit by opportunities in the filling of his creel. But as the number and the skill of our fly fishers are continually increasing, the question still remains how the breed of British *Salmonidae* can be kept up to meet the growing demand. Every true brother of the angle who pursues his pastime in a liberal and unselfish spirit ought, therefore, to direct his attention to the breeding and feeding of these fish, valuable as they are at once for sport and for the table. And it is important at the outset to draw attention to some conditions of this twofold problem which seem to be but imperfectly understood.

In the first place, the fact must be recognised that it is easier to keep up the number than the size of the trout in our best streams. Modern agriculture with its demand for thorough drainage tends to diminish the ordinary volume of water in our brooks and rivers. Fifty years ago, when there came a heavy spell of wet weather a great extent of spongy moor and meadow land along the watercourses imbibed and held up a large proportion of the rainfall. The spate came less suddenly and lasted longer, and in ordinary weather the banks continually gave out water to keep up the stream. Now it is either 'a feast or a fast.' The well-laid drains flush the rain water rapidly into the streams; the floods come down sooner and last for a shorter time, and the ordinary level of four-fifths of our trout rivers is very much below what it used to be when agriculture, though more thriving, was less scientific.

This diminution in the volume of water means, of course, a reduced supply of insect food for our trout. Nor is this all. Farmers and millers combine in many districts to keep the weeds close cut, and every weed-cutting destroys by wholesale the larvae of those insects on which the trout depends most for his ordinary food. As I walk along some well-known beck and see huge heaps of water weed drying in the sun, I feel sorely tempted to use a naughty word when I think of the millions of possible Ephemerae which have 'closed their little being without life,' hopelessly entangled in the ruins of their green abodes.

I know more than one trout stream where the Mayfly has disappeared within the last ten years, and have heard of sundry others. Of course this implies a diminution of the average weight of the fish in such streams, supposing their number the same. A fortnight's steady feeding on the grey and green drake used formerly to produce a marked improvement in the weight of the trout as well as in the colour of their flesh, so that those taken in the latter half of June with the black gnat or red-spinner were altogether a 'superior article.' Now, the larger fish are not at their best till the end of July or beginning of August, and the number of those which never get into condition during the fishing season, but remain, like the Ancient Mariner, 'Jong, and lank, and brown,' is steadily increasing, except in a few favoured reaches where there is a good depth of water with a strong sedgy border. I may remark by the way that the *Phryganeae* appear to suffer less from excessive weedcutting than the *Ephemerae*; doubtless because their larvae crawl about more in open spaces, and, from the protection afforded by their 'cases,' are better able to extricate themselves when hauled ashore in a mass of weed. The orl flies and caperers, for instance, keep their ground better than the more delicate flies of the Caddis family.

Reverting now to what I have called the twofold problem of breeding and feeding an increased stock of trout to meet the increased demand, I may state without hesitation that the difficulty in breeding fish in sufficient numbers will be far more easily overcome than that of feeding them up to a respectable size and condition. No doubt the shrinking of our brooks already alluded to has damaged many of the best spawning grounds, and exposed others in an increasing degree to the depredations of that worst class of poachers who destroy the fish on the redds. But, on the other hand, artificial breeding has for some years past been better understood and more extensively practised in the United Kingdom; and though we are still far behind the United States – and probably behind Canada – in this department of pisciculture, yet I think the Fisheries Exhibition certainly gave a stimulus to trout breeding which will not only keep up the tale of fish in well-stocked waters, but restore a fair head of trout in streams whence they have almost disappeared.

An interesting article published in the 'Standard,' on the breeding establishment at Howietown, shows that by the judicious outlay of a very small capital, millions of small fry may be yearly brought into the market at moderate prices and yet with a handsome profit to the breeder. We may, I think, assume that for the future there will be little difficulty in obtaining any reasonable quantity of stock trout from this and similar establishments. The chief question for the purchaser will be what size of stock will pay him best.

For a preserver who has, in connection with his own trout stream, the requisite appliances for 'hatching out' eyed ova, or feeding baby fish just freed from the umbilical sack, trout, in one of these two stages, will probably be the best investment. But for turning directly into the river the stock should be yearlings not less than five inches in length. They are easily moved if two conditions be borne in mind. First, the vessel in which they are carried should be smooth within, to prevent bruising, which is apt to set up fungoid disease; and, secondly, the water should be kept in motion, aërated, in fact, to suit the breathing of the fish. This, indeed, is the one indispensable condition for keeping the trout, in north-country phrase, 'wick and heerty' on their journey. The late angling editor of the *Field* told me, as the result of his own experience in transporting fish, that he knew no better vessel for the purpose than the ordinary glass carboy used for chemicals. Its merit, I presume, lies in the perfect smoothness of the interior. Such a vessel, however, is fitted only for a small live cargo. As the removal of trout in large numbers becomes a more familiar process, we shall doubtless see in general use travelling tanks much like a modern watering cart, but provided with mechanical means for keeping the water in motion.

My attention was first drawn to this subject many years ago, long before I had discarded the spinning minnow for the fly. I used to carry about a score of live minnows in a common soda-water bottle – just the glass carboy on a small scale – which I planted neck upward in my creel, with a notch in the side of the cork to permit free change of air. They never ailed anything as long as I kept moving; but if I sat down for a meditative weed – and where can this be better enjoyed than in a shady nook by the waterside, '*Propter aquae rivum sub ramis arboris altae*' ? – every minnow – out of pure cussedness as it seemed – would sicken in five minutes, and if I failed to notice the first symptoms would be 'an unpleasant demp body' in a quarter of an hour. Like minnow, like trout.

Some twenty years later, when I had been long familiar with the causes which made repose so fatal to my bait fish, I was actively engaged in a society for preserving the Thames about Marlow. Systematic poaching had made such havoc with those fine streams that a Thames trout had become a rare and almost legendary fish; and when we had put down our poachers and properly staked the 'ballast holes,' where they murdered our fish with the casting net, we found it necessary to restock the river. I obtained a goodly lot of trout from a Buckinghamshire stream some twenty-five miles distant, and had them brought to Marlow by no better conveyance than open tubs in a common cart, with floating boards to check splashing. The road was luckily a rough one, and the driver had strict orders – to say nothing of an extra fee – to keep continually at a jog trot, that the water might not stagnate. The fish all arrived at the Anglers' Inn, Marlow (long may it flourish!) in perfect health, though sundry of them were large fish, weighing from two to three pounds.

Our committee were then sitting, and after a glance at the tubs I went back to join them, taking it for granted that the trout would be at once turned in below the weir, according to instructions previously given. But after some ten minutes it struck me as odd that I had not seen any of the tubs carried past the window. Jumping up and calling to the rest to follow me I ran to the cart – not a minute too soon. Half the fish – and all the large ones – had already sickened and were gasping side up. We hurried them in hot haste down to the water, and the fresh stream just saved their lives, one fish only proving past recovery. Five minutes more of still water, and the whole cargo would have been lost; as it was, the introduction of those trout restored the breed which had become almost extinct in that fine reach of the river.

They were turned in, if I remember, about the end of August, after a season during which I could only hear of three trout killed by fair angling from Marlow Weir to Spade Oak. In the fourth season after, I took some forty myself, though hardly visiting the river twice a week.

I have told this story at some length to illustrate the necessity of keeping the water aërated by motion when stock trout are being transported; but it may point another moral, *viz.* that it is desirable to use sizeable fish for restocking exhausted streams.

Let me add here, that I am by no means fanciful about stocking water, whether pool or stream, with what is called a 'fine breed' of trout. Such a breed results from centuries, perhaps, of superior feeding, and trout of such a race, if removed to waters where the dietary is less generous, will be apt to 'dwindle, peak and pine,' or at best will lose their distinctive superiority. On the other hand, fish taken from a hungry water and turned into one where the bill of fare is more liberal cannot fail to thrive. I have seen many notable instances where tiny brook fish, which at home would never have exceeded four or five ounces in weight, have been removed into a large sheet of deep water, and have there become large and good – worthy of an angler's respect and affection. I will mention two examples. On a high moorland beside Lartington Hall, on the borders of county Durham, runs a small burn – the same which, after gathering its dark peat-stained waters, plunges down romantic Deepdale to join the Tees above Barnard Castle; 'scenes sung by him who sings no more.'

On this moorland a large pool was formed, of perhaps thirty-five acres, its formation aided by the course of the burn. The moss-hags which had quaked along the winding banks of the streamlet were scooped away till the gravel below was reached, and the peaty soil was used to form a raised barrier round the extensive hollow, so as to deepen the waters still farther. About five years after this artificial lake had been formed and stocked from the bit burnie that fed it, I had the permission of the owner, George Witham, Esq. – a name then well known in the scientific world, but my tale is some forty years old –   to try the fly one summer's evening on its waters. I was very fortunate, either in my day or my choice of flies, or both; for though I had been told that the fish could rarely be coaxed to rise, I killed in a short evening's fishing, with my Scotch lake flies, eleven trout, of which the smallest weighed above a pound, the largest two and three-quarters.

I made a yet heavier basket in a rough afternoon the following year. Finer fish I have rarely seen, small-headed, hog-backed, and strong on the line. They took the fly in the grandest style; showing snout, back fin and tail, and coming down on their prey with such certainty that I missed but one fish in each day. The water, as well as parts of the bottom, being darkish, and the depth considerable, their outside hue was clouded gold rather than silver, but they cut as red as trout of the Thames.

I know a similar instance in a deep reservoir on the Brown Clee Hill, fed by a petty brooklet. The fish in the pool are Patagonians, and not more large than good – those of the brook of the small dimensions suited to their residence. Thus there is but one step between the two questions of breeding and feeding. A well-fed trout will, generally speaking, be a good trout, and a large range of water will supply its inhabitants with at least a respectable dietary. In this way mills do the angler good service; the fish in the mill dam have, so to say, a larger pasture, and mostly weigh heavier than those in the shallow reaches of the Thames.

The first and most obvious method, then, for counteracting the causes to which I have pointed as tending to reduce the volume of our streams and the amount of trout food which they supply, lies in deepening and widening portions of those streams. This can be easily done in many of our brooks, by raising barriers to hold up the water, and by enlarging and deepening portions of their courses at the small sacrifice of a few square yards of poor soil adjoining a natural hollow in their beds. The fish in the artificial pools thus formed will be better fed and consequently larger than those in the ordinary shallow course of the brook or 'pelting river' – to borrow Shakespeare's phrase – which favours the multiplication of trout but fails to supply them with abundant food.

Of course we must remember that trout water, whether pool or river, may easily be overstocked. In the course of a ramble through an unfrequented part of Lochaber, I once came upon a tiny tarn, fed by a burn which, though of the smallest size, afforded excellent gravelly bottom for 'redds.' I made a few experimental throws over it, and each time landed a fish on every fly. I added two small hackles to my ordinary cast of three, and had five troutlings hooked in as many seconds. I made a dozen more casts, and each time took five fish. They were so greedy that they would have the hook, so small that I had no difficulty in sending the whole quintett flying.

Had I had any object in further slaughter – a feud with the cook at Inverlair, or an extensive contract for potted trout – I could easily, with the aid of my gillie to unhook the fish, have taken a thousand brace of these hungry fry in a day. Mine were perhaps the first artificial flies they had ever seen, for the tarn in question lies quite off the beaten track, though near Lochs Treig and Ouchan, which would have naturally attracted any wandering angler in those regions. But such a case of overstocking I never witnessed.

Within a mile or two, and on the same stretch of moorland, but at a lower level and where the depth of peat was far greater, lay another tarn of four or five acres in extent, which had no 'feeder' or possible breeding ground, and must have been casually stocked by some violent overflow of a neighbouring burn. I had heard of large trout in this, and tried it from mere curiosity, having never seen anything more dreary and unpromising, less like a Christian tarn than a reach of the Styx. I basketed five or six only; not that the fish were shy, but simply, as I fully believe, because they were few. They were all nearly of a size, above a pound and under a pound and a half; their outside colour pretty much that of a red Indian, and not unhandsome. But when sent up to table they proved simply uneatable, having the 'peat reek' so strong that I tasted one merely from a sense of duty, and dealt with the mouthful as Dr Johnson did with the hot pudding – 'A fool might have swallowed it.' Nothing better in flavour could have been expected from a mere turf hole, but the weight of these fish may illustrate what I have said of 'range of water' as conducive to size.

There are many large pieces of water, either altogether unused or given up to baser fish, which would carry a good head of trout It is always assumed that these require running water, or at least a pool fed by a stream or spring. But if turned out young they will grow surprisingly in water absolutely stagnant but for a passing breeze or shower. I know a small pond in the East Riding with no feeder or outlet, much resembling the chalk ponds on the Hampshire Downs. It is irregular in shape, but in area about equal to a circle of thirty yards' radius; shallow at the margin, but deepening to a small island in the centre; the ground shelving towards it for some distance, so that a heavy rain soon tells on its level. Its ordinary inhabitants are numerous tench and gold-fish, with a few minnows of extraordinary size. Into this pond the owner, who is not only a skilful fly fisher but much interested in pisciculture, turned a few small trout from the Driffield Beck as an experiment. Two or three years after I often saw a good fish rising near the little island, and about four years after the stock were turned in one of them was taken weighing 4 lbs. 7 oz. I did not see the fish, but was assured that he was in good condition.

He was turned loose again after a hasty weighing, but he had seen his best days, and in the following season was finally drawn out a mere living skeleton. Under the circumstances we can hardly 'wonder a great trout should decline.' The wonder lay in the dimensions he actually attained.

In another case I stocked with tiny trout, caught with the hand from the very smallest of Kentish brooks, a little pool of about twelve yards by five, formed merely for picturesque effect in the beautiful grounds of 'The Hollands,' near Tunbridge Wells. Here there was a sort of feeder, but so small that an ordinary pitcher might during nine months of the year have received all that flowed in the course of a minute from the 'little Naiad's impoverished urn.' In the third year afterwards I tried the pond thus fed with extemporised tackle – a hazel stick, a line of Irish thread, and a glass minnow which happened to be travelling in my portmanteau. In less than half an hour I took two trout weighing lb. each; both well fed, handsome fish, firm and pink-fleshed.

I mention these facts because I would fain see trout more generally introduced into ornamental waters. For instance, I feel assured that the sheet of water in Battersea Park, if judiciously stocked with small fish from a small stream, would carry a good head of trout, whose movements would divert many a toiling artisan, unused to any nobler fish than a half-grown rudd. There are many of our canals in which trout might thrive. Within a few fields of the Driffield Beck a notable example may be seen in a canal connecting the town of Driffield with the Humber. Oddly enough, the natives always call it 'the River.'

Some forty-five years ago, in very bad fishing weather, I wanted to carry home to Hull an extra lot of fish, and thought I would try the river head at an hour when, according to my experience, brook trout are hardly awake. I took a fair stock of minnows with me, and made my first cast in the morning twilight, soon after four o'clock. Between that hour and seven I got three and a half brace of trout, averaging more than a pound and a half, and decidedly better fed fish than those usually caught in the Club water even at that date, when minnows and May flies still abounded. A finer dish I have rarely seen; but I was grievously vexed at not being able to beguile one 'most delicate monster,' weighing, I am sure, full nine pounds, who more than once followed my minnow but was too wary to take it. Two years ago I saw a seven-pound fish from the same water, in perfect condition, and I suppose a score or so of heavy fish are caught there yearly; but there has been a great falling off in numbers. The size and flavour of these fish I attribute to the abundance of food.

All along the course of the canal, and especially about the locks below which the trout are mostly found, the small scale fish seem to crowd the water, and one might fancy a trout revelling without effort in one perpetual feast.

If the Driffield folks had only enterprise enough to turn in, say, three hundred brace of stock fish every year, there would be more first-rate trout – first-rate both as to size and condition – caught in that short stretch of inland navigation than in an equal length of any English river with which I am acquainted.

There are doubtless other canals in which similar, though not equal, results might be attained. I remember formerly hearing of some good baskets made in one near Chirk. Of course, where there is a strong head of pike trout will stand but a poor chance; otherwise, a canal carried through a good trouting country ought itself to be 'troutable.' It is, I repeat, a mere question of food, which will generally abound in large bodies of fairly clear water.

No doubt the angler in a canal, or in one of those waste reaches of water which border so many of our railroads, must forego the poetry of his craft. Not for him are the '*liquidi fontes et mollia prata*' – the gushing streams and flower-enamelled meadows which contribute so largely to the enjoyment of a fly fisher's ramble by brook or river. Yet to an artisan escaped from the weary town on a long summer's evening or a rare holiday, his sport will bring its own enjoyment and even its surroundings, if not distinctly picturesque, will have a certain rural charm. The level line of water along which he plies his craft has at least its green fringe and its border of fields to rest and refresh his eye; and if along with a few fish for the 'missis' he can carry home a bunch of marsh marigolds or forget-me-nots, a yellow iris, or a spike of purple loose-strife for the 'kids', he will be well pleased with his humble trophies.

Philanthropy in our England takes a thousand forms; an association for stocking the open waters nearest to our towns with the best fish they are capable of feeding would be a beneficent and popular novelty. And I feel sure that if ever the experiment be tried on a large scale, no little surprise will be felt even by experienced anglers at the ease with which trout will adapt themselves to waters apparently unpromising.

I have pointed out, under the general head of 'Flies,' the chief ingredients of that insect diet on which trout so largely subsist. But as that diet is, for reasons already mentioned, becoming scantier in many of our best streams, we should do well to study the means of supplementing it with other kinds of food. It is, I am afraid, useless to attempt restoring the larger Ephemera in waters whence they have died out, drainage and weed cutting remaining the same. The flies are too delicate to be fit for breeding after a long journey, and it would be difficult to obtain the larvae in sufficient quantities to give the experiment a fair chance of success. As regards the *Phryganeae*, there are some neighbourhoods where a few sharp lads might gather 'caddis' almost by the bushel for turning out in the adjacent trout stream. But this could only be worthwhile in a land of spring ditches and shallow drains, and even then it is by no means sure that the stock of flies could be permanently increased. In streams where the trout run large much might, I think, be done by providing them with cheap fish dinners. A trout over two pounds weight generally becomes 'piscivorous' if he has a chance, and never attains so large a growth as when he is abundantly supplied with minnows or other small fry. It is true that a kind of 'stall feeding' may be pursued with great success.

About the year 1840, a distinguished officer informed me that at a Waterloo Banquet which he had recently attended there were served up two trout nearly of a size, from the preserves of Sir Home Popham, near Hungerford, which together weighed 36 lbs. These fish had been fed on chopped liver, and my informant assured me that no salmon could be better eating. But a few years afterwards I heard of a still heavier specimen, weighing 23 lbs. 7 oz., sent up to London from the same neighbourhood.

This, as far as I know, was the largest specimen of *Salmo fario* on record in the British Isles.

A fish of twenty-one pounds is said to have been caught in the river Exe. I remember the capture – with pike tackle – of one over fifteen pounds in Marlow Pool, and have heard of other fish from the Thames that weighed eighteen pounds. The Driffield Club used to exhibit a stuffed seventeen-pounder, caught in days when there was a periodical migration of countless minnows up the various feeders of the 'Beck,' pursued by flights of the small black-headed tern or 'carr-swallow.' But till I hear of a rival candidate for first honours, I shall still say to that noble trout of Hungerford, '*Tu maximus ille es.*'

The system of feeding which gave him and sundry other stately 'bulks' – like Arac's brethren – to the market was briefly as follows. Two adjacent tanks – for the eaters and the eaten – were supplied by a running stream, and now and then a large hooped landing net with small mesh was dipped into the reservoir of bait, and its contents handed over to the cannibals hard by. Then ensued a grand scene: a dozen speckled giants appeared, rushing, plunging, gulping, walloping, till the last victim had disappeared, when tranquil digestion became the order of the day. Under this system of training, a trout on a large scale, caught lank and lean after breeding, might easily double his weight in the course of the season. It should, however, be remarked that much will turn on the smallness of the fry. Trout are sadly indifferent to family ties, but they will thrive on their infant grandchildren or great-grandchildren, whereas the occasional assimilation of an adult son or daughter will not keep them in condition. The heaviest meal will not fatten when it takes ten days to digest. Hence the great value of a good supply of minnows in a trout stream. Easily caught and greatly relished, they tend to check the practice of infanticide among elderly trout, while they are fattening from being readily digestible.

I have roughly guessed at two pounds as the weight beyond which a trout should not be wholly dependent on insect diet; but they sometimes take to the minnow very early. I remember watching a fish on the upper waters of the Frome extremely busy among some fry just where a small drain joined the stream. I was fly fishing, but, failing to raise him, I caught a tiny stickleback, clipped off the spines, and threw it to him on a double worm hook like a fly minnow. He took it instantly, and on landing him I found that, though weighing little more than three-quarters of a pound, he had actually forty-six small minnows in his maw, the uppermost freshly swallowed, while those farthest down were more than half digested, and perhaps more numerous than I made them out by the tale of backbones. This fish, though he had taken to a minnow diet so young, was very thick and firm-fleshed.

But it is for keeping up the condition of really large fish that an abundant supply of minnows is especially desirable, and I would strongly urge proprietors and angling clubs to lose no opportunity of obtaining additions to the local stock. There are plenty of small streams and spring ditches where minnows abound, with no trout to keep their numbers down, and it will be best to obtain them from a great variety of waters. Care must of course be taken that no fry of 'scale fish' find a place among them.

Next to the minnow in value as food for trout comes that very delicate little fish, the stone-loach, or 'beardie,' the delight of every urchin who has 'paidlit in the burn,' where it is found cuddling cannily under the shady side of a stone. Elderly trout pursue the loach most greedily, and seem to prefer it even to the minnow. I have never known the experiment tried of introducing it into a trout stream, though I have known several in which it was quite at home. But from the great variety of brooks in which it thrives, ranging from Scotland to Devonshire, I think such an experiment would be well worth trying. It would succeed, I feel assured, wherever there are plenty of gravelly shallows, broken by stones from the size of a fist to that of a brickbat.

The 'miller's thumb,' or 'bull-head,' has nearly the same habits as the loach, and is relished by trout in spite of his spiny shoulders.

Again, there are certain small crustaceans, popularly known as 'fresh-water shrimps' (*Cammarinae*, I think, is their learned name), which are found in fine sand in sundry streams known for the firmness and flavour of their trout. But of the habits of these queer little wrigglers I know nothing. I have merely a general impression that they ought to be classed among 'movable feasts' for trout, with a vague hope that some brother angler with equal zeal and more knowledge will succeed in introducing them to new waters for the fattening of underfed fish.

It is well known that small shell fish form a large part of the diet on which fish thrive in many celebrated lakes. Loch Leven may be mentioned as a case in point, though the area of the weed beds from which its trout pick their favourite food has been greatly reduced. The gillaroo seems to owe his special excellence to the same 'hard meat,' and I have little doubt that his distinctive gizzard is merely an organ developed in the course of many generations to aid in the crunching of shell fish. But I have never seen it suggested that the trout of our brooks and rivers have the same taste for these rough morsels. There is, however, one genus – that of *Limnaeus* – several species of which might, I think, do good service in a trout stream. One especially looks as if it would be 'catawampously chawed up' by any trout of good taste. The shell is very frail, with a wide transparent lip; and in warm weather you may see them by hundreds floating over the surface of a weedy pool with this lip upwards, surmounted and overlapped by a tempting expanse of soft, fat body, most inviting to any hungry fish. They are, it is true, chiefly found in still pools, but would thrive in the slow sedgy reaches and quiet backwaters of large streams.

This is not a mere conjecture of my own. A valued friend, the late Mr. Morton Allport, of Hobart Town, to whose judgment and energy Tasmanian pisciculture owed much of its success, imported a number of these shell fish soon after the introduction of English *Salmonidae* into the island, and watched their multiplication with great interest. He found that they would thrive in quiet streams, and showed them to me clustering round a bed of the English water lily. They were, in his opinion, excellent food for both trout and perch.

I have yet one more form of trout diet to mention which may surprise many of my readers. I speak of a certain very small leech, never, I believe, found in rivers, but abundant in sundry lochs. I must confess myself utterly ignorant of the laws which determine the habitat of these delicate crawlers, but I have found trout literally gorged with them who were far above the common standard in colour and flavour; and were I about to establish a normal training school for *Salmonidae*, I would stock my lake or reservoir with a few hundred of these *hirudines*, obtained, e.g. from Llyn Manwd, near Festiniog.

I have gone into these details from a conviction that the trout fishing of the future must turn in great measure on the question of food, and that any and every means should be tried to increase the supply. In dry seasons, the upper waters of our streams require especial looking to, when they are too much shrunk tp attract the fly fisher. It is occasionally necessary to move large numbers of the fish down the stream as its sources fail; but, short of this extreme case, a palliative may be adopted – more wholesome, I admit, than savoury – by a keeper who will condescend to details.

A few of the crows, magpies, stoats, or cats, that have fallen victims to his professional zeal, may be hung on branches overhanging the water holes in which the fish are gathered to keep their enforced Lent, and a goodly shower of gentles will greatly soften the rigour of the fast. In fact, no source of supply should be overlooked.

Few anglers are unacquainted with the annoyance of frequent wasps' nests along the bank of the stream they are fishing. I have myself more than once been driven to ignominious flight from a promising pool, and the thought has come into my mind, 'I hope when that nest is taken its fragments may be thrown into the stream.' If anyone asks, 'Why, what's that good for?' I reply with Shylock, 'To bait fish withal!'

GRAYLING

I have thus far spoken almost exclusively of trout. The grayling, however, deserves more than a mere casual notice, and Cotton's ghost might haunt me if in writing of 'fine and far off' I ignored the fish he loved so well.

And indeed, 'for my own particular,' I greatly admire the grayling, who, I think, is less prized than he deserves. His beauty is the least of his merits – yet how beautiful he is! Taken out of season – in June, for instance, or early July – the dull yellow-brown of his back and sides is not attractive; but when he has recovered his condition, and adds the charm of colour to his always graceful shape – when he shows a rich dark tint down to the mesial line, and silver mail as bright as that of the salmon in level lines below, while his lofty back fin, like some 'storied window, richly dight,' transmits the sunshine through purple, red, and gold, no lovelier prize, save the rarely caught red char, can grace an angler's creel. The curious vegetable fragrance, again, whence he draws his name of *Salmo Thymallus*, contrasts agreeably with the ancient and fish-like smell which clings to other finny captives.

For the table, I should place a well-grown grayling in autumn or winter above the average of river trout, while the 'shetts,' or two-year-olds, are in season all the summer through, and if judiciously fried are nearly equal to a smelt in flavour.

Cotton is in a measure right when he calls him 'the deadest-hearted of fishes,' making 'no great stir' on the hook. He bores steadily down toward the gravel, working mostly up stream, but rarely making a sudden rush or attempting to weed himself. Yet even this dispraise needs some qualification. In small streams I have several times encountered grayling who fought for their lives with all the dash as well as the doggedness of lusty trout, though I have never met with the like in a large river. I might make a fair guess at the cause of this difference, but prefer to record the simple fact.

I have seldom fished for grayling with any lure but the artificial fly. To me, indeed, the crown of all fly fishing is a bright breezy day on the Teme or Lug about the middle of August, when the grayling are coming on and the trout not yet gone off. The sport is varied but almost continuous; there is seldom a reach to be 'skipped' on your river-side beat. From the dashing rapid haunted by trout you ascend to the steadily running ford, from two to four feet deep, in which you know that the grayling lie thick – 'not single spies, but in battalions.' At the top of this again you come on a deep pool, with foam- flecked eddies where the trout reassume their sway, while on the confines of these different reaches you may hook either trout or grayling or both together. A brace of the former with one of the latter, or vice versa, make rather an exciting complication.

This delightful chapter of 'dual' captures ends with the first week of September; but there still remains a good spell of grayling fishing *pur et simple*. They draw together more and more in the quiet fords, and feed more boldly and continuously.

Sunshine sometimes appears to improve the sport, and on 'a glorious day in the golden-bright October,' with the most ordinary care in casting towards the light, you may not only take fish after fish along sixty yards of water, but on reaching the end may retrace your steps and fish it over again with equal success. When grayling are rising freely you may fill your basket in perfectly smooth water by a long cast with the finest gut.

A few words as to the style of casting which should be adopted may not be amiss.In the first place, I care very little for up-stream or downstream fishing when grayling are my object. I cast right across the ford, with just a shade of upward tendency. Whether in working the stream I shall move up or down its course will be matter of convenience depending principally on the sun and wind.

Grayling being chiefly found in the lower and broader reaches of the river, and affecting the mid-channel rather than the sides, cannot be reached by the up-stream cast unless you are wading deep, and not always then. If you wade you had better move up stream yourself to avoid disturbance, but you will still, I think, succeed better by throwing across than ahead. Grayling being, as I have said, gregarious, you will of course greatly improve your chances by fishing with at least two flies, and in a fair-sized river I seldom use less than three. Here the cross throw has an obvious advantage. I have killed doublets a dozen times a day, with now and then three fish at a cast.

'Fine and far off' should be the fly fisher's maxim with grayling even more than with trout. But not the less must he study to throw as little shadow as possible. The grayling lies chiefly in the open, and is easily to be approached under cover, so that everything may depend on your being on the right or wrong side of the water.

It should be borne in mind that the grayling shoots upwards at the fly almost vertically, and, if there is any eddy, often misses it Throw over him again and again no matter how quickly; you will have him at last. I remember killing a good fish at Leintwardine at his eleventh rise. As to the life-like working of the fly I have already said my say, and I will only add that in grayling fishing I repeat my cast more frequently, *caeteris paribus*, than when throwing for trout.

Of flies I have but few on my list, some of which I have named already as favourites with trout. Generally speaking, grayling flies should be small and of a marked character. Wren-tail with an orange body – a grand killer in Derbyshire – the fern fly, ant fly, silver blue and orange tag, with a small but showy red spinner for the evening, are all that I should specially recommend.

Though I care little for grayling fishing except with the fly, I ought fairly to mention that the heaviest fish are caught with other lures. I have heard of very large fish out of season taken with trout flies in summer in the Test and Avon. But, putting aside these worthless captures, grayling of the very largest size are chiefly taken by 'sinking and drawing' with the artificial grasshopper, or with worm or gentle. For myself – and I think I have scored pretty heavily – the largest grayling I ever took with the fly weighed but two pounds and three-quarters, nor do I remember to have ever raised a larger.

They run much in sizes, and in the streams of Shropshire and Herefordshire, where I am most at home, the September fish, representing the well-grown 'shetts' of the previous year, run close upon three-quarters of a pound, while those a year older weigh about a pound more. These latter are really noble fish, and give excellent sport with fine tackle; yet they fall far short of those killed with the gentle, especially when combined with that attractive lure, the 'artificial grasshopper.'

The heaviest basket I ever heard of was made at Leintwardine by the late Sir Charles Cuyler – a sportsman who had, I believe, no superior with the gun and very few with the rod. The exact weight, taken at one bout with the 'pointed' grasshopper, I cannot recall, but the best nine fish weighed twenty- seven pounds.

The grasshopper, as I tie it, has a plumpish body, ribbed with alternate strands of green and golden floss silk, with a narrow strip of fine quill or straw laid lengthwise on each side. The hook is about the size of that used for a small green drake, and along the back of it is lapped a small slip of lead, to facilitate sinking. Care should be taken that the bulk of the grasshopper may be chiefly at the back of the hook, in order not to interfere with the hold, and there should be room for a couple of gentles or a small worm-tail.

As the large fish suck this in after a most gingerly fashion, it is usual to have an inch or so of a small-barreled quill, something like a miniature float, sliding along the line, just far enough from the hook to be always kept in sight during the process of 'sinking and drawing.' When a fish takes, this is seen to make a slight but sudden downward movement, so that the angler's eye gives him warning before his hand can feel the touch.

Were I deliberately pot fishing without regard for the daintiness of my favourite sport, I could easily – especially in a bright low water – increase my take of fish by 'pointing' my fly hook. An ant's egg serves the purpose well, being both cleaner and lighter than a gentle. I remember early on a July morning mentioning this to a friend who was driving me over to Leintwardine. W — had little hope of sport; the river was low, the fish shy; the grayling especially, he told me, were sulking in shoals at the bottom of the deep pools.

'Were it not for your club rules,' said I, 'which you tell me are so very strict, you might pick out a few of those fellows by pointing your fly hook with an ant's egg.' he replied that it was not to be heard of, yet methought was rather curious as to the forbidden process.

We parted shortly after at the water-side, and before we met again in the afternoon I had a grand basket of trout. The river was so low that every stake showed; the fish came strong on the feed, and behind every stake I could see the suck of a goodly snout, so that a long cast up stream with my two-handed rod was absolutely murderous. W— had done very little with the trout, not having fished so 'fine' or so 'far off,' and having been unlucky in his choice of water. But there were two or three really handsome grayling in his basket, against which I had nothing to show. I had killed the only one of decent size which I had seen rise during the day, and even he was no great things. Could it really have been *mea maxima culpa* that I had taken no fish like those before me?

W— answered my questions as to the fly he had used with an admirable steadiness of countenance; but when 'still I gazed, and still my wonder grew,' he could stand it no longer, and burst into that cheery ringing laugh which his many friends round the Clee will recall so well and so regretfully. It was impossible not to join chorus as he just articulated, 'Ants' eggs.'

The gentle, used by itself on a very small hook and thrown like the fly, is very killing, especially after Christmas, when breeding time draws near, and the grayling grow sluggish and dainty. The worm will kill through autumn and winter, and is easier to manage than the grasshopper, as you may give your fish more time. But, after all, give me an open ford, a clear cast, and the artificial fly.

This irregularity of 'location' is very puzzling, especially when we consider how closely some of the streams whence they are absent resemble others in which they abound. The hypothesis which regards the grayling as a foreign fish, imported by the monks at some unknown date, seems quite untenable. It is, however, more to the purpose to inquire whether these valuable fish might not with advantage be introduced into many waters where they are hitherto unknown; and on this question I have no doubts. Let us have grayling in as many counties as the nature'of the streams will permit – at all events, in many more than at present. There are some first-rate trout streams into which, on the principle of 'letting well alone,' I should hesitate to introduce them, for fear of seriously reducing the supply of trout food. It should, however, be remembered that in shallow, rapid reaches of water, and wherever the stream is violent as well as deep, grayling will not rest. Nor do they ever work up stream, having (unlike the trout) a tendency to drop down from the upper stretches of water when these grow shallower till they reach the fords, when they find themselves at home – calm, even-flowing reaches, of moderate depth and speed. Thus the effect of their competition for food is necessarily limited, while the advantage of their neighbourhood to the trout – as, for instance, in the best Derbyshire streams – is found not only in the possession of two game fish for sport or the table instead of one, but in the extending the legitimate angling season through the autumn and winter months.

I have myself had no experience in the artificial breeding of grayling, and cannot pretend to say whether their introduction to new waters would be best achieved by this method or by moving a considerable number of moderate-sized fish. But with our present knowledge and appliances either plan might surely be carried out with little difficulty. If the fish are to be transported alive, the best time for their compulsory migration would probably be the very close of the year, that they may have the advantage of cool weather for travelling, and time to settle down in their new quarters before the breeding season.

There are however plenty of other streams, from the lowlands of Scotland to Kent and Sussex, where the grayling might be introduced with every prospect of success. Among those nearest to London I should name the Stour, and perhaps the Darenth. The Driffield Beck below Wandsford Mill seems exactly fitted to carry grayling side by side with trout, but I do not pretend to enumerate the streams in which the experiment should be tried. I wish rather to set angling clubs and riparian proprietors to work in what seems to me a most promising field. Especially let it be remembered that the grayling is rather a northern than a southern fish, and beyond the British Isles thrives best in high latitudes. I do not see why we should not have our finest specimens from the north of Scotland. At present I know but one stream where 'Thymallus' has been naturalised during the present generation – the Corve, a small tributary which joins the Teme at Ludlow. There may, however, well be others, as in a conversation a few years since with the Editor of the *Field*, he told me of some grayling which he had recently transported by rail with perfect success. These fish, however, were destined for a southern stream.

Here I might fairly lay down my pen; but age has its privileges, and holding with Cicero that the greatest of these is 'authority,' I am tempted to add a few miscellaneous hints on matters interesting to the angler, trusting that with a few, at least, of my readers, to whom I shall not be, like one of my ancestors, a mere *nominis umbra*, they will carry some weight.

And, first, as to tackle. Never buy a cheap rod; it may be admirably finished, but the chances are against its being thoroughly seasoned. It is only the great houses' that can afford to keep their staves long enough in stock to insure durability. Green-heart, and some American 'arrangements in cane and steel,' are now much in fashion, and I believe on report that you may now obtain a rod of greater power – especially for throwing against the wind – than those which have contented me. Still, sound hickory is not to be despised.

If you wish your rods to last long – and the two on which I depend have been in use fifty and twenty years respectively – look carefully to them at the end of the season. Let them be revarnished and relapped in the winter, and have all the rings save those on the butt moved some points round, so as to shift the strain and obviate any tendency to a permanent bias or 'cast ' in the wood. A splice rod has more perfect play than a jointed one, and is worth setting up if you live on a river; but otherwise the jointed rod of the present day, with ends carefully brazed to prevent swelling in the socket, and patent ferrules to save the awkward process of lapping the joints together, is a handy tool enough for practical purposes. On a wet day it is a good precaution to rub a little oil or deer's grease round the rim of each ferrule.

As for the reel, good ones are now as plentiful as blackberries. The circumference should be large and the barrel short, so that a single turn may gather in or release many inches of line. Multipliers might be pronounced an abomination, did not the proverb forbid our speaking ill of the dead. Anglers generally place the reel with the handle on the right, but I suspect the opposite practice is preferable; the control of the fish will thus be left to the 'better hand,' while the left will suffice for 'pirning in and 'pirning out.'

With regard to reel lines, I still adhere to the old silk and hair, but I can well believe that oiled silk, sufficiently tapered, is better in a high wind. Its weight, moreover, is a constant quantity, while that of silk and hair varies unpleasantly in rain and towards what I heard a Lancashire keeper call 't' faag eend o' t' dey.'

As to the gut collar, the question of 'tapering' is yet more important; in fact, perfection in casting cannot be attained unless this be' fine by degrees and beautifully less.' I have never bought any as perfectly adjusted as those I have tied for myself. But the graduated arrangement of the links is delicate and laborious work – more trying, I think, to the sight than even the dressing of flies, and the difficulty of the task of course increases with years. It is a good plan to have the gut sorted beforehand into distinct sizes – thick, medium, fine, and finest – and to tie a good many collars at one sitting when your eye and hand are in. Be very careful with your knots, and never attempt to make one till the gut has been thoroughly soaked in tepid water. Pay a high price for the best gut, particularly for picked samples of the finest. Engine-drawn gut is generally worthless; single hair is far preferable – indeed, were not the docking of horses so universal, it might be often used with advantage, as it falls more lightly, reflects the light less, and when taken from an undocked stallion is of such a length as to reduce the knots to a minimum.

The best chance of obtaining first-rate hair would, I think, be from some of the dray teams of great brewing firms. In some of our open northern streams good hair is invaluable. But it must be used with caution. Hair is very elastic, but will not bear a continued strain like gut. Leave it tied at a stretch, and it will shortly break. Hence, with even the strongest hair you must play your fish with a lighter and, so to say, a more variable hand than when using gut tackle. As for creels, a small one may do for brook fishing, but for use on good waters let it be roomy – enough so to hold at least twenty-five pounds of fish. I have not been specially privileged in access to the very cream of trout streams – have never, for instance, fished at Stockbridge or in the renowned Lathkill – have never had a day in the water at Cheynies, immortalised by that genial sportsman, Anthony Trollope, or in the upper waters of Foston Beck, admirably preserved by Colonel St Quintin. Nor, again, have I ever had leisure to pick my days, but have taken my chances of a holiday or half-holiday when they offered. Yet I have not infrequently filled a basket of the size recommended till it overflowed into my pockets.

By the bye, I think the form of the creels in general use a great mistake. They should be made much longer at bottom, so that a good weight of fish may be laid out without their pressing on each other, or being disfigured by bending. In an ordinary basket, the undermost fish on a good day are grievously crushed by the last comers – a sorry sight when laid out.

Questions of dress come near to those of tackle. A broad-brimmed stiff felt hat is your best thatch for all weathers. Wear woollen from head to fool, and knickerbockers with the thickest Inverness hose rather than trousers. If you have to wade, you must clothe your nether man accordingly; but do not wade oftener or longer than is absolutely necessary, especially when there are other anglers on the stream. If you 'establish a raw' on your foot, don't lay it up and 'swear at large,' but wash the place carefully, and clip away the loose skin. Then mix the white of a fresh egg with a few drops of brandy, and lay it over the bare place with a feather. When the spirit evaporates – as it will in a few minutes – a fine transparent film will be left. Repeat this process three or four times, and you will have a perfect artificial skin, which will neither wash off nor rub off. I have done a long day on the moors with such a false cuticle on heel and toe without pain or even inconvenience.

But your fly fisher must be fed as well as clothed; and though by virtue of his healthy calling he ought to make a substantial breakfast, somewhere towards 2 p.m. (generally the slackest time of the day) he will feel that Nature abhors a vacuum. Something he must have in his pouch

> Quod interpellet inani
> Ventre diem durare.

What that something shall be must depend on his taste and the state of the sideboard. But if he inclines to the sweet simplicity of sandwiches, let him make them of ham sliced very thin, and overlaid with marmalade. The combination may seem startling, but will be found most palatable, particularly in warm weather. A layer of unpressed caviare, again, with a squeeze of lemon and a sprinkling of mustard and cress, though less substantial, has a pleasant relish.

As for fluids, during many years, when I was well up to the mark as a pedestrian, I found nothing better in a long day by moor or river side than an occasional mouthful of cold tea. But I would mention for the benefit of those who, like myself, are in the down-hill of life, that I have found a great resource against fatigue in a pocket flask of the 'Vin Mariani.' It is an extract of the 'coca leaf,' the sustaining power of which (see Kingsley's 'Westward Ho!') has been for centuries known to labouring men in Central and Southern America. There are many preparations, but I find this the best and pleasantest. It is procurable from Roberts, the Bond Street chemist.

The luncheon disposed of, there remains a high and doubtful question – shall Piscator smoke? I think the ayes have it. For myself, in spite of King Jamie and his modern supporters, I cannot dispense with my water-side cigar, especially on a hot afternoon. No one, I think, can fully appreciate the effect, at once soothing and restorative, of a well-timed weed, who has not enjoyed it in a tropical climate. Often after a weary ride through Australian bush, the glass standing at 110° or even 120° in the shade, my pulses throbbing and every nerve ajar, I have thrown myself from my horse, set my back against the shady side of a huge gum-tree bole, and after a few whiffs of a ready cheroot have felt myself calmed and refreshed 'beyond the Muse's painting.'

Even in England there is many a sultry afternoon when the fly fisher, after four or five hours on the water, will enjoy the fragrant leaf with similar zest. And, luckily, the hottest part of a summer's day is usually a time when the fish are little on the move, so that he may have his smoke out without sacrificing his sport. Indeed, if he means to make a long day in July or August, he will often do well to prolong his rest, and while away an hour or two with a well-chosen pocket volume of Horace, for instance, or Boswell's 'Johnson,' or Percy's 'Reliques' – anything that may be engaged by snatches, without continuous reading. There are times of sultry stillness when to offer a fly to the sulky low-lying trout is as useless as whistling jigs to a milestone. Nevertheless, the angler at rest will do wisely to keep his ears open, and to cast an occasional glance out of the 'tail of his eye' up and down the stream. Three or four heavy rises seen or heard in succession may give him unexpected notice that the fish are astir again.

And here let me remark, that there are few questions concerning trout at once so interesting and so difficult of solution as that which touches the times of their feeding; the hours and days when they are likely to take freely. To the first part of the question it is easy to return a general answer; subject, however, to frequent exceptions, due to what seems like pure caprice or 'cussedness' on the part of the fish. As a rule, from the beginning of April to the close of the season the surest hours for sport are those from nine to twelve.

In spring, however, the fish often continue rising freely far into the afternoon, whereas in summer, unless strong wind or heavy showers come to freshen them up, they mostly go off the feed between one and two, coming on again after a longer or shorter interval, and rising boldly from an hour before sunset to an hour after – as long in fact as you can see to throw. This, however, is only in warm weather; if a dry cold wind comes up late in the afternoon your evening cast will disappoint you. Yet this only holds good as far as the Border; in the northern counties of Scotland trout are almost invariably astir on a good ford towards dusk in July and August.

Looking far south again, I may remark that in Devonshire during the spring months something may always be done between 2.30 and 4 p.m.

So much for the 'happy hours.' I have still to inquire what constitutes a good fly fishing day; and my attempt at an answer must involve a sweeping confession of ignorance. Most anglers indeed will agree in praising a day of chequered cloud and sunshine, with a strong yet soft breeze from the west or south-west; and there is no doubt that on such a day good sport is generally attainable and the fly fisher's craft is plied under the pleasantest conditions. Yet on shy waters I think I have made my heaviest baskets in a stiff nor'-wester with a dark sky and frequent bursts of heavy rain. The fish are thrown more completely off their guard and take the fly without misgiving as a battered and half-drowned insect. Larger flies, too, and stronger gut may be safely used.

Yet this only brings us to a conclusion which might have been taken for granted a priori; *viz.* that roughened waters and dimmer light make it more easy to deceive the fish. But an east or north-east wind very rarely produces the same satisfactory results. This may in part be due to the smaller show of the fly when the wind is 'snell and keen;' yet this explanation hardly meets the case, as trout often take very well when flies are scarce. We may, however, assume it is a general though unexplained rule that a moist air is better than a dry one.

In waters with which we are familiar something may be learned from the colour of the surface. I was fishing long ago with my brother in Loch Fruchie, and taking fish, such as they were, very fast. Suddenly the old boatman said, 'Ye may pit doon yer gaud noo.' My brother to humour him at once laid down his rod. I being, rather what Mrs Tabitha Bramble calls an 'imp-fiddle' in such matters, merely asked why? 'She's the wrang colour' was his brief answer; and certainly, though the breeze continued, the aspect of the loch had become dull and sullen. I fished on, however, and in the course of the next hour caught one small fish, when the veteran very pointedly said to my brother – ignoring me as unteachable – 'Noo, Mr John, ye may tak yer gaud again.' And sure enough, the hue of the lake had grown brighter and livelier, and the fish came on the feed again.

I have borne this lesson in mind ever afterwards, and have certainly found that when the wavelets on a rippled pool show a blue or blue-black tint, there is sport to be had, but when they wear a dull leaden colour the fish sulk. Why they do so is another matter, as to which this deponent sayeth not. Again, after a rough stormy night, trout seldom rise well before eleven o'clock; this, however, is probably owing to their having been on the feed all night.

The worst of all days, undoubtedly, is one when a thunderstorm is threatening but delays to burst. The clouds are piled in heavy masses, and every break in their array shows a lurid light gleaming through, of an indescribable tint between amber and lilac; the air is hushed and still but for an occasional hot gust, which seems to come from nowhere in particular. You feel oppressed yourself, and hardly wonder that 'the springing trout lies still.' Indeed it is a common apology for an empty creel that 'there is thunder in the air.'

But in truth when the storm actually breaks over you it gives you a grand chance of sport. I shall never forget a short bout of fishing which I enjoyed one evening just above Wansford Bridge. I had been early on the stream, though well aware from the aspect of the sky that my cake was dough till the threatened elemental war was fairly let loose. I worked my way doggedly down the beck, casting from time to time, as on Sam Weller's theory I might have eaten oysters, 'out of sheer desperation.' A few little fish I certainly took – they always will come when you have to put them back – and one solitary pounder, who must have been either eccentric or life-weary to rise on such a day.

But it was tedious work – the heat oppressive, the air dead. Even my attendant boy lost his faith in my star – took short cuts and long rests. I spun out my luncheon, smoked more than was good for me, and though I still held on for the heavier water below, I often doubted my weather forecast, and wished myself 'taking mine ease in mine inn.' But the stillness was at last broken by distant mutterings of thunder; the clouds banked up higher and higher, and just as I had reached the open water between Wansford mill and bridge the storm was upon me, with deafening peals and a slanting deluge of rain. Luckily I was waterproof, having one stiff cape over my shoulders and another buckled round above my hips and protecting me as far as my knee-boots.

The wind was too furious to permit casting, but as it blew

directly on my back I had simply to let out as much line as I wanted and let it fall as I could. Never did I see good fish rise so fast. The fly was seized as soon as it reached the water, and the only difficulty in killing the fish lay in the violence of the wind. In less than an hour and a half I basketed twenty-one fish weighing twenty-eight pounds. This could not have been done within the time had I not, in anticipation of the wild weather, been armed with stronger gut and a larger fly than usual. Four-fifths of the fish were taken with the blue-bottle, an excellent fly towards the close of summer, when the natural insect goes daft (to use the Yorkshire phrase) and cannot keep itself from 'the drink.'

Many similar experiences have led me to the conclusion that in bright, shy waters a thunderstorm sets the big fish feeding 'audaciously.' And it seems probable that the sudden changes in the mood of the fish which every angler must have noticed are due to the electrical condition of the atmosphere. It often happens that trout all at once cease rising, the river which just before was alive with rises becoming absolutely dead. In such a case an old hand will sit down and wait. Days may be better or worse, but there is hardly ever a day, except on a thick, rising water, when the fish do not come on the feed at some time or times which the wary angler will not let slip. 'Tout vient it qui sait attendre.'

Even odder than the sudden sulking of trout is the fit they occasionally take of 'short rising,' when after every promising break you feel only a slight twitch, and never succeed in hooking your fish. Whether this is due to some ocular deception which makes them miscalculate their rise, or whether for the time they are merely amusing themselves with the fly, like 'MacFarlane's geese, that liked their play better than their meat,' I cannot pretend to decide. The fit seldom lasts long, and while it does it tries the angler's temper sorely. I remember once in a Devonshire brook raising from twenty to thirty fish in succession without a single capture. The sky changed, and I took seventeen without a miss.

This may show that after several failures a fly fisher should not conclude too hastily that he has 'tailored' his fish. They may never have had the hook in their mouths. When trout rise short, it is a good rule to give up striking altogether, and be content with keeping a taut line till some determined fish hooks himself. If your fly be not hastily plucked away, a trout who has merely nibbled at the wings or tail may at a second or third rise 'go the entire animal.'

If you hook a fish foul – and the symptoms are not to be mistaken – risk your tackle rather than slacken your hold. He will never dislodge the hook unless by your timid handling. I once hooked a three-pounder near the tail – luckily on an open stretch of water – and held on to him till in his struggles down stream he swung in to the shore and was cleverly netted by a friendly looker-on, who had continually shrieked to me to 'give him line.' He dropped off the hook the instant he was netted, and I showed my friend with pride that there was a small scale on the point of the hook below the barb. The fish had been literally killed by the hold of the mere tip of the steel on his tough skin.

But I am running riot in old reminiscences. Happily, they are at least cheerful and blameless records, and raise no 'accusing shades of hours gone by.' No doubt, the fly fisher has what Mrs Ramsbottom calls his 'little Piccadillies;' he does sometimes fish a little beyond his liberty, and perhaps on a very bad day when he has landed a trout barely up to the mark in point of length gives the benefit of the doubt to the creel and not to the fish. But on the whole I have found my brother anglers worthy men and pleasant companions, with whom acquaintance readily ripened into friendship.

Their quiet converse with nature seems to smooth down asperities of character, and they move 'kindly men among their kind.' There are few of them, too, who have not during their devious rambles noted something in the field of Natural History which they can impart in conversation. Speaking as one of the fraternity, I think the caution we most need is the time-honoured *Ne quid mimis*. The fly fisher's art is so interesting and so many-sided that its votaries are too apt to fancy themselves justified in making it a business instead of a recreation. I have known very clever men who devoted some eight months of the year to a series of 'fishings,' and to salmon gave up what was meant for mankind.

I am by no means sure that I should not have fallen into the same error myself but for the blessed necessity of work, early laid on me and scarcely abating with years. But I am very certain that had I done so I should have penned these pages, the records of my experience as a fly fisher, with regret instead of pleasure.

If I may venture a few 'more last words 5 to my brethren of the angle, they shall be echoes of a farewell uttered long ago.

Finally, pursue a liberal sport in a liberal spirit. Help a brother angler freely, especially when less able than yourself to afford a well-stocked fly book. Neither poach yourself nor encourage poachers by purchasing fish procured by doubtful means. Spare small fish (except in those over-stocked waters where all are small) and large fish when out of season, but not past recovery.

Abjure lath fishing, cross fishing, netting and spearing, and renounce salmon roe except to thin the trout near the spawning beds of salmon. And when you have filled your creel, maintain the old repute of the brotherhood by a liberal and not exclusive distribution of your booty.

So may your intervals of well-earned relaxation by lake or stream be welcome and fortunate. So may genial skies and soft showers add freshness to the air and beauty to the landscape. So may hand and eye work truly together, whether you wield the fly rod or lay it aside for the pencil. So may you return home unjaded from your sport, with a light heart and a heavy basket – happy, above all,

> To know there is an eye will mark
> Your coming, and look brighter when you come.

H. R. Francis.

4

Chalk-Stream Fishing with the Dry Fly, and May-Fly Fishing

CHALK-STREAM FISHING WITH THE DRY FLY

That different rivers require different styles of fishing, or, in other words, that the highest art as practised in one locality is occasionally almost useless in another, may now, I think, be laid down as an angling axiom; certainly it is a rule recognised in practice by, at any rate, most fly fishers of experience. On one river trout will take the fly 'wet,' on another it is almost essential to use it 'dry;' whilst on some waters, like the well-known lakes of Westmeath, for example, the only time when anything worth calling sport is to be had is whilst the 'fly is up,' that is, during the season of the appearance of the May fly, and then the lure must be the natural insect itself used with a blow line. The extent to which these differences may exist in different streams is often only found out by the fly fisher through the disagreeable experience of empty baskets, on first visiting a new locality. Many and many a time has an angler, skilled in all the niceties of trout fishing in his own Highland streams, been utterly baffled when he first essayed his luck with the well-fed, not to say pampered, fish of Test, Itchen, or Kennet. And it is not difficult to find the explanation. The character of the clear chalk streams of the south is entirely different from that of the rocky mountain rivers and peat-stained torrents of the Highlands, and consequently the habits of the fish are also widely different.

The chalk-streams are wonderfully prolific in insect life, far and away beyond anything of which the trout of Scotland or Ireland have for the most part any experience and besides the numberless flies bred in our southern streams, there is always an abundant store of larvae, shrimps, water snails and other trout food which find their habitat among the weeds, to say nothing of minnows and small fry on the gravelly shallows. So that, with a large choice in their feeding, the fish soon wax fat and dainty, and while a trout in a rapid mountain or moorland stream has to be on the look-out all day long for anything edible which comes within his ken, and even then has hard work at times to keep himself in respectable condition, a chalk-stream fish is always picksome and hard to please, and will only take the fly when the natural insects are sailing down in goodly numbers. At other times he is either sheltering among the weeds, or else busy with bottom or mid-water food.

In many streams a judicious cast of three flies thrown into likely spots with a light and skilful hand will bring fish to the creel fast enough, but this kind of fly fishing for chance fish is seldom productive of any sport on a chalk stream. When, however, there is a heavy rise, and every trout is busily engaged in taking fly, it will be noticed that the fish take up a favourable position just beneath the surface of the stream, and feed steadily and persistently in the most quiet and deliberate manner possible.

A movement of a few inches, a careful scrutiny, and a gentle unobtrusive 'suck' describes exactly the usual manner in which a chalk-stream trout takes his surface food. It is quite unlike the rush and the splash with which a Scotch or a Devonshire trout leaves the shelter of a submerged rock to secure the passing fly, and everything combines to make it difficult for the angler to keep out of sight, as well as to put the fly over the fish in an effective and natural manner. When a chalk-stream fish is feeding at the surface, the angler's fly is always brought into comparison with the natural insects floating down, and little sport is to be expected unless the artificial fly is most skilfully made and skilfully handled. It must be sufficiently neat and natural in appearance to deceive any fish, and it must be thrown so as to float 'cockily' like the real fly it is intended to imitate.

Frequenters of chalk-streams fish almost exclusively with a single dry fly, and only when the fish are visibly feeding at the surface. The angler selects his fish, gets behind him (that is, below him), and prepares for a cast up stream. Then taking two or three false casts in the air to judge the exact distance, the fly is thrown with the intention of making it alight gently a foot or two above the rising fish and exactly in his line, for a well-fed chalk-stream trout will rarely go even a few inches out of his way for a passing fly. If the fly falls short or wide, it should be left till the line has floated some distance to the rear of the fish, when it must be picked off, whisked through the air two or three times to dry the wings and hackle before a new cast is made. If there is no clumsiness several trial casts may be made before the exact distance is found, and the fish will go on rising undisturbed, but the slightest bungle on the part of the angler is fatal and puts the fish down for the next half hour. If it be remembered that most of the best fish lie close to the bank and that the fly has to be sent down floating naturally correct to the very inch, it will be seen that there is room for great exercise of skill, and to succeed even moderately well requires a vast amount of practice.

It will always be a moot point how far it is necessary or not to present to rising fish an exact imitation of the fly on which they happen to be feeding. And the greater the experience of an angler the less will he be inclined to lay down the law on this and kindred questions: he will have learnt that his preconceived notions, based on extensive observation and practice, have frequently been completely upset by some sudden and unintelligible caprice on the part of the fish.

The anglers one meets on a chalk stream generally have some interest in entomology, and it is the exception for a skilful fisherman not to know something of the natural flies which tempt the trout to the surface. On the other hand, it is generally admitted that with a shy fish it is half the battle to put the fly right at the first cast; in other words, a fish is often thrown off his guard completely by a well-directed fly, no matter what, so long as it comes down exactly in the right spot before his suspicions are aroused by seeing a foot or two of glittering gut pass over his nose half a dozen times. So that there is a certain amount of truth in the saying, 'It is not so much the fly as the driver' though the originator of this Hampshire maxim is himself quite as famous for his practical knowledge of flies and fly tying as he is for his skill in handling a rod.

But the angler who really desires to get the most enjoyment out of his sport will never be contented with the utilitarian view which measures a day's sport solely by the weight of the basket; he will always have powers of observation keenly developed, some at least of the instincts of the naturalist will be present, and the marvellous profusion of insect life – which is the peculiar characteristic of the chalk streams – cannot fail to excite his interest. And, other things being equal, there can be no doubt that the entomologist always has a great advantage over the man who knows nothing and cares nothing about the habits and life history of the flies of the streams he frequents. Moreover, there are some days, as all experienced anglers will admit, on which any efforts however skilful appear to be useless until the right fly is found. Then possibly, after an hour or more of fruitless whipping, the spell appears to be broken, and fish after fish falls a victim to the attractions of a single fly, the only pattern in the angler's store which for the time possesses any charm.

A certain amount of fly fishing entomology may, of course, be learnt from books, but the only knowledge which can be really useful is that which the fisherman acquires for himself by his own habits of observation. The novice should, therefore, make a practice of studying the flies by the water-side; he will soon learn to recognise some flies at a glance, but, however proficient he may become, it is hardly likely that he will ever be able wholly to dispense with the useful habit of dipping up from the water a few of the natural insects, rather than fish for a moment in doubt or hesitation. To readily recognise the fly on which the fish are feeding, and to be able to match it with a good imitation of his own making, gives a peculiar pleasure and confidence: if to this the angler can add the consciousness of skill and dexterity in the use of his rod, he may wander from stream to stream independent of local fancies and piscatory heirlooms, but with a good prospect of sport wherever he may find a rising fish.

The following is a list of the most useful flies for chalk-stream fishing. It does not profess to be exhaustive, but it will be sufficient, I think, to guide one who is strange to this style of fishing, and to enable him to equip himself with such flies as most southern anglers consider necessary. Several of these flies have already been described by me in the '*Fishing Gazette*,' but recent experience has suggested slight modifications in a few cases. However, the patterns here given have all been put to frequent trial by experienced anglers on the Test, Itchen, Kennet, and other streams, and may all be relied on.

I begin with several dressings of the best of all chalk-stream flies:

THE OLIVE DUN

Body: Olive silk. I know nothing better than Mr Aldam's 'gosling green,' but it wants most delicate handling, and great care should be taken not to have too much wax on the tying silk, or it will darken the floss and spoil the fly. A ribbing of fine gold wire is an improvement.

Wings: Dark starling.

Legs and Whisks: Hackle stained olive – not too yellow, but a dull brown olive.

Body: Quill dyed olive, with or without gold tag. Wings and hackle as before. This pattern admits of several shades, and is, perhaps, the best all-round pattern that can possibly be used in Hampshire, from one end of the season to the other. It is always worth a trial. It is sold in thousands, and slays its thousands every year.

The same pattern as the last, with light brown fibres of hare's fur tied in for legs. Very good in April, and an excellent floater.

Body: Leveret's fur dyed olive, ribbed with gold wire.

Hackle and wings as belore. This is known as the 'rough spring olive.' A useful variety.

Hook, 0 and 00.

THE INDIA-RUBBER-BODIED OLIVE DUN

This is a 'detached-bodied' fly (figured in the illustration annexed, the numbers corresponding with the numbers of the flies in this list), and if carefully made is a most killing pattern in April. Every year since I first discovered its merits on the Winnal Club water at Winchester I have found it useful, frequently killing with it when the usual favourites have been tried in vain over rising fish. The rubber body was not my own idea, though I believe I was the first to try it and prove its value.

The fly is made lighter or darker according to the colour of the rubber, and wings and hackle must be chosen to match the body. The hackle should be of a brownish olive to harmonise with the body, which, when held up to the light, has a translucent appearance, as like to the body of a natural dun as it is possible to obtain. It is only in the early spring that I ever do much with this fly, and then I use it on a No. 00 hook.

It is extremely difficult to tie it small and delicate enough for summer use, but I have killed with it in August on a 000, the smallest size made. For late summer and autumn I generally adopt horsehair bodies, as the hair can be dyed different shades, and can be used of a pale watery hue which cannot be got in India-rubber. I am never without a few of these detached bodied duns, and they have again and again procured me sport when all else failed; but it must be distinctly understood that they are only killing because of their close resemblance in colour and transparency to the natural insect.

Some people seem to think that it is the detached projecting body which makes the fly attractive, and so they tie detached bodies of quill and silk, which are, of course, dull and opaque, and very inferior to hair or rubber. In fact, I consider it is labour wasted to tie detached bodies except of translucent material; and if silk or quill be used, it is far better to use it on the hook in the ordinary way.

HARE'S EAR

Body: Hare's fur ribbed with gold, and fibres picked out for legs, winged with dark starling. This fly is a great favourite on the Test.

Hook, 0 or 00.

THE RED QUILL, GREY QUILL, AND GINGER QUILL

Body: Undyed quill.

Legs arid Whisks: Red hackle.

Wings: Darkish starling. The grey and ginger are generally dressed with lighter wings.

Hook, 0 or 00, usually the smaller size.

The Red Quill is, perhaps, the best all-round evening fiy that can be used in the summer months.

THE IRON BLUE

This fly comes out thickly on some parts of the Test; it is less common on the Itchen, and in some places it is rarely seen at all. When it does come out the fish generally refuse everything else. It varies a good deal in colour, but I believe the best general dressing to be:

Body: Quill, dyed a dark blue with a violet shade. Some prefer mauve silk with mole's fur.

Legs and Whisks: Dark honey dun, the natural fly having yellow tips to its dusky blue legs.

Wings: From the breast of a water hen, or from the tail feather of the greater titmouse.

Hook, 00 or 000.

THE 'LITTLE MARRYAT'

This is a fancy fly well known at Winchester, and indeed it is a prime favourite all over Hampshire. It bears a close resemblance to some of the pale watery duns which are always to be seen in warm weather. It begins to be useful at the end of April, and if dressed of suitable size it will do well from May to September, and will often kill the best grayling in October.

Body: Very pale buff opossum fur spun on light yellow silk.

Wings: Medium starling.

Legs and Whisks: The palest feather from a buff Cochin China cockerel.

Hook, 0 or 00.

THE RED SPINNER

Of all the numberless patterns which have been devised to imitate the gauzy transparency of this fly, I believe this to be the best; of late years it has been most successfully used in Hampshire, and is known as the 'Detached Badger.'

Body: Detached, made of reddish brown horsehair, and firmly whipped to the hook with strong well-waxed silk.

Legs and Wings: A 'badger hackle' dressed buzz. This hackle is difficult to obtain, and is of a rusty grey in the centre (almost black), with bright shining golden tips.

Hook, 0 or 00.

WICKHAM'S FANCY

One of the most useful flies that can possibly be used, whether for trout or grayling. It is always worth a trial, though what the fish take it for it is impossible to say. It is a very attractive, bright looking fly, and an excellent floater, but it sometimes does wonders in rough, wet weather, when dry fly fishing is hopeless. It should be made as follows:

Body: Gold tinsel ribbed from tail to head with red cock's hackle.

Wings: Dark starling. Landrail makes a nice variety.

Hook, 00 to 1 or 2.

FLIGHT'S FANCY

This fly hails from Winchester, and it is very useful towards the end of April, when the olives are beginning to get lighter in shade; and all through the summer months a small 'light' may be resorted to with confidence when delicate duns are about.

Body; Pale yellow, or primrose, floss silk ribbed with fine flat gold tinsel.

Wings; Light starling.

Legs and Whisks: Pale buff, or, for a change, honey dun.

Hook 00 or 000.

With this list of flies a fisherman may consider himself well equipped for the first two months of the season, and there are many days in every month of the summer and autumn when these same flies tied smaller would be found sufficient to insure the best of sport.

I do not believe in dividing artificial flies according to months, and a good comprehensive assortment of spring patterns will, with slight modifications, always be of general use at all times and in all weathers. Still, there are some very favourite flies which do not appear before May, and as these sometimes entirely monopolise the attention of every feeding fish, they must be added to the list. I leave out the green and grey drake, as they are not found on every water, and almost every angler has his own special pattern: but, in my opinion. May flies are frequently tied too large, and I believe, whatever pattern be adopted, the best sport will be obtained by small flies.

THE BLACK GNAT

The natural fly has a long, thin, shiny black body, not a bit like the fluffy little lump usually seen in the imitation. Then the wings are long and lie folded quite flat (not sloped like those of a sedge or alder), and projecting over the tail end of the body, showing a shiny, metallic, gauzy film, in strong contrast to the black body, and which cannot be imitated by feather.

This is how I make my pattern. On a 00 or 000 hook I put a longish body of black ostrich herl, which has first been stripped. Then I cut a strip of pike scale the proper length and shape to represent the two folded wings and tie it flat on the top of the hook, taking care to show the projecting bit above mentioned. Then over and in front of the wing I take two or three turns of a small black starling's feather, and the fly is finished. It does not float very well, but in fine still weather it is very effective; and the pike scale, tied as I have described, will stand a great deal of whipping.

Those who object to the pike scale wing can substitute starling feather, but the fly will be less lifelike, and on a hot August day certainly less killing.

THE SEDGE

The last two or three seasons this fly has not preserved its reputation as a standard pattern for late fishing on a summer's evening. It has been a mystery to many who used to look upon it as a never-failing resource. A few years ago it killed splendidly at Winchester; and I remember seeing a man come to the Old Barge stream, at eight o'clock one evening in August, and kill five brace of good trout with his favourite sedge. He rarely used anything else in the evening; and I, myself at that time fished it with more confidence than any other fly. But I have done very little with it lately, and my stock of sedges has not wanted replenishing for a long time.

When the trout and grayling return to their old tastes, the following will probably be found the best dressing for the sedge and its variations:

The Silver Sedge, which I believe is no sedge at all, but an imitation of the small grass moth which flutters about in the meadows by the riverside.

Body: White floss silk, ribbed with silver; hackled all over with buff or light red hackle.

Wings: Landrail.

Hook, 00 to 1.

THE RED SEDGE (OR, SEDGE PROPER)

Body: Red fur from hare's face, or fox's ear, or from the reddest part of an opossum skin. Rib it with gold thread and wind on a red hackle from tail to head.

Wing: A ruddy feather from a landrail's wing.

Hook, 00 to 1.

The Big Sedge: This is the local name, but I prefer to call it the 'Cinnamon.' It is a fat, toothsome morsel, nearly an inch long, and answers capitally on a moonlight night, when it is

warm, still, and free from mist. I have killed many heavy fish with it, especially in September, during the harvest moon.

The dressing I prefer is the same as that given for the red sedge, on a No. 2 hook, and winged with the reddest part of a cock landrail's wing, or, better still, with one of the under covert feathers of the peahen, which are very faintly mottled with a darker shade of brown.

Though true to nature, I think it is a mistake to dress the body thick, for the fly is apt to be heavy and lumpy, and so float badly.

THE ALDER

Is very useful in June, and on some rivers will kill in the May-fly season better than the drake itself. It is in great favour with the Fairford anglers, and the natural fly is very plentiful on the Colne.

BodyBronze-coloured peacock herl.

Hackle: Black, or a dull-coloured feather, with black centre and ruddy tips.

Wings: From the tail feather of a hen pheasant.

There is another very good variety known as the 'Button/'or 'red-winged alder' which should be dressed as before, only that the wing should come from the red tail feather of a partridge.

Hook, No. 2.

THE BROWN QUILL

Very useful in August and September.

Body: Some light quill dyed in Judson's light brown. Very good imitations have been produced by taking ordinary peacock quill and bleaching it.

Legs and Whisks: Ginger.

Wings: Medium starling.

Hook, 00.

THE INDIAN YELLOW

Body: A delicate brown silk ribbed with bright yellow.

Legs and Whisks: A rich buff.

Wings: From the under wing-feathers of a young grouse.

Hook, 00.

This fly has a very prominent reddish brown head, which may be imitated by a couple of turns of dark orange silk.

The grouse feather is the right colour exactly, but it is very soft, and makes a poor wing for floating. It is a pity some other blue feather cannot be found suitable for this fly and the next.

THE BLUE-WINGED OLIVE

This fly is larger than most of the duns of the summer months and generally makes its appearance just at dusk, when it sometimes comes out in myriads.

At Winchester in September I have seen the river covered with it, and rising fish only a few yards apart as far as one could see. Some of the heaviest fish I have ever killed in Hampshire have been taken with this fly; still I have never been satisfied with any of the imitations I have yet devised.

The body is of delicate greenish olive, legs a pale watery olive, and the wings distinctly blue, like those of the Indian yellow. I have made the body of silk, wool, dyed fur, ribbed with gold, and with quill of different sorts. I hope someday to hit off the right shade in dyeing fibres of the condor's wing feather, and also to discover what will make the best wing. Possibly the blue feather from a merlin hawk's wing might do, or perhaps the coot's wing might solve the mystery. It must not be a soft feather which sucks up water and gets sodden directly, for the natural fly sits up and rides cockily on the water, and no half-drowned imitation can ever do much execution. I am convinced we have not got the right pattern yet.

Hook 0 or 00.

THE LITTLE SKY BLUE

This is a splendid grayling fly in August and September; in fact, all free-rising fish take it well in the warm autumn mornings from ten to midday.

Body: Pale straw colour, of silk, quill, or fur. I have killed well with all three, but silk I like least, as it changes colour after it is wet much more than other materials. Legs and Whisks: Light honey dun.

Wings: A pale delicate blue, best imitated with a jay's wing feather.

Hooky 00 or 000.

THE RED TAG

This is generally regarded as a grayling fly, but at times it does wonderfully well among trout. The brighter the day and the hotter the sun the better does this fly succeed. It is not generally known that when trout are 'smutting' – i.e. feeding on that tiny black midge which baffles all imitation – they will often take a small red tag ravenously. On one of the hottest days in August 1884, fishing at midday, I hooked eight large trout with the red tag, and this on a piece of water which it was usually considered hopeless to fish before dusk. As for grayling, when they are lying basking on the gravel in about two feet of water, the red tag will almost always bring them up. I have had splendid sport with it on many occasions. This is the dressing:

Body: Peacock herl, short and fat, with a tiny red tag of floss silk, wool, or scarlet ibis feather. Floss silk looks very well when it is dry, but it shrinks up when wet, and often loses its colour; I have always found wool much more killing.

At the shoulder should be wound a dark, rich, red hackle.

Hook, 0, 00, or 000.

THE JENNY SPINNER

This is the transformation of the iron-blue dun, and is one of
the most beautiful and delicate flies to be found by riverside.
It is often seen dancing up and down in thousands after a hot
day, and the fact that it is by no means uncommon on rivers
where the iron blue is scarce, leads me to think that some other
summer duns (possibly the little sky blue) turn to this delicate
transparent spinner. It is impossible to see it on the water, and
at best it is a most difficult fly to imitate. For these two reasons
sport with it is somewhat uncertain.

It should be dressed with a detached body of white horsehair
tipped with a couple of turns of mulberry silk and white whisks.
Tie the body to a 00 or 000 hook with mulberry coloured silk
to show the head and thorax of that colour. Wing it with two
hackle points from a very pale blue dun cock, almost white,
and let the legs be of the same colour. Or it may be dressed
buzz with a pale grizzled hackle, like the red spinner, No. 6.

THE INTERMEDIATE

I use this name to denote a class of delicate flies which I use
with considerable success in summer fishing.

Everyone must have noticed how the different duns seem
to run by different gradations from one kind into another, so
that sometimes a fly picked off the water cannot definitely
be named according to any of the standards of classification,
and yet it bears a considerable resemblance to several flies we
are accustomed to call by name. I have found it very useful
to tie various horsehair detached bodies of pale and delicate
tints, and then match these with wings and hackle; choosing
different shades of honey dun, light buff, or olive for legs, and
varying the colour of the wings so as to suit the rest of the fly.

I take immense pains over these patterns, and, by constantly
studying the changes in the natural insects, am enabled to

produce delicate and life-like artificials which frequently bring a good fish to my basket after he has steadily refused to be tempted by other flies.

This list is, I think, comprehensive enough. Some will think it needlessly long, and others will miss some favourite pattern of their own special fancy. But, in giving my opinion on the subject of flies, I have described those which my own book contains, and a supply of which I always like to keep up to working order. If they are dressed of suitable size, and are used with fine gut, they will suffice to give sport if sport is to be had. Anyone who fails with such a list as this will, I am convinced, find fly fishing generally an unprofitable pursuit

H. S. Hall

MAY-FLY FISHING

The true May-flies of the British angler belong to the order *Neuroptera*, to the family *Ephemeridae*, and to the genus Ephemera. In the majority of the colder and more rapid English streams, such as the Test or Itchen, *E. danica* is the predominant species, while in the more sluggish rivers or lakes *E. vulgata* is commonly found, and more rarely *E. lineata*. These three – the only English species – may be recognised by minute differences in size or colouring, slight variations in neuration of wings, or in the markings of the thorax or abdomen, etc., all of which are no doubt of considerable value to the scientific entomologist, as enabling him to separate the species, but are of no practical use to the angler for the purposes of his sport When he finds in this country one of the *Ephemeridae* of large size, with wings erect dotted with four or five dark spots and tinged with a delicate shade of yellowish- grey green, with body of a pale straw colour marked in the lower segments with a few brown streaks, the thorax of a deep brown-black with a pale sepia blotch in the middle of the back, and the three setae of nearly equal length, and especially if he finds this insect on the water at the end of May or early portion of June, he may be certain that it is a specimen of the Green Drake, or subimago of one of the above- named three species. Having once seen the subimago, he will find no difficulty in recognising the same insect after the further metamorphosis to the imago, Spent Gnat, or Black Drake.

Not only are the three species so closely allied and so similar in appearance that, for all angling purposes, the imitation of any one is quite near enough to serve as an imitation of all, but, beyond this, their life-history is, as far as known, identical, whether in the immature larval stages when under the water; or the subimago rising from the surface of the stream and flying to the shore; or the perfect insect, the imago, under which form the reproductive functions are exercised.

The eggs, when deposited on the surface by the female imago, sink to the bottom of the river, and after the lapse of a certain time the young May-flies are hatched out in the form of tiny active larvae. It is probable that the comparative temperature and depth of the water, and the surrounding circumstances tending to increase or diminish the quantity of light and sunshine, may have some effect in retarding or advancing the period intervening between the deposition of the eggs and the birth of the larvae. Having succeeded in hatching the eggs of *Ephemera danica* in captivity, I am in a position to give some precise data, which, however, must be taken as showing the result only with this particular species under particular conditions of light and temperature. A number of eggs taken on June 9, 1887, hatched on August 15 in the same year, a period of sixty-seven days.

The new-born larvae at once commence digging their way into the mud by means of their tusk-shaped mandibles and forelegs, and form tubular horizontal galleries of a diameter only slightly greater than that of their bodies, but, according to the observation of Pictet, not sufficiently large for them to be able to remain in these retreats while growing. As they increase in size they desert the galleries previously dug and form fresh ones; as, however, they always affect water of a certain depth, in rivers subject to sudden floods they are obliged to change their quarters from time to time in order to preserve these conditions.

As the larva grows it sheds its outer skin many times, some further development of the various organs taking place with each moult. The entire larval existence is passed in comparatively still portions of the stream, buried in the mud at a depth varying according 1o the temperature; thus, in very cold weather it has been found burrowing more than three feet in the river-bed, in the early spring at a depth of about eighteen inches, while at the commencement of June it is only an inch or two below the surface. It is quite possible that this statement may give rise to some controversy, and instances will be given of these larvae being found in fast-running stickles, or shallows, and on hard clean gravel, and on this evidence anglers will be asked to discredit the careful observations of naturalists repeated over and over again during the last century.

There is, however, no doubt that some considerable number of May-fly larvae are from time to time found in rapid water where there is not sufficient mud to cover them. This seeming anomaly is, to my mind, quite capable of being explained. Every flood, every cleaning of the river, every disturbance of the mud, and every cutting of the weeds must of necessity set adrift a certain number of larvae; these are unable to progress against or even across the stream, and the moment they find they are being carried down, instead of exhausting their strength by vain efforts to stem the current, they let themselves sink to the bottom, and crawl along until they find a suitable place, in which they once more commence their burrowing operations. Hence the occasional presence of larvae on hard gravelly scours; and, of course, the greater the number of May-flies on a river, and the more frequent the causes of disturbance, the more numerous are likely to be the occasions on which the larvae and nymphs are found on what must be considered unsuitable ground.

After a certain number of moults the wing-covers attached to the thorax become visible; at first they are transparent and very small, but gradually grow larger and become darker in colour as the development of the wings folded up within them progresses. From the time of the first appearance of the wing- covers the name nymph is applied to the immature insect, but, beyond that it has grown larger and slightly darker in colour, and that the mouth organs and branchiae are further developed, it has altered very little in appearance from the new-born larva.

Before treating of the next change, from nymph to subimago, there are two points requiring consideration, and on these two points, unfortunately, very little reliable information can be obtained. They are firstly: the length of time intervening between the depositing of the eggs and the appearance of the winged subimago on the water; and secondly: the nature of the food on which the insect subsists during the larval and nymph stages.

When, with the kind assistance of a friend, I first succeeded in hatching May-fly eggs in captivity, we entertained strong hopes of being able to work out these two important questions of the life-history. Much time was consumed in daily microscopic examination of the eggs as the gradual development of the embryo proceeded. To provide as far as possible in captivity the same circumstances and the same surroundings as the larvae would have experienced in the natural state, mud, gravel, and weeds from the river were distributed in the troughs in which the eggs were hatching. A grave cause of anxiety was that, of course, we could only use London water, and very possibly in the filtration which it undergoes the most necessary food for the young larvae might be removed. All our efforts, however, were in vain. In a few weeks, out of many hundreds of thousands of eggs hatched not a single living specimen could be found.

Although much disheartened at this first failure, and having been in two consecutive seasons since prevented from trying the experiment again, I do not confess myself beaten, and fully expect some day to succeed in rearing full-grown May-flies from eggs hatched in captivity.

There are, however, sufficient data to justify the positive statement, that not less than two years elapse between the laying of the egg and the appearance of the winged subimago on the water. Every year since 1886 I have searched in the mud during the drake season, and have invariably found two sizes: one, quite near the surface – the nymph just on the point of changing to the subimago – and the other, much deeper in the mud, a half-grown larva without any trace of wing-covers. In no single instance was a larva found either in an intermediate stage or smaller than the half-grown specimens, and hence the evidence may, I think, be deemed sufficient to establish the fact that the time occupied in the growth of the winged insect from the egg is two years, and no more.

As to the food question. Pictet declares that he has discovered remains of small insects or aquatic worms in the alimentary canal of the larvae. An earlier authority – Swammerdam – says that he has only found 'terre glaise,' or clayey earth. Pictet's observations are, as a rule, so accurate and so reliable that it would be an act of presumption on my part to cast the least shade of doubt on any word he has written, yet, as far as my own experience has gone, a number of autopsies performed at various times, and many microscopic examinations of the larvae in various stages of preparation and mounting, have failed to bring to light anything beyond semi-digested vegetable and earthy matter. Yet the formidable mandibles of the larvae and the other fully developed mouth organs seem eminently fitted to deal with living larvae or insects, although Pictet throws doubt on this use for the mandibles, as he distinctly states, when speaking of the galleries in the mud in which the larvae live – '*Flies fouissent avec leurs mandibules et leurs pattes antérieures, un peu semblables à celles des courtilières.*'

The nymph having now arrived at the period of its existence when it is on the point of undergoing the metamorphosis from larva to subimago, is worthy of careful examination. It has at this stage, when viewed under the microscope, a very curious appearance. The outline of the nymph itself is unchanged, but the entire margin, whether of body, legs, or setae, has a semi-transparent appearance, within which is seen a dark opaque insect, very similar in contour to the nymph itself, but more slender in all its proportions. The head with the antennae and eyes, the thorax and legs, the abdomen and setae, are each distinctly visible within the corresponding organ of the nymph; and the wings are neatly folded up and packed inside the wing-covers.

Submerged about an inch under the mud, generally among the roots of the weeds, the nymph works its way out of the soil and rises in a series of jerks to the surface of the water. On arrival there, under normal circumstances, the larval skin is split longitudinally up the back of the thorax by a violent effort; through this aperture the thorax of the subimago first protrudes, followed by the head; next the legs struggle out; the abdomen and setae are then drawn out, and lastly the wings emerge one after the other from the wing-covers, and are unfolded and extended. The subimago remains a few moments floating on the surface of the water, or supported on the nymph-shuck, until the wings are dry, and then, as the Green Drake, flutters before the wind in a heavy laboured flight to the shore, unless in the meantime it has fallen a prey to one of its many enemies among the fish or the birds.

The above is the natural order of the metamorphosis under normal circumstances, but very frequently the exact sequence is destroyed by some slight accident or mishap. Thus, as an example, some nymphs will reach the surface too soon, and float many yards down before the splitting open of the larval envelope can be accomplished; others, again, will have partially or even entirely emerged from the shuck before reaching the top of the water, and may possibly be drowned or fatally crippled in the wings. Again, in many ways the order in which the various organs will become detached from the exuvium can be altered: the wings may be drawn out of the covers before the abdomen and setae leave the larval skin, or possibly one or more legs on one side may get entangled, to extricate which a very decided effort may be required.

Such organs as are only of use in the mud or the water are shed with the exuvium; among these may be noted the mandibles, the powerful digging claws, and the branchiae, whose function it is to separate from the water the air required by the nymph for respiratory purposes. The hairs which fringe the antennae, legs, body, and setae of the nymph are absent from the winged insect, the antennae are much shortened, and the mouth organs are generally atrophied. The setae of the subimago are somewhat longer than those of the nymph.

The subimago having flown ashore, finds shelter from the sun on blades of grass, sedges, or among the leaves of trees, and after a period of from twenty-four to thirty-six hours – the length of time being greater or less according to the temperature – the final change to the imago or perfect insect takes place. As a preparatory step, the subimago fixes its claws firmly to some solid body, such as a wall, or post, or bough of a tree; its outer skin is then distended and splits up the back, the head and legs are drawn out, then the abdomen and setae, and lastly the wings. As the wings of the imago are withdrawn from the outer skin which formed the exterior surface of the subimago wings, these latter collapse at once, so that the exuvium left by the imago has, to a certain extent, the same outward appearance as the nymph-shuck, the most apparent distinction between them being the presence on the nymph-shuck of the branchiae, arranged on each side of the back of the abdomen at the joints.

The hairs with which the surface and margins of the sub-imago wings were covered are absent from the imago; the setae and forelegs in this last metamorphosis have become much longer, and this increase is more marked in the males than in the females. Thus, according to the dimensions given in the Rev. A. E. Eaton's 'Revisional Monograph of Recent *Ephemeridae* or may-flies,' the most modern and reliable entomological work on the subject, the setae of the female increase from about 16-19 mm. in the subimago to 24-26 mm. in the imago, while in the case of the male the setae, in the subimago measuring from about 17-21 mm., extend to as much as 36 or even 41 mm. in the imago.

The male imagines are seen dancing up and down in the air in clouds, and the moment a female appears a number of them start in pursuit of her. Sexual intercourse takes place in the air during flight, the male lowermost. To quote the words the Rev. A. E. Eaton:

> Darting at his mate from below, and clasping her prothorax with his elongated foretarsi (whose articulation with the tibia is so constructed as to admit of supination of the tarsus), he bends the extremity of his body forwards over his back, grasps with his forceps the hinder part of her seventh ventral segment, and with his outer caudal setae embraces her sixth segment. These two setae exhibit near their origin a strongly marked articulation, where they can be deflected abruptly so as to lie forwards over the back of the female, parallel with one another between her wings. Meanwhile the couple gradually sink, the female not being quite able to support herself and mate, and by the time they reach the ground, if not before, their connection is usually terminated.

The fecundated female, after resting awhile, repairs to the water and, hovering over it, just touches the surface from time to time as she drops part of the eggs.

The only purpose for which they seem to have existed in the winged state, viz., that of perpetuating the species, having been accomplished, both sexes fall almost lifeless on the water, with their wings extended and lying flat, and at this period of their brief existence are usually designated by anglers the *Spent Gnat*.

The immature May-flies at the earlier stages being burrowing larvae living in the mud ('*larves fouisseuses*,' as Pictet styles them), do not to any great extent serve as food for the fish. A certain number are occasionally found during the spring in the stomachs of trout, but it is probable that when an autopsy reveals the presence of any considerable number of these larvae, it is due to some disturbance of the mud of the river having set the larvae adrift, and, naturally, a hungry trout finding a quantity of palatable food such as this within his reach would, if possible, gorge himself with it. I know, from undoubted evidence, that from one fish in the Kennet more than one hundred May-fly larvae were taken in spring, but considering the enormous quantity of May-fly present in this river, it is not surprising that after a flood or during weed cutting a fish should find hundreds of larvae helplessly carried along by the stream.

The first stage at which the trout can get the chance of feeding freely on the Ephemera is when the nymph is working its way out of the mud and swimming to the surface of the water for the purpose of effecting the transformation to the subimago. When this first occurs the fish seem afraid of an insect so much larger than the forms of life which have previously formed their staple diet. After a time, attracted by the great quantity of these creatures, they gradually become bolder, and, after trying an occasional one and finding them to their taste, soon commence to chase the active nymphs, taking them eagerly, with a loud splashing noise and much movement beneath the surface of the water. Before long a fish in the act of seizing the nymph is surprised to find it elude his grasp, and to see the winged insect emerge from the shuck on the surface of the stream and leave the empty exuvium behind. The next time this happens he will possibly take the subimago, and thus he gets his first impression of the May-fly itself. This exuvium must, however, be a succulent morsel, as not infrequently the fish will take it in preference to either the nymph or the subimago.

If only fishermen could be persuaded to leave the trout alone at this stage, they would in a few days get thoroughly well on to the Green Drake, and feed on the floating fly with a sense of security. It is, however, vain to indulge in any hope of inducing the modern school of anglers to practise this degree of patience and temporary self-denial, although if they would only once try the experiment their sport would no doubt be so improved that they would have no cause to regret it. As it is, every proprietor or lessee of a fishery, and equally every member of a club or subscription water, expect the keeper to send them a telegram at the very first sign of a May-fly. Without a moment's delay, each and every one of them must postpone every engagement made, whether business or social, and hurry down to the river-side. At once the eager angler must put up his favourite pattern and keep casting it over the feeding fish: a few – very few – he kills, some he pricks, and many more he makes so shy that they will not rise for another week, and thus never do get thoroughly well on to the fly at all. As well might one try to stem the rising tide as hope to convince fishermen that it is good policy to leave the trout alone and let them feed in safety for a few days on the winged insect; and as, above all, it is my desire to make this chapter of practical use, I suppose it is necessary to pander to the taste of the fly fisherman, and try to teach him how to catch the trout while they are taking the nymph.

It is not difficult to discriminate between the rise of a trout taking the May-fly itself on the surface of the stream, and the movement of one taking the nymph swimming upwards through the water. When feeding on the nymph the fish is bulging, that is, darting backwards and forwards, to the right and to the left, driving a heavy wave before him and making a loud flooping noise as he snatches at his prey, but very seldom taking it on the surface. On the other hand, when taking the subimago he is poised close to the surface, in midstream occasionally, but more generally on the edge of a run behind weeds, or in a favourable corner close under the bank, quietly and gently sucking in flies one after another as they sail smoothly down over his nose.

When the fish are bulging, perhaps the best pattern of all to use is a hackle fly dressed as follows:

Hackle: A well-marked darkish feather from the breast of an Egyptian goose. If one is insufficient, use two.

Body: Pale maize-coloured floss silk, ribbed with a strand of peacock herl of a pale cinnamon colour at root – the pale portion of the herl at shoulder, and the metallic point showing about three turns of a dark rib at the tail end. A strand of white condor with blackish point is perhaps preferable, and certainly stronger.

Whisk: Three or four strands of brown mallard.

Hook: 3 or 3 long.

It is a difficult fly to dress owing to the stubborn nature of the Egyptian goose hackle. The accompanying plate gives a good illustration of the size and general appearance.

This fly should be fished floating, but not too dry, as it is intended to imitate the subimago when only partially withdrawn from the shuck, but not altogether clear of it.

If the Egyptian goose pattern is not successful, the following may be tried:

Wings: Rouen drake dyed a somewhat brown green. This shade is usually known as the 'Champion,' being the colour of the wings of a pattern the late John Hammond of Winchester dressed, and called by this name.

Head: Bronze peacock herl. Hackles: The first a grey partridge dyed in strong tea, and the second a pale ginger cock.

Body: Straw or maize husk, ribbed with fine flat gold and crimson tying-silk.

Whisk: Brown mallard.

Hook: 2.

Over bulging fish it should be fished only moderately dry, and flat, not cocked. The same pattern fished quite dry and cocked is a very good one – in fact, perhaps the very best – for fish taking the Green Drake.

It may be varied by omitting the tinsel and ribbing the body right down from shoulder to tail with the crimson tying-silk and ginger hackle.

With these two patterns of Champion, and, for a change, one dressed precisely like them, but with the wings dyed of a more greenish hue, and the two following imitations, any fisherman can travel all over the kingdom, and kill the trout wherever and whenever they are really feeding on the subimago:

Wings: Canadian summer or wood duck.

Head: Bronze peacock herl.

Shoulder Hackle: Hen golden pheasant.

Ribbing Hackle: Pale ginger cock.

Body: Straw or maize husk, ribbed with crimson tying-silk.
Hook: 2 or 3.

Wings: Rouen drake, undyed, which is better than the ordinary mallard wing, as the markings are more distinct.

Head: Bronze peacock herb

Shoulder Hackle: Hen pheasant, slightly dyed a pale medium olive.

Ribbing Hackle: Blue Andalusian cock.

Whisk: Brown mallard.

Body: Straw or maize husk, ribbed with pale olive tying-silk.

Hook: 2 or 3.

For imitating the spent gnat there is no pattern to approach Mr. Marryat's, dressed as follows:

Wings: Four dark grizzled blue Andalusian cock hackles set on horizontally quite flat, and at right angles to the hook-shank. If dark Andalusian hackles are not obtainable, it is far better to use ordinary black hackles than light duns.

Head: Bronze peacock herl.

Shoulder Hackle: Grey partridge.

Ribbing Hackle: Badger.

Body: White quill or white floss silk, ribbed with a strand of peacock herl which is cinnamon- coloured at root and dark at point, or condor, as in the Egyptian goose pattern, the dark portion showing about three turns at the tail end of body.

Whisk: Brown mallard.

Hook: 3 or 3 long.

The sizes of hooks given in all the above patterns are those of the ordinary eyed hooks.

A few words will suffice to indicate the rod and tackle which will be found most serviceable for this class of fishing. A moderately stiff single-handed glued cane rod of eleven feet, in two or three joints, will be a far more comfortable weapon to wield than any double-handed one, although if there are any conditions under which a double-handed rod could be preferred, it would be when fishing the floating May-fly; yet it is not so handy to use, cannot throw any longer distance, and is powerless against the wind when compared with the single-handed rod. If the built cane be deemed too expensive, a greenheart rod of the same length and character can be substituted.

A good bronze or ebonite revolving-plate reel, large enough to hold at least forty yards of line. A pure silk solid plaited line, moderately stout and parallel through the central portion, but tapered for the last five yards at each end; this dressed in pure boiled oil, according to Mr. Hawksley's improved plan, and occasionally rubbed well over from end to end with red deer fat to make it float. Gut cast not too fine – in fact, moderately fine undrawn for the point, tapered gradually to quite stout trout gut at the loop by which it is attached to the reel line. With a landing net and basket, the gear is complete.

As to hooks, the argument that is applicable to show the advantage of the eyed hook for small flies is strengthened tenfold in regard to the larger sizes. I would, however, offer one word of counsel: do not be persuaded to buy May-flies dressed on hooks any larger than those specified for the patterns given, nor, in fact, for any May-flies. Nos. 2, 3, and for the outside limit 3 long, are quite large enough. A small May-fly will often hook and kill a fish which will only splash at and refuse one of the monstrosities frequently foisted on the unwary by the tackle- makers.

Having rod, line, cast, and fly together, the next point to consider is how to use them. I would premise that, without washing in any way to be dogmatic, all the experience gained during many years has tended more and more to convince me that, whatever may be the case with imitations of other Ephemeridte, with the May-fly it is of the greatest advantage to fish dry or floating. The only stages at which it is possible for the natural May-fly when taken by the fish to be entirely submerged is in the nymph state just before changing to the subimago, and the spent gnat, which when quite dead may possibly, after some lapse of time, become sodden and sink, although on this latter point I am inclined to think that it is far more likely to shrivel up and become disintegrated on the surface of the water. If, however, the angler desires to fish it under water or sunk, he must omit that part of the instructions relating to drying the fly.

The first cast to learn is the ordinary overhanded one, in which the hand holding the rod is raised so as to carry the rod backwards a short distance beyond the perpendicular, feeling the line all the time, and, after a decided pause, just as the weight of the line commences to bend the rod-top backwards, the hand is brought forward and down again with a slightly increased velocity. The motion of the hand throughout is smooth and without jerk, and should describe a slight curve – the object of this curve being to prevent the line when travelling backwards from coming in contact with the rod, or the line itself when coming forward. If the fly is dry the cast on the water may be at once completed, but if not, the backward and forward motion must be repeated a sufficient number of times to thoroughly free the hackles and wings of the fly from moisture.

At times some difficulty is found in drying a Mayfly sufficiently. In this case one of two things has probably happened: either the fly is thoroughly sodden, when it is as well to put up a new one, and leave the other to dry in your hat, after coaxing the wings, etc..., into position with your fingers; or the wings have got turned down and caught under the bend of the hook, when the fly will neither dry rapidly nor float well. As the hand comes forward the rod-point must be lowered, and the line delivered at a level of about a yard above the water. The hand is then slightly checked, and the fly falls lightly and without splash. The checking of the hand serves a twofold purpose: firstly, causing the fly to land on the surface without disturbance, and secondly, delivering it with plenty of slack line, which, as shown later on, will prevent or retard its dragging.

If it is necessary to make a very long cast, the hand when travelling back must be raised above the level of the head, so as to lift the line as high as possible behind. This is called the steeple cast. , It may be laid down as an axiom that the distance an angler can cast is limited by the length of line he can keep in the air behind, with the addition of a few yards he can slide from the hand while delivering the fly; hence the advantage of steepling when trying to make an extra long throw. It is also necessary to steeple when there is a bank or bushes immediately behind the angler; even with very long grass it is often useful.

If the wind is dead in the face of the fisherman he must use a somewhat shorter length of gut, and follow the previous instructions for casting, up to the point of delivering the fly; but when the arm attains the angle of 45° with the plane of the water it must be -well extended, the knuckles turned down, and a cut made downwards and towards the body, the elbow being at the same time raised and the rod-point carried down to the level of the water. If accurately timed, this back motion acts as a check, and the result is that the line is extended in the teeth of the wind, the fly travelling out straight, and falling lightly and without disturbance. This is called the downward cut.

For fishing against a very light wind, or across any breeze short of half a gale, no style of casting is to be compared with the underhanded or horizontal cast. As may be inferred from its name, it is a cast made underhanded or with the rod held in a horizontal position. The movements are precisely similar to those of the overhanded cast, except that the rod is in a horizontal instead of a vertical position, and the motion of it is in a direction parallel to the surface of the water instead of at right angles to it, as in the case of the overhanded cast. The line should be returned under and delivered over the rod.

There are many good reasons why the underhanded cast should at all times, where practicable, be used by the angler who desires to be successful. With it he can throw against a moderate wind or across a strong one, and his fly will in the majority of cases land on the water cocked, or floating with its wings up in the natural position. This last is a very essential and important point when dealing with shy fish, and with no fly and in no style of angling to so great a degree as with the May-fly. Besides these advantages, there is another which, if possible, is even of greater consequence than either, viz., that with the horizontal cast the fisherman himself will work more easily keeping quite low down, and, whether returning, casting, or drying the fly, neither his rod nor its shadow is ever nearly so visible to, and consequently likely to scare, the fish.

There are only two difficulties to overcome when commencing to learn the underhanded cast. The first is to get over the cramp caused by the alteration in position of the hand and the strain on a set of muscles which are scarcely used at all with the overhanded cast. The second, that from the fact of the rod-point, and therefore the fly, travelling along the arc of a circle of which the hand is the centre, and the plane of which is parallel to the plane of the water, it is far more difficult to place the fly accurately over the rising fish than with the ordinary overhanded cast, when it is directed in a straight line down on to it. Both of these difficulties are, however, overcome by practice and perseverance, and having once mastered this cast, the angler will never fail to use it in preference to any other. It should also be noted that with this cast a fly can be placed under overhanging boughs, or up under a bridge, where it would be an utter impossibility to do so by any other means.

If the beginner finds that, without being himself able to specify the cause of his non-success, he is not progressing, and if he cannot get a friend who can cast to tell him of his faults, as a general rule, and in all styles of casting, he may safely infer that he is getting into the habit of either using too much force, or of casting and returning too quickly; very possibly he may be falling into both these errors.

Wherever possible throw up stream, and let the fly come down to you; the fish when feeding are invariably poised with their heads looking up stream waiting for the flies to float down to them, so that when fishing up you not only present the fly to the fish in the more natural manner, but being below them have a better chance of not being seen yourself. As the fly comes down to you, it is necessary to draw, in slowly by hand a part of the slack line, otherwise this slack line on the water is likely to retard the effect of striking so much as to make you miss the fish. The line must not be drawn in too rapidly, or a decided pull or drag on the fly will be caused. Where it is impossible to fish up or across, the only plan is to drift from above or cast down stream; just as the fly is descending check it so that it falls short of the full cast, and, lowering the hand, then let it float down to and beyond the fish without drag before recovering. It should, however, be remarked that when drifting every angler must expect to miss a great proportion of the fish he rises, and, further, he must not be surprised to find that the first cast over a rising fish will in the majority of instances either rise him or set him down altogether.

There are in every reach of every stream places where the dry- fly fisherman may confidently expect success with a rising fish, and others where he may with equal confidence predict failure. As a fundamental principle, the artificial fly should float down to a feeding trout in precisely the same direction and at precisely the same pace as the natural one. This is merely tantamount to saying that the object of a scientific dry-fly fisher should be to so manoeuvre his artificial fly as to make it as far as possible copy in its movements, as it should in its appearance(those of the natural insect. The natural insect emerges from the nymph-envelope on the surface of the stream, and as far as it drifts down on the water is carried along at the same speed and in the same direction as the run in which it happens to be when first clear of the shuck. Under no condition is it very likely for a shy fish like a trout to take a fly deviating from this natural course, and the more a river is fished the shyer the trout become, and the less likely they are to forgive a mistake in this respect.

Wherever the run of the water has the effect of causing the artificial fly to drag, there the fisherman is likely to find himself foiled in all his efforts to rise the fish, and the place should, as a rule, be avoided. On the other hand, wherever the run of the water causes the artificial fly to follow exactly the course taken by the natural, there a rising fish is likely to be tempted by a good imitation delicately and accurately placed. As a general rule, wherever the action of the water on the line causes the artificial fly to deviate in pace or direction from that which the natural insect would follow in a similar position, a wake is produced behind the fly, and this is technically termed dragging.

There are three conditions under which dragging may take place. A fly may travel either faster or slower than the natural insect, or in a different direction from it.

The fly travels faster than the natural insect in a place where the angler has to throw across the stream, and where the most rapid portion of the current is between him and the spot where the fish is feeding. The fly then drags because the action of the stream on the line causes the fly to travel at the pace of this the more rapid stream, instead of at the rate of the portion of the river where the fly is floating. It further has the tendency of dragging the artificial fly more or less across the normal direction of the stream. This form of dragging can be obviated, or at least delayed until the fly is below the feeding- place of the trout, by throwing the line in a curve with the convex side directed up stream, and until the pressure of the water has deflected this curve into a straight or concave line no drag can take place. In a very wide stream, with the current throughout nearly uniform in force, the same tendency to drag exists, and the same remedy can be applied.

Another place where the artificial fly travels more quickly than the natural insect is where the fish is rising on a smooth glide immediately above a rapid run, and in this case the drag can be delayed until the fly is below the fish by throwing a very slack line – that is, placing the fly with the last yard or so of the gut extended, and the upper part of the cast and a portion of the reel line loosely or in curves on the water. The check referred to in the instructions for making a cast is the most effective method of producing this result, and it is far easiest to accomplish when wading in a direct line below the fish.

If a fish is rising in a slow running bay, the artificial fly cast with a tight line will be carried down at the pace of the faster stream outside, and in this case again the slack line is the only means of preventing the drag. With a strong wind blowing straight up stream a fly cast in the ordinary way, and fished from directly below, will be dragged down by the extended line, from the moment it reaches the water until it has floated a short distance, and thus left slack line below the fly. To prevent this keep the point of the rod well up until the fly has landed on the water, then at once drop the hand and rod-point so as to slacken the line.

When the lower part of the reel line lies on an eddy, it will cause the fly to drag by making it float more slowly than the pace of the stream. Slack line will naturally delay this. When drifting or using the half-drift, the line as it commences to tighten delays the pace of the fly, and thus causes it to drag. Plenty of slack, lowering the hand as the fly travels, and even walking slowly down the bank, will retard this.

In a small eddy where the natural insects float in a direction opposite to the general run of the stream outside, a fly must drag; but in a large eddy it is sometimes possible to cast up the eddy and let the fly drift down it, thus placing oneself apparently in the position of throwing down stream.

Dragging owing to the fly drifting across the natural run of the stream is a very usual cause of non-success. Perhaps the strongest example of this is when casting to a fish rising under and close to the opposite bank: the moment the line is extended the fly begins describing a segment of a circle, of which the rod-point is the centre and the length of line the radius; and here, again, the slacker the line the longer the drag is delayed. It is strange how often fishermen fail to notice this class of drag, and wonder at their being unable to get an offer from a fish rising freely, and in a place apparently so favourable. It is in a case of this description that the advantage of a well- fatted line is most evident, as it floats down with the fly, while the ordinary varnished silk line sinks and causes the fly to drag.

The result of all consideration of the question of dragging tends in one direction, and the lesson to be learnt cannot be too strongly impressed on the minds of anglers who wish to be successful, and are therefore alive to the fact that to learn this or any other art they must continually study to find out their mistakes. One often hears approbation expressed of the casting powers of various fishermen; in the words of the majority of their admirers they are loudly praised for throwing so 'straight a line.' I cannot conceive a stronger condemnation. In almost every possible position where drag is likely to occur, the remedy suggested is a slack line, and I believe that the straight line is often a cause of failure in wet as well as dry fly fishing, the drag taking place beneath the surface of the water, especially in fast streams.

When to cast to a rising fish is at times important. In changeable weather, for example, select a moment when the sun is covered by a cloud, in hot bright weather wait, if possible, for a light puff of wind to ripple the surface. When the natural flies are floating down in droves of some six or seven, with intervals, and especially in the case of the spent gnat, a trout will often take every one passing over him; in such a case do not select the interval, but rather strive to let your artificial fly come down the first of a drove. With very shy fish on a calm day taking only an occasional fly, it is sometimes a good plan to wait patiently, and just as he rises cast into the very ring he has made; if he misses the natural it is almost certain that he will come at the artificial, and even if not, he will often turn round and seize the imitation as well as the living insect. After such a fish has leisurely taken the fly and gone down into the weeds to ruminate is perhaps the very worst moment to select for throwing to him.

Above all, remember that the first cast over a rising fish, before his suspicions have been aroused, is the most likely one to kill him. If it were possible to gauge the probability of tempting a trout under any circumstances, and reduce the problem to a question of odds, I should say that if at the first cast the odds are three to one against rising the fish, at the second they are ten to one, and at the third or any subsequent cast fifty to one. If you wish to kill shy fish, take as your guiding principle that delicacy and accuracy combined in the first cast, before the trout has caught a glimpse of either the fisher or his rod, is the great desideratum.

Do not cast except to fish feeding or poised near the surface on the look-out for food. Mark accurately the precise spot of the rise, and when doing so do not forget that the ring made by the trout is carried down at the pace of the stream; thus, though you cannot place the rise too high, you may easily place it a yard too low down; and this is a fortunate circumstance, as it is a fatal error to make your first throw too high up and bring too much of the gut, and possibly part of the reel line, over your fish's nose. Crouch down and keep well out of sight; crawl up to the place from which you can most conveniently reach him. On a puffy day move during a catspaw, wait during the calm interval, and cast during the next catspaw.

Use the horizontal cast wherever possible, and at the first attempt place the fly, quite dry and cocked, lightly on the water so that it will float down over the feeding-place of your fish accurately and without drag. If you succeed in rising your fish, strike from the reel – that is, without holding the line in any way; remember it requires very little force to drive the barb of the hook home, and any excess is worse than useless. While playing your fish, keep on taking him down stream so as to drown him as quickly as possible, and at the same time take him away from his lair, where every impediment by the assistance of which he is likely to break you is well known to him. Do not attempt to net your fish until he is exhausted; the best indication of this is that he turns on his side on top of the water. More big fish are lost by premature attempts at netting than from any other cause. Sink the net deep and draw him over it, then gently raise the net and draw him ashore, but do not attempt to lift him out at arm's length. If sizeable, give him his quietus with one smart blow at the summit of the spinal column; if undersized, return him gently to the water.

If you cannot succeed in rising your fish, and determine to seek for one feeding elsewhere, retire from the water with the same caution you exercised when approaching; still keep well down, crouching or kneeling; again remember to move during a puff of wind and wait during the calm intervals, and altogether be most careful not to show yourself and thus make him still shyer than he is already, and this as much for the sake of the next fisherman who may try him as for your own. Note particularly that at all times when moving, whether crawling up to the water or beating a retreat from it, the slower and more deliberate the motion, the less likely you are to scare the fish.

Every one of the principles I have striven to inculcate apply with equal force to dry fly fishing of every kind and description, whether with duns, sedges, or May-flies, and most, if not indeed all of them, are equally applicable to trout fishing with the sunk or wet fly.

There are, however, certain special points and precautions necessary when fishing the May-fly. Remember that all the volumes of matter written to prove that May-fly fishing is an easy pursuit, to be followed in a dilettanti fashion, lounging along the river bank in full view of your fish, have no application to the chalk streams 'that trout feeding on it are not, to use the witty expression of a first-rate performer, willing to 'take anything, chucked anyhow;' that during the drake season fish are just as difficult to catch and as unlikely to forgive a mistake as at any other time of the year. The largest fish in the river are generally feeding, and are the special objects of the angler's attention, and the larger the fish the more experienced and shyer they are likely to be, and consequently more easily scared or set down. The same accuracy, the same delicacy, the same freedom from drag, the same careful stalking, the same care to keep out of sight not only the angler, but also his rod and line, are just as necessary then as in any other part of the season.

Do not cast too frequently. If a fly floated accurately twice or thrice over a trout is not taken, either rest the fish Until he has taken another natural fly, or, if too impatient to do so, go on to another, and return to him a quarter of an hour later on. During the rise of May-fly fish often take up their quarters in unexpected places; a very favourite one is in a small run between a weed patch and the bank, or in the slack water immediately below a bank of weeds, and, especially when taking the spent gnat, in almost stagnant water. In fishing stagnant places leave the fly on the water as long as it floats, as a trout will frequently cruise round and round such a place, and after some minutes suddenly come up and take your fly. Above all, do not neglect small carriers or tributary streams, as the very largest fish are occasionally killed in them with May-fly. When taking the spent gnat trout generally travel more or less, and it is well to note the direction in which they are moving when they rise at the natural, and cast well above in that direction. Note that the very best conditioned and largest trout in a river generally feed on the spent gnat, and rise very quietly and with no more commotion in the water than the mark of a minnow. It may be laid down as a rule that the best fish usually feed well on the nymph and spent gnat, and badly on the subimago.

The reason probably is that when they are well on the nymph and take, or try to take, an occasional winged fly just out of the shuck, they are often baulked by the drake managing to fly away just at the moment they are rising; hence they avoid the subimago, and keep on feeding on the nymph. After a time they find very few nymphs, and then naturally come on to the imago, which, lying flat on the water with its wings extended, is unable to fly, and falls an easy prey to the trout.

Although, as a rule, the spent gnat is more plentiful on the water in the evening, and even sometimes after dark, yet occasionally trout during the day will prefer the imitation of it to that of the Green Drake. A week or more after the fly is over, trout taking duns will often be tempted by a spent gnat: it seems as if the memory of the flavour lingers in their minds. In wet weather great execution is sometimes wrought with the May-fly. Though heavy work to dry the fly thoroughly, it is none the less necessary to do so, and a perfectly dry cocked May-fly on a rainy day is almost certain death to a rising trout. It is, of course, more difficult to cast against the wind with a May-fly than with a small dun, but with a short length of gut and the use of the horizontal cast or downward cut it can be done.

A half-hour before the hatch of the drake, the Alder or Welshman's Button are often taken, and at times these or the Kimbridge sedge are taken in preference to the May-fly itself, even during the thickest of the rise. Sometimes, with a good show of the Ephemera on the water, none of the many patterns known will rise the trout. In such a case try Flight's Fancy dressed on a 00 hook, or, if this should prove unsuccessful, the Wickham or Pink Wickham on hooks 0 or 1. If this will not tempt them, as a last resource try a sedge dressed large on hook No. 2 or 3. Perhaps the best pattern of sedge is that known as the Kimbridge, dressed thus:

Wings: Woodcock.

Body: Pale condor, nearly but not quite white.

Hackle: Pale ginger cock, carried down the body from shoulder to tail. It should be fully hackled, and if one hackle is insufficient, two should be used.

If, after all, you cannot rise the fish; if all changes of fly are useless; if you cannot throw accurately against the wind; if the trout keep coming short, and you either do not touch them or at best only hook them lightly and they get away; if the hooked fish weed you and break; if hook after hook snaps off at the barb; if you get cast after cast broken, or perhaps finish up by smashing your favourite rod short off at the butt ferrule, one parting word of advice. Do not swear at the river or the fish in it; do not abuse the hook-maker or fly-dresser; do not rave at the rotten gut, or heap blasphemy on the head of the unfortunate man who made your rod. All this is childish, useless, and unsportsmanlike. Probably your non-success is due in most respects to your own shortcomings.

You cannot rise your fish with any pattern of fly in your book, because, in all probability, he has seen you or your rod waving over the water, and is fully alive to the fact that he is being fished for. You cannot get your fly out against the wind, because you hurry your rod and use undue force, or because you will not finish the cast with rod-point close down to the water. You fail to hook your fish, because you strike too soon or too late. The fish weed you, because you lose your presence of mind when they are first hooked, instead of resolutely dragging them at once down stream over the top of the weeds, or giving them plenty of slack line, according to circumstances. Your casts and hooks are broken, because either you do not test them, or else you put undue strain on them.

As to the fracture of that pet rod, it may be due to a thousand-and-one causes besides the roguery of the rod-maker. Perhaps you hurry it too much. Perhaps every time you get a small piece of grass or weed on your hook you lash a long line backwards and forwards, with great violence to try and force it off. Perhaps, when you get hung up in a weed or sedge you try to pull it off with a furious jerk of the rod, instead of taking the line quietly in your hand and drawing it gently away. Possibly, too, in such a position as one of the foregoing dilemmas you cracked the joint almost through yesterday or the day before, and the least strain today is sufficient to complete the fracture. In fact, I would preach one text only: Keep your temper and be patient if you would succeed, not only in May-fly fishing, but in any other fishing, any other sport, or, in fact, in any walk of life or occupation you may pursue.

Frederic M. Halford